"As if governed by an internal life clock, and intricately tied to ancient maps used by wayfarers who precede us, the practice of pilgrimage is universal across cultures and spiritual traditions. In *Into The Thin*, Stephen Drew's deeply personal account of walking The Camino, we travel through numinous landscapes and holy stopping-places, auspicious moments shared between pilgrims, and timely teachings found in his own process of loss and grief, introspection and discovery, purification and renewal. Lace-up your boots and answer the call of The Way. Your life will be enriched by walking with this seasoned traveler of roads."

–Frank LaRue Owen, author of *The School of Soft-Attention*

"Along the Camino de Santiago Stephen Drew's body and spirit are in continuous conversation to the rhythm of footsteps as he walks up mountain slopes and along ancient town streets, past cathedrals and cafes, through forests, wheat-fields and vineyards. In this 'crucible of pilgrimage' physical challenge illuminates trials of the heart. "

–David K. Leff, author of *Canoeing the Allagash*

"I got chills when I read the first sentence of *Into the Thin*. This is a book for those who aren't sure where to begin (or how to begin again), and it's for those who have an inclination that beginnings don't always look like we think they should. Drew offers an eloquent glimpse into that thin place where joy can well up from deep sorrow. Walk with the author on a pilgrimage into the heart and soul of what life can be like when you answer the call toward resilience. You'll be changed, and glad for the journey."

–Heidi Barr, award winning author of *Woodland Manitou*

"Stephen explores the idea of how a pilgrimage, begun on the side of a road in rural Connecticut, led him to experience the spiritual world in walking the Camino de Santiago de Compostela. The proximity I felt to his words was more than geographic…It was hearing my own inner voice. Please find time to read Stephen's book. Go on the journey. It will lead."

–Lee Cantelon, author of *The Words: Jesus of Nazareth*

"*Into the Thin* bravely reveals the life-changing inner journey that often accompanies a physical pilgrimage. Driven by a series of heartbreaking losses, fueled by the meditative act of walking across Spain toward the holy city of Santiago, and inspired by a host of new and interesting people, Drew draws readers toward "thin places" where the veil between spirit and body is light. This is an inspiring narrative of awareness, reflection, and resolve that will leave the reader looking at their own lives in new ways."

–Beth Jusino, author of *Walking to the End of the World: A Thousand Miles on the Camino de Santiago*

"It's tempting to say you don't need to walk the Camino after reading *Into the Thin*. Stephen Drew's vivid, lyrical descriptions of the landscape, the people, and the pilgrim culture take you there. But what's more accurate is, if you've ever dreamed of doing this walk (or even if you haven't), you'll come away with a strong desire to do so. I believe this story of heartache, grief, and humility is what this journey has always been about and remains so today. It's rare to accompany another person on a path of such intimate, beautifully written self-reflection. Drew is generous in his invitation; I urge you to accept it."

–Iris Graville, author of *Hiking Naked: A Quaker Woman's Search for Balance*

"*Into the Thin* describes a long walk on ancient paths across northern Spain. Stephen Drew vividly evokes the physical landscapes of his trek and the cast of fellow pilgrims he befriends along the way. But Drew also finds along the *Camino*, 'thin places' where answers may perhaps be found to mysteries, above all the mysteries of pain and darkness in a life, and how we may, if not overcome them, learn acceptance. *Into the Thin* is an honest and inspiring book."

–Robert McWilliams, author of *The Kiss of Sweet Scottish Rain*

INTO

A Pilgrimage Walk

THE

Across Northern Spain

THIN

STEPHEN DREW

HOMEBOUND PUBLICATIONS

Ensuring the mainstream isn't the only stream

Postal Box 1442, Pawcatuck, Connecticut 06379-1442
www.homeboundpublications.com

© 2020 · Text by Stephen Drew

First published in the United States of America
by Homebound Publications 2020.

Quantity sales. Special discounts are available on quantity purchases by corporations, associations, bookstores and others. For details, contact the publisher or visit wholesalers such as Ingram or Baker & Taylor.

The author has tried to recreate events, locales, and conversations from his memories of them. In order to maintain their anonymity, in some instances, he has changed the names of individuals and places, and he may have changed some identifying characteristics and details such as physical properties, occupations, and places of residence.

ISBN · 978-1-947003-76-7
First Edition
Front Cover Image © Stephen Drew
Interior Map © Lora Sutyagina
Cover Designed by Leslie M. Browning

10 9 8 7 6 5 4 3 2 1

Homebound Publications is committed to ecological stewardship. We greatly value the natural environment and invest in environmental conservation.

For Joan and Fred,
two who did their best.

———

Bay of Biscay

FRANCE

○ Bilbao

Saint-Jean-Pied-de-Port

Roncesvalles

Larrasoana

Pamplona

Puente de la Reina

Calzadilla de la Cueza

Hornillos del Camino

San Juan de Ortega

Santo Domingo de la Calzada

Los Arcos

Frómista

Condes

Castrojeriz

Burgos

Belorado

Nájera

Logroño

Ebro

Zaragoza
○

Duero

 INTRODUCTION

WHO KNOWS WHERE OR WHEN anything really begins? A first walk that sets off across the living room carpet toward the hopeful faces and outstretched arms of Mom and Dad, could eventually lead through to the high meadows of the French Pyrenees and beyond. Before all the different ways we found of moving ourselves from one place to another, there was always walking, ancient and perfect. So when difficulties come as they must in this life, it is often the elegant movement of the walk we resort to in search of our answer; a way to consider, to reflect, to center our troubled selves. Maybe on a country road, down a path, along a winter beach, or through a labyrinth, the walk has a way with the mind and the heart.

Saint Augustine of Hippo once coined a phrase in response to a philosophical conundrum. "It is solved by walking," he said. I read this quote not long after the darkness arrived during the long year of 2010; a time which I shared with my second wife and family, a time which begged for answers. The deaths of a close friend and mentor as well as my wonderful father-in-law, the health crisis of a step daughter, the suicide death of my twenty-eight year old son, and lastly the decline and end of my marriage, all conspired to create an emotional crucifixion. There was more, but these were some mighty big "its" to be solved, or reconciled, or at least made sense of …even if it just was not possible.

Seeking simplicity and a peaceful setting in the aftermath of all this, I moved to the bucolic small town of Morris in northwest Connecticut. At its center are the town hall, school, church, firehouse, the post office, a deli, and a smattering of other small businesses. For insight on local politics or information on that bad accident from last night, just go to the deli for coffee early and have a listen. They'll get to it sooner or later. The rest of the town features well-spaced homes and farms that surround Bantam Lake, as well as some lovely roads less traveled. Here, I found a simple, somewhat austere life, and fell into the practice of daily walking. In addition to being a sensible form of exercise for a man of a certain age, I have mostly found it to be unifying of body, mind, and spirit. It seems I also developed a bit of a local reputation, as many conversations with friends and neighbors often begin with, "I saw you walking the other day." I've come to love this beautiful place of four deep seasons and of people who wave and smile as they drive by.

During a long walk one very hot and humid August afternoon, I was suddenly and spontaneously called to the Camino de Santiago, the Way of Saint James. The Camino is a Catholic pilgrimage of about 500 miles (or 800 kilometers) and is usually completed in five to six weeks. People have been walking the ancient roads to Santiago de Compostela in the northwest of Spain for over a thousand years in search of redemption, release from burdens, forgiveness, and meaning; sometimes searching for the experience of God Itself. Typically, those who come to it have felt some sense of calling.

One effect of pilgrimage is that it slows life down. So it was more than a little ironic to me that this phenomena of calling happened in the space of time it took to walk a single step. One step only. As my foot lifted, the entirety of walking the Camino de Santiago and all of its attendant implications then entered my life as a complete reality. There was no sense of having a choice, no need to engage in decisional balancing, no need to even wonder how it could or would ever be. It simply yet definitely was now so as my foot returned to the ground. I remember I'd been leaning forward a bit as I walked and that suddenly my body had straightened, that some kind of sound had lifted from my throat. Fear spontaneously erupted with a flood of thoughts masquerading as rational. Reeling from this, I continued walking as the fear eventually waned. After a time came peace and stillness and a thought that did not express in voice, but if it had, would have sounded like a chocolatey-warm, soothing whisper. And it would have said something like this: "Live well. Be at peace. Follow your path. Know that when the rhythms of life allow, you will go. There is something there for you." I eventually returned home, got into the shower and wept. I had never known anything like this and frankly questioned my sanity, though the reality of it seemed undeniable.

The route I eventually took, the Camino de Frances, the French Way, begins in the town of Saint Jean Pied de Port in the south of France near the Spanish border. It traverses northern Spain from the Pyrenees Mountains, through the Basque country of Navarre and La Rioja, and crosses the vast Spanish Meseta into the region of Galicia and the city of Santiago de Compostela. It ends at the Cathedral there, in a crypt beneath the altar, before the mysteriously contained relics of Santiago, Saint James the Apostle of Jesus. The Camino experience is the epitome of pilgrimage; the movement in body, in mind, in deepest thought, and in Spirit. It is about a faith expressed in leaving home and all that is comfortable and familiar and soothing, to walk on ground unknown.

My first awareness of the Camino came in the mid-to-late 1980s, while living an essentially drunken and debauched life during the aftermath of the end of my first marriage, which also involved a year-old daughter and three-year-old son. It's how emotionally immature, alcoholic men in their late 20s respond to stress and rejection, so it made sense to me. In an effort to maintain a modicum of self-respect, I would attempt to do respectable things. Things like read books. I was mostly interested in American fiction writers such as Wolfe, Hemingway, Fitzgerald, Steinbeck, and the like. It was therefore unusual for me to borrow a copy of a non-fictional travelogue and love letter to Spain from a friend. I was attracted to its title, *Iberia*, written by a then very living James Michener.

Though I found it a rather tedious read, it brought me to a deep affection for Spain. Particularly appealing was his, more than Hemingway's, detailed account of the Festival of San Fermin in Pamplona, which features the famous running of the bulls. The notion of a drunken crowd of men being chased through the narrow streets of the Old City by six angry bulls was just about the most romantic thing I'd ever heard of. To run with the mob's abandon expressed a freedom of which

I could only dream. Desecrated living can make that sort of thing sound attractive. But beyond all that, the book revealed a Spain that was tragic, heartbreaking, frustrating, yet magical; a place where history, I would later find, is a very capricious thing. The last chapter, my beautiful reward for staying with Michener's book, was entitled *Santiago de Compostela*, where he described his own Camino pilgrimage in 1966, referring to it as "the finest journey in Spain." The idea of a mystical walk across the north of Spain through the depth of culture and time appealed to the wanderlust I had always felt, my deepest desire to see what lies around the bend. It never occurred to me then I would one day actually walk the Camino, but the first seed had been planted. The density of all that transpired in the interim greatly diminished my recollection, but it was always with me, latent and waiting.

Late in 2011, a little over a year after my son ended his life, my girlfriend Dianne called and suggested I have a look at an online trailer for a movie playing nearby. She would only say that the story might be difficult for me, but it looked like a lovely film nonetheless. I was intrigued.

I immediately gathered it was about a father whose son is killed while on a hike in Spain, travels there to retrieve the body, and takes up his son's journey. I saw what Dianne meant. But it also looked like a wonderful story of adventure, and I'm always up for that. Besides, I had learned well by then that pain will always yield to growth and healing. So off we went...to see *The Way*.

I was in tears within the first 10 minutes, the kind of tears that gently well and fall, quietly absent of any overt drama. They came then, and sometimes still do, from well-developed habit, and from the cool, still place within; the perfect place where ache and longing live. I tend not to dab at these tears. I prefer an air-dry. I prefer the full effect. Whenever the big black dog of grief comes to visit, this is how I welcome him. And each time we play together, it hurts a little less—just a little.

As I watched this movie, a kind of vague recollection unfolded. I realized this was all quite familiar to me, that I *knew* of this Way the characters walked. *Iberia...Santiago de Compostela.* Yet it still never occurred to me that I should walk the Camino. For this, I'd need to be put firmly out of mind.

I certainly was on a hot August day almost a year later.

Recovery from addiction and what created it produces an interesting effect that not many people experience. For most, life unfolds on a continuum through reasonably predictable passages and transitions from decade to decade. We come to self-govern and view the world through the development of certain ideas and paradigms, an operating system that allows us to negotiate life with at least some measure of competence. But what if the operating system goes awry? What if a key answer to life (alcohol intoxication for me) turns out to be...unsustainable? And what if this unsustainable answer turns out to be all rolled-up into identity and how the world appears to be?

If the unsustainable is to be turned aside for survival (and it is), then inherent in that process, a lot must change (and it does). As the new answer forms and the old is left behind, the personality, motivated by survival, molds and adapts to a very different view of every experience. A radically different interior landscape develops and a new self emerges. Something fractured becomes whole. Old friends not seen in a while begin to say things like, "Something about you is really different. Can't quite put my finger on it but…"

In my case, as with most, this happened over quite a bit of time. My Rome wasn't built in a day, but was built exceedingly well. I didn't get my old life back after the drinking. I got a new one. So here's the thing: I've actually lived two very different lives in one. And it was only the new life that could ever have accepted and embraced the Camino; that could ever have heard its call. The old one was simply sealed off from any goodness and therefore doomed.

This experience of pilgrimage on the Camino de Santiago came perfectly and precisely as I began my seventh decade, a time when one realizes there are some things to consider— maybe even some things to pass on. There has been a voice gathering from some essential and mystical place. It wants to speak of things like crucifixions and resurrections, of redemption, of journeys within and without, about the breaking and healing of the human heart, and about the improbable becoming real. It wants to speak of romance and adventure and conquering fear; of finding the freedom of heaven right here between the lines of life.

Seems I have a thing to say.

 PROLOGUE

A S THE TRAIN CAME TO A STOP, the window framed the station sign for Saint Jean Pied de Port. Almost four years had passed since being called here to walk the Camino de Santiago. There are times when language comes up short, when the best words will be utterly banal and vacuous. But now there was only the loaded anticipation I felt as this long awaited object of my heart's desire was finally here. There had already been a few of these moments: earlier in the morning in Bayonne with this last ticket in hand, the day before while riding the trains south from Paris and Bordeaux, the gentle nudge of pushing-back at JFK two days and 3700 miles ago, and the click of the lock on my front door at home. But here I was at last with 800 kilometers of walking and the depth of myself before me.

Stepping onto the platform, I slipped on my pack and walked toward the street in the sunlit cool of a late April morning. I wandered over to where some fellow passengers had gathered around a large map of the town. After realizing it made no sense to anyone, I followed a group that looked like they just might know where to go. Virtually everyone walking from the train station was a pilgrim, easily recognizable with backpacks, wearing hiking shoes, zip-off pants, and layers of quick drying shirts. Though comfortable among them, I spoke to no one yet, listening instead to the rich mélange of language as we made our way.

We continued along through the streets of Saint Jean looking for the "old city"—the section of town behind fortress-like walls. The idea of a fortified town was a relic from medieval times when building walls was all that could be done to create some sense of sanctuary. Other than the white stone sides and reddish tile roofs of all the homes, the neighborhood outside the walls looked rather suburban-American to me, and I found this surprising. Eventually our walk delivered us to the gate of the old city at the base of Rue de France. In my excitement, I walked past the hotel where I had reserved a room, but it was too early to check-in anyway. To finish convincing myself I was actually there, I took a very deep breath and decided to explore the town of Saint Jean Pied de Port…in the south of France… in the Pyrenees Mountains.

There was an odd familiarity with my new surroundings. During my research, I had immersed myself in books, maps, and videos of the Camino. I walked to where Rue de France ended at Rue de la Citadelle. Turning right would take me downhill to the river and beyond to the starting point of the Camino. Turning left would take me uphill past the pilgrim office, and ultimately to the highest point in town where the Citadel was located. I opted for a left, passing the pilgrim office which was closed until 2:30, and continued climbing the narrow, cobblestoned street past hostels, shops, and restaurants. At the top of the hill, the Citadel gradually revealed itself. Though most recently used as a school, its original purpose as a fortress was evident. Built during a time of religious wars and Franco-Spanish conflict, it was an imposing, foreboding structure, with embattlements and high, thick walls. The views of the surrounding area were spectacular, from the tightly packed roofs of the old city, outward to the more generous spacing of suburbia past the walls, and beyond to the lime green patchwork of farmland that leaned against the more distant Pyrenees Mountains surrounding the town. The place seemed charged with the energy and echoes of those who had been there. It was alive, and I knew walking the Camino de Santiago would hold much more of the same.

Returning down the hill, I realized I was quite hungry. I retraced my steps to Rue de la Citadelle and wandered down the street until I came upon a bistro that looked warm and friendly. It had a take-out counter near the front, empty blond wooden tables and chairs just beyond, tile floors, funky art on the white stone walls, and rough-cut wooden rafters overhead. The aroma of freshly baked bread filled the air, and the staff was smiling as they worked.

"*Bon jour*", I said to the pretty, reddish haired, middle aged woman who greeted me as I entered. She smiled and replied "*Bon jour*", then in lightly accented English asked me if I would care to eat inside or out.

We went through the door at the back of the restaurant that led to a terraced outdoor dining area. It was carved into the hill topped by the Citadel and I was seated at a table that allowed a view just over the rooftops toward the mountains.

I set my pack on an empty seat beside me and felt the warm sun and the cool, gentle breeze. Before me was the menu...in French.

At the next table a diverse looking group of four Americans, three men and a woman, held an animated conversation. Given our minority status here, it should have struck me as more of a coincidence than it did. One of the men glanced at my pack and from the brand instantly deduced where I might be from. It was a trick I'd remember for use in the coming weeks.

"Hey there! Care to join us?"

Relieved, I stood up.

"Love to, thanks—name's Stephen."

I sat directly across from Robert who had invited me, a heavyset 30-something from New York City. Next to him was Sarah, heavier as well, also from New York, in her late 20s with light purple hair and a simple lip piercing. She seemed to be Robert's traveling companion. At the end of the rectangular table was Harold from Albuquerque, in his late 40s with the weathered look and wiry build of an experienced backpacker. Next to me was the youngest, Nick from Baltimore, pale with a slight frame and mildly effeminate affect. They all greeted me warmly, and to be accepted in the company of fellow pilgrims gave me the feeling of belonging.

They were already eating, and as I glanced around, everything looked delicious. They were sharing two bottles of wine that were well on their way to being emptied. Robert asked if I'd care for some wine and a menu suggestion. I passed on the wine, but noticed the meal he had ordered was a sampler of local meats and cheeses which he described as "superb" and I trusted it was. Ordering problem solved, I placed my attention on my companions.

Feeling strangely safe with this group after our introductions, and perhaps by virtue of being the oldest, I dove right in.

"So what is it," I asked, "That brings us all here?"

Robert answered readily. Gesturing toward Sarah, he said, "We're here to basically graze our way across the Camino, however long it ends up taking. I guess it's a summer of wandering.

"Travel is so fucking cool...just the best," Sarah chimed in. "The Camino looks like it might be hard, but it's totally doable. It was my idea to start here. I wanted to do the whole thing and see the Pyrenees."

Robert smiled slightly. "I was pushing to start in Pamplona or maybe Logrono, but I gave in." Then he said laughing, "She's got a way."

"I saw that movie," Nick said softly, "had to come here." And then looking toward Sarah, "Same here—had to walk the whole thing." ("That movie," the almost universal reference by pilgrims to *The Way*.) "I'm a little freaked about tomorrow though," he allowed.

There was a pause, and Harold said gently, "You'll be fine. You look to be in decent shape. Keep it light, don't push too hard, and you'll be okay."

"You've walked a lot?" I asked Harold.

"Oh yeah. Last 20 years or so I've done at least one major through hike a year."

Robert asked, "Your first Camino?"

"It is," Harold replied.

"Why the Camino now?" I asked.

Harold thought for a moment, looked at me and grinned. "It's just a really good walk— been on my mind for a while now. I guess I felt a pull. And you?"

Noting that no one had gone too awfully deep, I followed suit.

"Guess you could say I was called here," I replied, smiling. "Seems I've got a few things to work through…you know, maybe a broken heart and a few highly questionable personal behaviors. That kinda stuff."

They all laughed. I found myself hoping they'd not press further, and was thankful it went that way.

The remainder of our conversation centered on the 25 kilometer trek before us tomorrow; a day that promised a long, steep climb of unspeakable beauty through a high pass in the Pyrenees, along with the constant threat of instantly and radically changing weather conditions. The Camino presents its most difficult stage on the very first day, and we had all resolved to take the more scenic and challenging Napoleon route instead of the somewhat easier Valcarlos route. As the most experienced world traveler among us, Robert had researched the route thoroughly. He found that the *auberge* (dormitory accommodation) at Orisson, eight kilometers into the walk, always filled-up in advance, so he booked beds before leaving home. As the result of his foresight, he and Sarah had the option of bailing out there should the conditions turn ugly. The rest of us were committed to the full walk across the Spanish border into the village of Roncevalles before any shelter would be found. I didn't realize it, but my first lesson of the Camino was revealing itself.

Pilgrims come to the Camino with infinite motivations and purpose. Rarely, if ever, will one find a person who is there for the simple hell of it. It's always deeper than that. But my research about the pilgrimage suggested there are two very broad classifications of those walking: tourists and seekers. Though there are many shades of each, both would have to be considered noble inclinations if for no other reason than for the sheer effort involved in walking 800 kilometers. Besides, most "tourists" end up finding more than they had planned. I had become aware that not surprisingly, pilgrims can be at least mildly judgmental of each other; that even the most pious will fall into this unfortunately ubiquitous human condition almost instinctually. So here in this moment, in my very first encounter with fellow pilgrims, I felt myself slipping into the abyss of judgment. Un-pious me. I resented that this...this *tourist* anticipated the possibility of difficult weather and made plans accordingly. So from my fear of this very contingency, I judged him—friendly and inviting him. Screw him and the purple haired girl. I am a seeker. There will be noble suffering. My God, the crap that goes through my head when a little fear creeps in. Fortunately, I've come to know when my interior life gets muddy. It just doesn't feel good to me to be this way and the fear is always a give-away.

Reminded of his kindness and confronted with my pettiness, I said to him, "That's just good looking-out, dude. Nice." He smiled and nodded. Score one for peace and love.

We lingered together for a while enjoying the warmth of the afternoon sun, and laughed easily even as we spoke nervously about what lay ahead. I admitted to myself and to them that I dreaded pain and uncertainty and most of all, failure. For many on the Way, the days just before beginning the walk can be a time of doubt, fear, and worry, when we must at last confront the first of a million steps. But there is a power in any group as has been proven to me so often, and collective courage trumps individual fear every time. As I stood up with every-one to leave, I felt confident and competent and ready to begin walking my Camino.

I checked into the hotel, tucked in just behind the town wall. Rustic and old-world, it was dim inside with a tired, well-worn charm to it. I took my key, and climbed the creaking stairs to the third floor to find a humble, mauve colored room with a full sized bed, cramped bath, and balcony with a view over the wall to the mountains. Tossing my pack on the floor, I stepped onto the balcony, sat on a patio chair, and propped my feet on the rail. Thick, low, steel gray clouds started to overtake the mid-afternoon sky, and served as a reminder of an ominous rumor young Nick had mentioned about weather coming in for the morning. We had been almost dismissive of it. There is *always* weather coming in; this is the Pyrenees! But these clouds carried more than just the possibility of rain. They carried the promise of a new way of life to be lived for a while; a way that accepts what is, plans for only the most essential things, and wishes for little. I wondered how I would honor what awaits me, whatever that might be, and what it would all come to mean.

Every pilgrim receives the Credencial de Peregrino, or Pilgrim Passport. It is the official document for those who travel the Camino. I sent for mine a couple of months before leaving home. It identifies the traveler by name and country of origin, as well as by international passport number. The Credencial folds accordion-style and contains 56 blank panels that will be stamped at the starting point of the Camino, and at each stop along the Way. Almost every meaningful place has its own stamp or *sello*. For a Pilgrim starting in Saint Jean Pied de

Port, all of the panels are full by the day of arrival in Santiago de Compostela. There, the Credencial is examined for continuity. When the final *sello* is affixed, two beautiful documents are then issued: The Compostela, with the pilgrim's name written in Latin, stating the Camino was completed for either spiritual or cultural reasons, and the Certifcado de Distancia, which states the kilometers walked based on the starting point. I grabbed the Credencial from my gear, and feeling a little restless, headed off to the Camino Office for my first stamp, a scallop shell to affix to my pack, and some general guidance for the coming day.

Emilie, in her early 30s with a kind face and soft brown eyes, greeted me warmly as I sat before her and handed over my Credencial. While she stamped it, I selected a scallop shell from a basket, leaving a five Euro donation in its place. The shell is the pilgrim's symbol on the Camino, and though there are some fantastic stories about how that came to be, the idea of the fluted fan of the shell representing all the roads leading to Compostela appealed to me the most.

After showing me the starting point of the Camino on a map of Saint Jean Pied de Port, Emilie advised me that weather for tomorrow on the high Napoleon route was unsettled, but she anticipated it would be open despite the possibility of strong winds and rain.

Sensing my apprehension, she smiled and said softly, "You can do this. You'll see."

Somehow I believed her. She described the route, and the only warning she had concerned the descent into Roncevalles after about 20 kilometers.

"You will see a dirt path to the left, and a road to the right," she said. "Do not take the path. It is too steep and slippery. The road will take you there in only a little more time."

After leaving Emilie, I found a pilgrim boutique. The shop-keeper was giving a customer a tutorial on the proper use of walking sticks, so I joined their conversation. He assured us it would save wear and tear on the legs walking uphill, downhill, and even on level ground if used as he suggested. I bought two, and as I was paying for them, he commented that once I used the sticks, I'd not carry a pack without them again.

For the remainder of my final full day in France, I wandered through town and observed life as it arose around me, honing the essential skills for what lay ahead: to live without agenda or expectation and to be fully available to whatever may come. Later, at dinner alone in a café alongside the canal, I looked at my Credencial once more and on the back fold found the *Spirit of the Camino*. It summed things up quite nicely.

Welcome each day—its pleasures and its challenges. Make others feel welcome. Share. Feel the Spirit of those who have gone before you. Imagine those who will follow you. Appreciate those who walk with you today.

I woke at six o'clock on the first day of walking; still dark as night, and I realized it was midnight at home. Though I'd had some difficulty falling off, it had been an uninterrupted sleep, and I was grateful for that. Placing my feet on the cold wood floor, and turning the bedside light on, I prayed a silent prayer of surrender to the pilgrimage.

I wanted to leave in the pre-dawn light, the vague, gray light that speaks of beginnings and new things, a light that invites but promises nothing, a light seemingly intended for the relatively few—my kind of light.

After leaving my room key at the empty desk in the lobby, I stepped out into the street, shouldered my pack, and made my way to Rue de la Citadelle in the cool, dark, lonely morning. I walked down the hill and across the canal bridge, able to see almost the entire narrow street before me as it faded to a point. The tapping of my sticks on the street echoed on stone walls and shop windows as I moved through the silent sleeping town of Saint Jean Pied de Port toward *le* Porte d'Espagne (the Spanish Gate) on the western side of the Old City. Beyond were the first steps of the Camino de Santiago.

CHAPTER 1

DISTANT COWBELLS ECHO through the lush spring-green foothills of the Pyrenees, and the air is laden as it often gets just before the rain falls. The fragrance of loamy earth rides on a light wind, and Cuckoo birds sing their reassurances to me as I climb on this ancient road toward Roncevalles. There are small pockets of pilgrims in front and behind, out of earshot, so the predominant sound I hear is my own labored breath. I am establishing a pace, and learning to coordinate my use of the walking sticks. I've accepted the first days of the Camino are about the body finding its way, its rhythm, and adapting to what is being asked of it. Yet I feel I'm learning to walk again, and there is a measure of this that feels almost spastic.

The grade had been very steep since setting off but has now flattened some after a kilometer or so. It's as if I am being buttered-up for what lies ahead. I'm walking in foothills, but as the views gradually widen, I can see mountains ahead. The feel of the breeze is becoming noticeable now, telling me it will soon rain. I don't believe these cows of France. Not for a minute.

Almost all of them are standing. Shouldn't they be lying down with rain on the way? I wonder if the few that have lain down are the older, wiser cows, silently waiting to be proven right. The pack cover is on, and the folded poncho is hooked over my waist strap. Apprehension is nipping at the edges of my every thought. Still, I do my best to focus on walking, for now there is little else but my legs and the sticks, the weight of the pack, my breath, and the beauty that is all around me.

The Camino turns sharply to the left, almost a switchback, as the grade launches. As if on cue, the rain begins, first as an ever-so-light tapping on the plastic pack cover—so light it would seem unworthy of any degree of real concern. It quickly becomes insistent and forces out the remaining vestiges of denial. Hurriedly, I don the poncho as the sky opens full-on, and within the space of ten or so steps, I am walking in another world. The wind that has come with the rain is in my face, driving sheets of water on the paved road toward me. With each step, it feels as though I'm walking waist deep in a swimming pool. I have slowed to a crawl in the climb, the wind, and the water. I must focus on the step before me, and before me, and before me. Time itself becomes distorted and slows. Looking inward, I find fear of failure creeping in, but determination is holding its own at least for now. Those who have gone before me have been explicit: *No matter what, just keep walking.* And so I do. The hamlet of Huntto eventually creeps into view and hope lives.

There is a café in this beautiful place set on a hillside and overlooking a valley, though the rain is currently obscuring the view. Under an overhang, amidst the outdoor tables and chairs, pilgrims have crammed themselves into every conceivable space. Attempting to have coffee or food now would be absurd. I stare out blankly at the downpour and contemplate what might be next. I am five kilometers into a 25 kilometer walk and still 15 kilometers from the summit of the climb before descending into Roncevalles. My humanity beckons and I am feeling lost as the rain continues unabated.

*   *   *   *   *

I was given a surprise party on the day I turned 60 years old, a little over two weeks ago. My girlfriend Dianne and a benevolent little cabal that included my oldest friend and some other key players had conspired in observance of my birthday, and also as a send- off to the Camino. Over the centuries of this pilgrimage, it has been a tradition to send the *peregrino* on his way with the blessings of the community; to bestow faith and courage at the beginning of such a long walk from home.

This particular gathering of 30 or so dear friends was held in a stone, Tudor-style Catholic retreat house atop a hill near my Connecticut home—the perfect setting. Normally, I don't care much for being at the center of attention but this was different. It was very much about *us* before I ever walked into the room and the atmosphere there was as warm and familiar as a favorite soft blanket. Every face before me held a story I knew well, and every one of them knew what it was that I proposed to do. No one had ever suggested I might be crazy, though I couldn't make assumptions about their thoughts. All of them spoke only of their hope and faith and encouragement. So heartfelt were their words and gestures, I could only assume the pilgrimage would surely end well in the city of Santiago de Compostela, and I would arrive safely.

dark night of the soul   St John

Near the end of our time together that day, our host and my close friend Father John suggested we pray together, and handed us each a copy of *A Pilgrim's Prayer*:

O God, who brought your servant Abraham out of the land of the Chaldeans, watching over him in all his wanderings, and guided the Hebrew people as they crossed the desert, we ask you to watch over us as we walk in the love of your name to Santiago de Compostela. Be our companion on the way, our guide at the crossroads, our strength in weariness, our defense in danger, our shelter on the path, our shade in the heat, our light in darkness, our comfort in discouragement, our firmness in our intentions. So that through your guidance, we may arrive safely at the end of our journey, and, enriched with grace and virtue, may return to our homes filled with salutary and lasting joy.

Other than John and me, no one there had ever seen these words and our only guidance as we started to pray was that we "speak slowly and let the prayer find its rhythm." Yet not a single syllable was spoken out of turn, and I wondered how that could be. At the end I was moved to say to everyone, "It seems then, we go together."

* * * * *

A distant rumble of thunder interrupts my reverie. My eyes have been closed in reflection, but now I feel awakened and compelled to resume my walk despite the downpour and threat of lightning. So off I go—spastic legs and driving sticks, head down into the wind and rain. It seems to me as though this is the hardest thing I've ever done. Each step is a goddamn eternity. Just keep walking. No matter what, just keep walking. Every time I approach a curve, I pray for a crest in the road but there is none to be found. It only goes up. I think of my friends, of their confidence in me, my calling to be here, and I begin to wonder. Has the ego laid the ultimate trap? Have I been a fool? Crossing a country on foot? Has this whole thing been nothing more than an elaborate delusion? The self-doubt and fear of the absurdity of it all consume my thoughts as the rain and the climbing seem to drain my energy. My old friend desperation is lurking in the shadows of my consciousness. Perhaps this is the Dark Night that Saint John wrote about with his tale of purgation yet ultimate union with God.

In an obscure night
Fevered with love's anxiety,
(O hapless, happy plight!)
I went, none seeing me,
Forth from my house, where all things quiet be...

Onward on this ancient mystical road I climb, and underneath all of this chaos of mind and body there lies a growing sense of being informed of something, though I can't yet imagine what it could be I'm being told. My old Catholic sensibilities have me wondering about some sort of retribution. My more recent notions suggest a stripping of ego and the birth of something new and more authentic.

Ascent: Noun—

>*1. upward movement; a rising movement.*
>*2. movement upward from a lower to a higher state,*
> *degree, grade, or status.*
>*3. a movement or return to a source or beginning.*

After almost an hour's time and two more kilometers, the rain diminishes to nothing as the wind begins to gust. The solid overcast breaks up into fast moving clouds and I begin to dry out. There should be a little over one kilometer to Orisson and surely there will be food at the *auberge* there. My Spirit begins to sing again and my pace quickens. I see the valley views of the Pyrenees much better now and they are so huge, so utterly magnificent, that at one point I audibly gasp at the sight. The weather changes quickly in these mountains and it seems across the inner landscape as well.

As I enter the café of the *auberge*, the dry warmth envelops me as I peel off my poncho and pack and set them against the wall. Rustic and inviting with a stone wall and fireplace at one end of the room and café bar at the other, I feel relieved and at peace and oddly at home. There is a smattering of pilgrims eating and talking, and we smile at each other in the silent greeting of those who've suffered in similar ways. I order food: a fresh bacon sandwich, two chocolate croissants, and the first of several coffees.

I am soaking in the dryness and the fullness and the warmth. Pulling out my guidebook, I carefully study the profile of this stage of the Camino. I am eight kilometers from Saint Jean Pied de Port and have climbed over 700 meters. The summit of the climb is just shy of 1500 meters, and is 12 kilometers away.

The climb is flattening significantly—still upward, but not as steep. Clearly, the worst is behind me. After about an hour of rest, it is most definitely time to go.

Sheep are grazing languidly in pastures of a paler green here in the sunny high meadows, seemingly unimpressed by the gusting winds that now have my full attention. When I stop to look at them, they will not maintain eye contact. I choose to not take this personally, deciding instead that they are more likely aloof to pilgrims in general. I assign to them more intelligence than the cows that were so obtuse about the coming rain.

The ground up here is craggy and uncompromised and there are few man-made structures other than the road itself. The desolation of this place inspires me, and somehow I feel strikingly alone, yet part of it all. Though my pace is more brisk than it was in the monsoon below Orisson, I lean-in hard as I walk through winds of 70 kilometers per hour and more. Sometimes, a gust hits me from the side, and it rocks my body such that I have to catch myself. But I am in a newness of beauty so magnificent that it is almost difficult to accept, and besides, for me the wind is vastly preferable to rain.

The rhythm of any sustained walk is a peculiar thing. It seems the walking bones are connected to the thinking bones, and can lead me to either plumb the depths of my being, or simply notice the mechanics of my steps. I can focus on beautiful surroundings, or on the mildly psychotic meanderings of my consciousness. It occurs to me now that I'm more open to company during these early days when the pilgrimage is mostly about the body and learning the ways of the road. It only makes good sense to be available to the idea of a shared experience. There will be plenty of time for walking alone during the more contemplative experience of crossing the Spanish Meseta in about two weeks.

Despite the unrelenting wind, my body has achieved a kind of flow and this delights me. I am energized and more confident of finishing the day gracefully even though I haven't covered half the distance yet. Ahead of me I see a pilgrim whose walk is labored and slow, and I approach from his left. As I pass him our eyes meet.

"*Buen Camino!*" I say (the greeting between pilgrims on the Way). He breathily replies in kind as I smile and continue on.

Several minutes later, he appears from behind on my left and says, "Hey! Where ya from?"

"The States. Connecticut. I'm Stephen. And You?"

"I'm Greg—from Canada, out in BC. Hell of a day."

I expect to hear an "Eh?" but do not. "Yes it is indeed. A bit of everything so far, but what a beautiful place for a little stroll," I say with a grin.

"Sure is. You've got a good pace going there. Mind if I try and keep up?"

"You caught me in my second wind, Greg. Before Orisson, I wondered if I'd ever make it. I'd really like that very much. Thanks."

"I think you may be *my* second wind," he says.

I give a weighty moment's thought to the idea that being open to walking in company almost immediately gave rise to the appearance of Greg on the Camino, and I wonder if there is some kind of magic genie floating on the winds.

Greg has a youthful, athletic way about him for his 50 years. He speaks of his home in the shadow of the Canadian Rockies, about his love for playing hockey and hiking and skiing, of his wife, two sons ages 17 and 15, and 13 year-old daughter. I can tell he misses his family even though he's been gone only four days or so. They've never been apart for this long. He seems to be a practical man, yet I sense there is a dreamer lurking beneath his pragmatic veneer.

I sometimes wonder if it's true that the disembodied spirits of loved ones gone might exert some ethereal influence over our earthly lives. If so, then my son Keith would have been unrivaled in his effort to bring me here. It is equally true that my father, now almost three years passed, would have thought me to be insane for coming. The matter of fathers and sons has made my heart hurt for as long as I can remember. As both son and father, it is a relationship that has eluded me. Yet their memory walks with me now, as it has since their respective deaths. It seems we became closer when they left.

Son and father passed,
My hurt heart,
Their respective deaths,
Closer when they left,
Still all sounds so odd to me.

As Greg and I walk the Camino together, he shares his story of what brought him here. He begins by talking about how his father at the age of 63 had walked the Camino on this route, the Camino de Frances, completing the pilgrimage from Saint Jean Pied de Port to Santiago de Compostela. The most meaningful time on his journey was spent alone as he crossed the Spanish Meseta. I get the sense that he, like most pilgrims, returned home quietly changed.

Some years ago, his father was stricken with Lymphoma and at one point during the course of the disease, his prognosis was quite grim. During a quiet moment alone together, Greg's father told him that if he should die, he would want his ashes spread at a specific location on the Meseta. Of course, Greg assured him he would make it so. Fortunately, the treatment of the cancer was ultimately successful and his father recovered completely from his illness.

Shortly after, Greg says he felt a calling to walk the Camino to honor his dad and to express gratitude for his survival. Though he waited some years for life circumstances to allow this, his motivation and sense of purpose has been steadfast. His father will follow the journey from home in Canada as Greg posts on social media. Greg also tells me of his oldest son's desire to walk here with him someday, as the call of the Camino extends into their next generation.

I tell Greg how beautiful I find his story to be, though decline for now to fully share why. One learns to exercise discernment about disclosing these things, to honor the energy of the moment. When he asks about my family, I tell him about Dianne, that I'm twice divorced and have had two children of my own and three step-daughters. It's good enough for now, but perhaps a better opportunity will present itself before we eventually part. This kind of thinking serves to remind me that there are so many things that haunt me—things to be confronted on the long walk ahead.

We continue past the halfway point at Pic D'Orisson where there is a statue of the Virgin said to have been brought here from Lourdes by shepherds. Two more kilometers brings us to the gate that signifies the Spanish border as we press on toward the summit of the route. The approach to the top brings a short-lived squall of snow mixed with rain, and then at last the road begins to descend. We soon find ourselves at the cross-road that Emilie had warned me of yesterday. To our left is the steep and dangerous path, and to the right is the road she recommended...covered with a crusty, shin-deep snow pack and quite impassable. Some other pilgrims have gathered here as well, and looking at each other we speak the international language of the shrug as we set off down the slippery slope. Greg and I agree this is a true "Camino moment" where cir-cumstances allow only faith to follow.

We immediately descend deep into the tree line as the wind at last falls silent, and though it is certainly steep, we find nothing really treacherous about this path. In the quiet of the forest and finally past the exertion of the climb, we chat about the blessing and the mystery of finding each other as we did, and the shared energy of our walk together. We continue to wind our way down on this beautiful path for another four kilometers before the buildings of the Collegiate Church and Monastery at Roncevalles come into view through the trees. It is late in the afternoon, the air feels raw under a gray sky, and we are so very tired.

After checking in to the *albergue* (Spanish *auberge*), show-ering, and changing into clean clothes, I feel rejuvenated and set out to wander through Roncevalles while Greg rests. I stop into a bar for a snack before dinner where I meet Tim from New Orleans and Bill from Alabama.

Before he retired, Bill worked as a federal agent of some sort and his reluctance to elaborate much about this intrigues me. He is a wandering adventurer in his late 50s, handsome, and the picture of fitness. Most recently, he spent the winter living in Key West fishing for tarpon, barracuda, and small sharks from a kayak. He has dedicated his life to traveling the world in search of "real cool things to do." He learned of the Camino in a barroom chat the previous summer and thought it might work nicely into the springtime. He is here to experience the microcosm of northern Spain, to meet people from all over the world, and laughingly admits, "I haven't ruled out getting laid."

Tim is also retired, a portly man who looks a bit older than his mid-50s. He owned a corporate recruiting agency in New Orleans, and made a small fortune after Hurricane Katrina hit. It seems his niche was bringing insurance adjusters to town. After the dust settled, he decided it was time to pack it all in, sold his business, rented out his home, and set off to travel the world. He likes to refer to himself an "international homeless person" and maintains only a post office box back in New Orleans.

Both show me that there are ways to live in this world that are decidedly outside the realm of the conventional, and I promise myself to reflect on this some more.

I disclose my own story in a similar way as I did yesterday at lunch in Saint Jean Pied de Port, mostly in order to maintain the light spirit of the moment. It strikes me as a good reason to be vague once again. The remainder of our conversation is for the most part rather hilarious and after realizing that we all hold pilgrim meal tickets for the restaurant La Posada, we agree to meet there for dinner and more conversation. My sense is that Greg will get a kick out of these two.

I return to the *albergue* and find Greg in his bunk reading as I slide into mine below him. I fill him in on dinner plans and he readily approves. This place, an old monastery run by a Dutch confraternity, was recently renovated and set up to accommodate hundreds of pilgrims plus overflow as needed. As far as I know, it is the largest *albergue* on the entire route. There are three floors of about 30 cubicles containing four bunk beds each. At the ends of the long hallways on each floor are the bathrooms. We are sharing our area with two young ladies— one German and one Asian. Pilgrims are assigned beds in the order of checking-in. The German speaks some English, typical for many young Europeans, but the Asian does not, and so communication with her is difficult. Somehow though, we manage quite nicely.

Dinner turns out to be a party. Greg, Tim, Bill and I find ourselves joined by Heinrich, a tall and rather elegant gentleman from Hamburg, Germany who will turn 60 as he ends his Camino. He has a bone-dry sense of humor and an endearing way of misusing certain words when speaking in a heavily accented but quite understandable English. We're gathered in celebration of having survived the journey from Saint Jean Pied de Port through the winds and rain and snow, and agree to a man that it is at least one of the hardest things we have ever done. People have been killed on the Napoleon route, and Bill informs us that a man was literally blown off the Camino today in the strong gusts, falling some 15 meters down an embankment. Fortunately, he was not alone, and his fellow pilgrims dropped their packs and scrambled down after him to find he was not seriously injured.

Our collective thinking tells us that we have gotten past the hardest day the Camino presents, and all of our guidebooks agree that tomorrow's walk to Zubiri will be a piece of cake in comparison. My new friends decide that this calls for many more toasts, and at two Euros per bottle, the wine flows as I watch them all become a bit inebriated. Though not in the least envious of how they are feeling now (or perhaps in the morning), I decide it's time for me to leave and wish them a good evening.

Long before I came here I'd heard of the mysterious energy of the Camino, and though it remains enigmatic, I believe it touched me today. It's like a wispy, ephemeral current, subtle and perfect. It flows toward Santiago de Compostela from everywhere, neither pushing nor pulling. The pilgrim rides along on this current and it infuses the body when the more carnal energy wanes. It infuses everything, really. It has intention and it has intelligence. It has a thing to tell me. It is expressed in the wind at my back and the wind in my face, in the driving rain, and the warmth of the refuge. It lives in the air, in others, and in the inspiring answers to fearful thoughts. It shows itself to me in the peaceful eyes of standing cows and indifferent sheep, in the reassuring songs of Cuckoos, and in the holy act of ascension. I am relieved it has not forgotten me since it called as I walked along a country road in Morris, Connecticut.

The silent *albergue* is lit only in the red night lights now. I think of Dianne and fall fast asleep.

CHAPTER 2

A soft, echoing Gregorian chant slips into my dream. I open my eyes as the recorded chanting continues to drift through the dorm, and see the lights of the *albergue* coming on. Pilgrims are silently padding down the long passageway outside our cubicle, toilet kits in hand, towels tossed over their shoulders. Greg is shifting around in the bunk above me, and across the cubicle, the girls are still sleeping. As consciousness returns, I stretch and scan my body in search of pain or soreness from yesterday's trek across the mountain pass, but there is none. I feel wonderful.

I swing my feet to the floor, and as I stand Greg and I exchange "Good mornings." Not wanting to appear presumptuous, I ask if he'd care to walk together to Zubiri. Smiling, he says, "Of course—sounds awesome!" We immediately agree that we are not on a schedule and so there is no rush to go.

Our Dutch hosts hover near the doors of the *albergue* to wish us *"Buen Camino"* as we leave, and advise us that rain is predicted for the area today. On go the pack covers before we cross the courtyard and head toward the road. Greg and I decide to walk for a while before stopping for breakfast. Finding the painted yellow arrows that mark the Camino, we leave Roncevalles for the three kilometer walk to the next village of Burguete. We pass the infamous sign on the N-135 roadway: Santiago de Compostela—790(km). It is 8:00AM and we are walking the Camino de Santiago without a care in the world. Neither of us feels any effects of yesterday's journey, and I find this remarkable. Even the clouds are parting.

The walk today is living up to the description in the guidebooks as being lovely, forested, and with many flat sections. It is beyond delightful, and the village and café soon come into view. This is a very popular place for breakfast, and quite crowded this morning. It affords us the opportunity to chat with fellow pilgrims as we wait to place our orders at the counter. The mood is light and virtually everyone is smiling.

My body is craving carbohydrates. This strikes me as counterintuitive, for at home I eat mostly protein and vegetables. But I remind myself that it is time to listen to the body, so I tuck into a *grande cafe con leche* (a latte of strong Spanish coffee), and a chocolate croissant. The Spanish version of a chocolate croissant is about six inches long, three inches wide, and a few inches tall. It has a sweet, clear glaze on top and literally oozes chocolate from each end. I will likely taste these little orgies of fresh pastry in my dreams for the rest of my life, and hope with all my heart they are this good for the remainder of the Camino.

Greg and I visit a market as we leave Burguete for trail snacks and then continue our walk through beech tree forests and the villages of Espinal and Gerendiain. We stop after nine or so kilometers for another *cafe con leche* with our lunch. It seems an addiction to them is setting in. Lunch consists of the humble *bocadillo*, a sandwich of crusty bread with *jamon* (cured ham) and *queso* (cheese). These too, may prove to be addictive.

As we walk the Camino, Greg and I talk mostly of the beauty of our immediate surroundings, but also of our hope for what the journey ahead might bring to the inner life. I tell Greg about watching a pilgrim being interviewed in a documentary filmed on this route. He spoke about the simplicity of the life out here, of putting one foot in front of the other, swinging with the step and watching for whatever comes up in the rhythm of the walk. We remind each other that this part of our pilgrimage is mostly about the body becoming established in its walk, the placement of feet, the use of the sticks, and even discovering the finer adjustments of the pack straps so it carries well. It is about learning the pilgrim customs, how to find our way and a place to sleep, and how to be with those who do not speak our language. For now at least, this Camino of the Basque country is a carnal, earthy experience. We conclude that insight will eventually come, but for now it's really quite simple—we walk and we carry.

Burden—*noun*
   1. *that which is carried; load.*
   2. *that which is borne with difficulty; obligation; onus.*

When carrying the entirety of one's life possessions in a bag, it pays to be selective. My pack is rust-colored, with a rated volume of 48 liters and is of an internal frame design. I had chosen it from a dizzying array of similarly sized packs at the outfitter several months before I came here. My Camino research repeatedly warned against over-packing, and suggested a size ranging from 40 to 60 liters would prevent me from doing so. I tried on one pack that did not feel particularly comfortable, and then this one. It felt as if it had been built for my body. This was clearly *my* pack. Dianne was with me when I bought it, and I can remember her saying, "I can't believe that bag is going to hold everything you'll need to live for the two months you're gone."

"Yes," I said. "Exactly."

The general recommendation is that the weight of the loaded pack should not exceed 10 percent of the body's weight. This is trekking and not backpacking, so the absence of any camping gear makes for a lighter pack. When I left for the Camino, I weighed just below 200 pounds over a six foot frame, so rounding up would be about 20 pounds. I wanted less because I would likely lose weight.

I remember the final packing session in my living room the night before I left home. Every item, every article of clothing was spread out on the couch, and as I packed each I considered, almost prayerfully, if this was a need or a want. More than anything, I wished to honor the true nature of this pilgrimage, which for me, was to live minimally, absent of distraction.

It came in at 15 pounds. Adding an average water load of two liters would make it 17 or so.

Perfect.

At the very bottom of my pack I carry several small stones which together can fit into the palm of my hand. My plan is to leave these stones at a special place located at one of the highest points on the Camino, just beyond the village of Foncebadon in the region of Galicia, near the end. Like almost everything here, Cruz de Ferro (Iron Cross) has medieval origins. It was built as a pagan structure, essentially a wooden post about 30 feet tall, 18 inches wide at the base, and tapering to about 10 inches. As the Camino de Santiago became more popular and because of the religious implications, an iron cross was added to the top. Over the course of a thousand years of pilgrimage, it has become a holy place of deep significance as a repository of stones carried from home that represent burdens and troubles and things to be forgiven. This place has become part of the fabric of the Camino culture and experience. The stones I carry each represent an emotional burden I have borne alone or have shared intimately with others. And burdens, it seems, come in an infinite variety of forms.

Greg and I approach the final two kilometers of our 23 kilometer walk to the town of Zubiri and it turns out to be quite challenging. The Camino descends steeply, and due to springtime runoff, the path is mostly mud that covers shale. The sticks save me from slipping more times than I can count. Our walk is taxing, and every single step and movement must be carefully considered. The warning I received about the descent into Roncevalles would have applied more here. By the time we reach the bottom of this section, our shoes and pant legs are caked in grayish-brown mud. But before us at last is the welcome sight of the Rio Arga.

Crossing a Romanesque bridge into the town of Zubiri, we search for lodging and find a very nice private *albergue*, sharing a room with about nine others for 15 euros, plus five euros for a combined load of laundry. In the rear of the building is a long sink with scrub brushes for cleaning our shoes and also provides an opportunity for mingling with others. By late afternoon, our chores are done and we are showered. We head to the rustic and comfortable lounge area and post home for a while before heading out for dinner.

The modern-day Camino's infrastructure provides for excellent cell phone reception in most places and reasonably good wifi at the overnight accommodations. Knowing this before leaving the States, I have brought both a cell phone and a tablet despite my insistence on living with minimal distraction.

Cell phones just make good sense for practical safety if for nothing else. But mine functions far more as a compact camera than as a communication device. Virtually every pilgrim I've met so far is carrying one, and mostly for that purpose. I imagine that during the early days of cellular use, there was much judgment in the pilgrim community about the difference between "real pilgrims" and those who carry phones.

It has never been lost on me just how blessed I am to be here. From matters of finances to the life circumstances that are kind to allow, I know beyond question how fortunate I am to be able to check out for two months, travel to Europe, and walk across the north of Spain. It has not always been this way.

Not all that long ago, I was taught that giving freely in the spirit of abundance and of radical gratitude was an essential thing. What naturally followed was a commitment to share this pilgrimage as it unfolds through words and photos posted on a blog, though this still strikes me as being somewhat out of character. I've shared the blog address with all those who might have an interest, and especially those of whom I am so mindful for a variety of reasons. It is at its very core, an act of love and service, a gift. I like the feel of it. Despite my potential failure or success being so public, I simply cannot do this any other way. Though I really didn't want to pack a tablet, blogging with a smart phone is virtually impossible, so I found a light-weight device which so far has not proven to be cumbersome. It is my tool and not my master, and my hope is to keep it this way.

The morning of day three on the Camino begins simply enough with the room lights coming on—no Gregorian chants today. Despite sharing the space with nine other pilgrims, neither Greg nor I are aware of any snoring from last night (though we did use ear plugs to be on the safe side). Community breakfast at the *albergue* is hearty and quick. Well before 8 o'clock, we're heading back down Zubiri's main street toward the bridge to rejoin the Camino. Following the yellow arrows along the Rio Arga, we begin our walk to Pamplona on a beautiful spring day under a broken overcast sky. There is a gentle, cool breeze in the air.

About two kilometers into the walk, on a narrow stretch of the path, we come upon Heinrich who we had met at dinner in Roncevalles. He has been walking alone, and asks if we would mind him joining us. And so now we are three.

He is around six feet, four inches, with a very trim, athletic build. His expression is that of a most peaceful bemusement which combines soft blue eyes with an ever-so-slight smirk. He generally looks…pleased. Though Heinrich's presence is understated, with a mildly patrician affect no doubt owing to his German nature, he is open and available to us and others whom we meet. He will engage just about anyone in conversation. I notice how he walks. He is poetry in motion. He uses the sticks which are driven by a minimal movement of his arms, but the tips of the sticks find their place on the ground by slight movements of his fingers on the grips. His considerable height allows for a long stride, and in his economy of movement, he appears to glide along the ground. My own walking seems choppy in comparison, and as I try to imitate him, that vague sense of feeling almost spastic returns. I resolve to learn how to glide.

As we walk, Heinrich tells us of his business in Hamburg, a high-end health club he owns with a partner. His passion is playing drums in a band that specializes in American Pop and R&B music, and he has an endearing habit of singing random lines from songs they play (Greg and I both suggest he stick to the drums). After ending his pilgrimage, he plans to meet his wife in Barcelona, and from there they will travel to the island of Majorca for two weeks to celebrate his 60th birthday. Heinrich, it seems, just loves to have a good time.

We are trying to get Greg to say "Eh" like a proper Canadian, but he refuses despite our multiple entreaties. Heinrich however, has responded nicely to our requests for translations of profanity. Before we stop for a late morning lunch at a café by the side of the river, Greg and I can say "motherfucker" and "dog shit" in perfect German.

As our walk toward Pamplona continues, the now-narrow dirt path of the Camino turns sharply and we slowly climb a very steep hill covered in scrub brush. At the top, we find an L-shaped building divided into two distinct sections. One wing of the structure functions as an *albergue*, and the other is a Romanesque chapel with thick, windowless stone walls. The grounds in front of the building feature a large grassy area, punctuated by gardens that are populated mostly by daisies as well as tulips of almost every color. Pilgrims wait around the entrance to the *albergue*, queuing-up to check-in. I notice the chapel door is open, and after dropping my pack I go inside alone (pilgrim etiquette suggests leaving packs outside or in vestibules when entering places of worship). Greg and Heinrich are chatting in the gardens as they look about.

Whenever I enter churches I tend to look up. I wonder if this is merely an old habit of the mind or a reflex of the Soul. A taped Gregorian chant whispers through the place as if the white plaster walls and rough-cut stone arches are breathing. The space is lit mostly by candles. Some spotlights shine on the retablo. There are no pews, only a small open area before the simple altar. Just inside the door, seated at a small table, is an older woman who stamps Credencials and accepts donations. She smiles to welcome me.

An early childhood mystery of churches stirs in me. Nearly 60 years have passed, yet now I recall the faded memory of a deep scarlet red door with jet black hinge straps before me as my mother pulls it open and we walk into the cool dark quiet. The walls shimmer red in the glowing reflected candle light, and in the air there are traces of the thin, fragrant aroma of incense. Though we are alone, we are hushed because there is Something-So-Big in here. As she slides into a pew, I follow and watch as my mother settles onto the kneeler, her back quite straight, elbows placed atop the seatback in front of her, hands clasped under her chin. Her head is bowed as it rests on her hands, and her eyes are closed. Perhaps she has moved toward the Something-So-Big I cannot understand. I am sitting as she kneels, and we stay here for a child's eternity. I drink in this mystical place and all of its strange and inexplicable parts. As she finally stands to leave, I notice that every little sound we make echoes loudly, and the ceiling is so very high.

I return to the gardens with Heinrich and Greg, suggesting they have a look inside. As they do, I shoot some photos of the building and gardens, as well as the surrounding green, wooded hills rising sharply from the Rio Arga that are dotted with small clusters of buildings.

My new friends eventually rejoin me, and as we slip our packs on, Greg says simply, "Gentlemen…Pamplona awaits."

CHAPTER 3

From the countryside of the Rio Arga valley, the Camino delivers Greg, Heinrich, and me to the outer edges of the city. After about an hour of walking through the busy downtown, we are led at last to imposing medieval stone walls. We pass over a drawbridge gateway and enter Old City Pamplona.

Pamplona. I love the way the word moves through my mouth as I speak it, rich and round and full of Spain. In it, I hear an incantation of the elegant brutality of the bullring, the chaotic psychosis of crowded narrow stone streets echoing the music of the Basques, the words of Hemingway and Michener that seemed to call me here, and magical ideas of romance and adventure in a place so far removed from my home.

When I first came to know of Pamplona during those earlier years of dangerous living, I'd have never believed it should be an ancient spiritual pilgrimage that would one day bring me here; my drunken daydreams and fantasies of what I'll do "someday" transmuted to a forgiveness of the old ways. A miracle can be described as a divine intervention in human affairs, resulting in something remarkable. It is as if arrival in Pamplona, the capitol city of the region of Navarre, is in itself a pilgrimage, even if I'm only spending the night. For me it is a marking of the passage of time, of resurrection and redemption realized. To be here now, on the way to Santiago de Compostela, feels remarkable.

A place announces its essence in how it celebrates. Mardi Gras in New Orleans, New Year's Eve in Times Square, Carnival in Rio de Janiero, will all tell a thing or two about people in their place. Nothing speaks of Pamplona like the Festival of San Fermin with its infamous running of the bulls.

Pilgrims arriving between the 6th and 14th of July find a very different Pamplona than my friends and I do in late April, and most of them bypass the city completely as all the Camino guidebooks suggest. Every *albergue* is closed, other accommodations are completely booked, and the streets are choked with people dressed in white with red scarfs, most of who are drunk on Sangria mixed with cola. During the roughly one week festival, nearly two million liters of wine are consumed as the city becomes possessed and all its normal functions come to a halt. The Festival celebrates the life of Fermin, once the Archbishop of Pamplona, who was beheaded for his beliefs, thus the symbolism of the red scarf—gruesome perhaps, but oh so Spanish.

Each day, the highlight of the festival is the running of the bulls at 8:00AM, an odd time for a culture that is so nocturnally inclined. Six-or-so bulls are released onto a route that takes them over a 900 meter course to the bullring. Slightly further down the course from the bulls, is a group of runners, mostly men, whose purpose is to run ahead of the bulls, hopefully without getting gored or trampled. To participate, the runners must be in observance of some simple rules (there are no rules for the bulls). They must be at least 18 years old, cannot provoke the bulls in any way, nor be under the influence of alcohol (hence 8:00AM). Because there is no line of sight between the bulls and runners, a rocket is fired as the bulls are released, and the runners take off, looking over their shoulders as they go. Spectators are behind barriers, leaning out of windows above the streets, and filling the bull ring as they cheer on both bulls and runners. It is a mad display of courage and of reckless abandon; a celebration of the risk of life itself. Once the desire of my younger, wilder heart, it is no longer. These days, I find myself contented with other, more interior pursuits. Thankfully it has come to this. I'll leave the Bull Run of Pamplona to others.

My friends and I wander the streets of the Old City, half-heartedly attempting to follow our guidebook maps. But mostly we exercise our growing trust in the Camino to deliver us to the place where we will sleep tonight. And so it does. One room, three beds with a private bath for the humble price of about 10 euros each. The room is on the fourth floor of a hostel and has French doors which open onto a very small balcony that affords us a complete view of the theatre of the street below. The building directly across from ours seems so close that I could leap to it. There is no space between buildings and so looking up and down the street from the balcony reveals the near-perfect geometry of an urban canyon. Everything in sight, even the street itself, is immaculate and well kept. It is quintessentially Spain, and like most streets in Old Pamplona, seems poised for the night when it will fill with crowds and music and reveal the sensuality of the city.

It is mid-afternoon as we take turns in the shower and tend to our pilgrim chores. Fatigue from the 22 kilometer walk and extended trek through the city finally takes its toll, and before long we drift off for a nap. The muffled noise from outside the slightly-opened French doors lulls us to sleep.

Later we head out, and are greeted by a misty rain that has begun to fall. It adds a peaceful atmosphere to the subdued blue light of the waning day as Greg, Heinrich and I make our way through the early evening streets of Pamplona. *Siesta* is over and the shops and restaurants are all reopening. Spanish cities come alive in the evening, as whole families pour onto the plazas. Tonight we have no purpose in mind other than to wander aimlessly, notice everything we can, and find a place to eat.

It occurs to me that it can be difficult for men to become close. At least that's been my experience. Three days ago we were completely unknown to each other, yet two of us from North America and one from Europe have been placed together to walk for a time on a holy pilgrimage. Of all the possibilities, it is us. But I want to know more. I want to say more. I want to be close with them as I am with the circle of friends at home who gathered to send me off on this journey. To find this degree of closeness so quickly with these good men is probably an unfair expectation, but the high station of sharing the Camino with them gets the best of me, and so I get these ideas. Perhaps I'm just a bit too sentimental. For tonight at least, I'll blame it all on Pamplona.

Saturday morning dawns cool and crisp under a mostly clear sky as we leave the hostel. We are eager to walk today despite a late start, and in equal parts thankful and amazed at our lack of injury or soreness at the outset of this fourth day. After stopping for *café con leche* and croissants, we pass through a stone archway, and put the walls of Old City Pamplona behind us. Before us lies a 24 kilometer walk to the town of Puenta la Reina.

We leave the outer Pamplona city limits after crossing the well-manicured campus of the Universidad de Navarre, then passing through the small town of Cizur Menor, we enter the gentle rolling hills of the plains to the west. The Camino surface changes from pavement to a mixture of yellowish dirt and fine-gravel which crunches softly underfoot. It's good to hear my steps again.

Thin Places is a 5th century Celtic term used to describe locations in the world where the layers between matter and spirit are only paper thin, where conditions encourage the cultivation of inspired thoughts and mystical experiences, and where the veil is lifted ever so slightly in a timeless wisp of a moment. I've been considering this since sensing the energy of the Camino while walking in the Pyrenees, and realizing it's been with me since time itself began. It would be easy to declare the entirety of the Camino de Santiago a thin place and celebrate the mystery of it with each step. But there's more to it. There's always more to it. Thinness reveals itself from within, and if that's even close to being true, then place has less to do with it than perception. This walk is certainly moving toward Santiago, but more than that toward something finer. It is moving me into the thin that is close as my breath, a place where there really are no layers, and no conditions other than whatever awareness may come.

On either side of the Camino there is mostly early growth wheat, lusciously deep green and wet-looking and about a foot or two tall so that it waves as a light wind slides across its tops. Also coming to life on the plains are expanses of mustard plants, knee-high and of the most radiant golden yellow I have ever seen, that contrasts sharply against the wheat. I feel as though I might be dreaming all this, while my friends walk in silence, seemingly lost in their thoughts.

We soon find ourselves at a place that I know in my soul I will never forget. Heaven itself leans in close and whispers to look at this, and as we come upon it, each of us slows to a stop. Before us is an immense field of mustard plants, and the light is shining on them such that they seem to be illuminated from within as in an astral vision, casting a warm golden glow that fills the air and reflects on our faces like buttercups would beneath our chins. From the Camino, the field extends several hundred meters across, and about as deep. At the farthest edge of the field in the distance is an abandoned light brown stone church of Roman design. About 50 meters to the left of it, is a lonely ruin of sturdy stone walls without a roof that perhaps was once a monastery. The sky behind this scene is milky-blue with streaks high and white. Transfixed, I wonder if this is what heaven looks like, for I could spend eternity here in this perfect light. It's as if there is nothing left on earth to see.

We linger here for a while, and after shooting some photos, reluctantly gather ourselves to leave. I cannot really know what my friends' experience here has been, but safe to say it is unique to them—each pilgrim's way, his own. As for me, I have a sense of release at least for the moment, though I am certain the mystery will present again as another place, another thought, another pilgrim, another something. Pilgrimage is about movement over ground and through experience, <u>embracing and letting go</u>. Now as I walk away, moving on as the Camino would have me do, I look over my shoulder several times, and in the changing light I simply see a large field of mustard plants, an old church, and a ruin.

My friends at home, those Souls I carry in my heart, come close to mind now, more so than ever since that first day ascending the mountain pass. I am convinced it is their thoughts that mingle with this energy of the Camino to help carry me along almost effortlessly. We share this walk more than they will ever know. How I wish they could live for a moment in this pilgrim skin I wear.

There is a tall ridge a couple of kilometers ahead topped by a line of massive windmills, and the path is taking us ever closer to it. Looking to our right and behind us toward Pamplona, reveals an expansive patchwork of green wheat fields, squares and strips of golden mustard, and a sprinkling of villages and hamlets across the plains. A fleet of low thick clouds sails over, mottling the land below with deep shadows, and the wind picks up considerably as we near the top.

The infamous statue, an oxidized metal sculpture depicting a band of pilgrims making their way, comes in to view as we reach Alto de Perdon. At the top of our 400 meter climb, a plaque written in Spanish translates into "Where the way of the wind meets the way of the stars" (a nod to the mythical etymology of the word *compostela* as meaning *field of the star*). We pause here, enjoying the spectacular views. Looking westward,

Kingdom of events

I can see the end of today's walk, Puenta la Reina, just over 10 kilometers away.

Descending the western side of Alto de Perdon proves troublesome. The Camino is littered with softball sized stones, all loosely strewn down the path, and this requires us to be vigilant of the placement of each step so as to not risk rolling an ankle. Other than the occasional profanity, there is no conversation until a seeming eternity passes, and we finally reach the bottom of the hill. The effort is rewarded with a gentle descending tendency of the path as we pass through the green fields of the plains, and the lovely Camino villages of Urtega, Muruzabel, and Obanos. This stretch is so easy that we do not stop walking other than to take an occasional drink of water, but maintain a casual pace until we enter Puenta la Reina.

The Camino routes us directly into the parking lot of the first accommodation in town, a combination *albergue* and hotel. Greg chooses a bed in the *albergue*, with Heinrich and me each seeking private rooms. We come from diverse circumstances. Greg is very much a family man, the primary provider with children of high school age. He has responsibility to and for others, and is still quite engaged in his career. His is a life of noble constraint. He must also be aware of the time he is allotted here, and of finances. Heinrich and I have a bit more freedom being somewhat older, that phase of our life now behind us. I'm mindful of this now, and hope the difference in our choice of accommodations is not troubling for Greg. I would likely have joined him, but I've committed to telephoning friends back home at 1:00AM our time, and need to set an alarm for that hour—impossible in the communal *albergue*.

After a round of laundry and a shower, I walk about on my own for a while and explore some of Puenta la Reina before meeting the others for dinner.

The town grew up around the six-arched roman bridge over the Rio Arga, financed in the 11th century by Queen Muniadona to alleviate the need for a ferry crossing on the increasingly busy pilgrim route, hence the name which translates to Bridge of the Queen. Puenta la Reina is primarily known as the place where other routes join the French Way to form a single road.

I saunter through the town in the slight chill of late afternoon, noticing how strange it feels to walk without carrying my pack or using the sticks. *Siesta* is now over and locals are filling the areas surrounding the cafes, many greeting me as I pass with a seeming obligatory *"Buen Camino."* I can easily forgive their weariness of the *peregrino* as they have seen so many.

The ornate façade around the doorway of Iglesia de Santiago catches my eye. After stopping for a moment to appreciate its detail, I open the door, finding the church full as a Saturday evening High Mass is being celebrated. The intricate gold retablos behind the main and side altars are brilliantly lit and soaring organ music fills the air. I observe discreetly for a short while, and it is striking to me just how deeply present in worship these Catholics of Spain seem to be. I feel as though I'm intruding on their experience, so I leave, hopefully without being noticed.

Eventually I find my way to the bridge, and walking on its original stone surface, feel my very soul touched by those who have walked here before, my pilgrimage now part of theirs. How many have walked these stones in the last 10 centuries of time at this place where different paths are joined into one?

Early in the 12th century, the Catholic Church declared that completing the pilgrimage during a year when the feast of Santiago falls on a Sunday, would result in a "plenary indulgence," meaning that beyond the temporal forgiveness of their sacrament of confession, existence in a state of purgatory after death for the cleansing of sin would be deemed unnecessary. Past the basic question of sin itself, there seems to be an implied arrogance to such a policy that I find distasteful. Still, I ponder how the purpose of walking to Santiago de Compostela has changed over time.

It is solved by walking, but what is "it"? I lean on the stone railing over the center arch of the bridge watching the river flow, and question if maybe I really am seeking absolution as did so many before me—if my old cradle Catholicism isn't exerting some subtle influence here. There had been years of indoctrination after all. *Bless me Father for I have sinned…it has been 46 years since my last confession. I have hurt for having been hurt and have disregarded the Golden Rule in favor of self-centeredness and made children and lovers weep and oh so much more than a few Hail Mary's will ever rectify. Yet even worse than what I have done is what I have failed to do.* So how about eight hundred kilometers? Will that do it? Can we finally call it even?

Sin: Noun—
   1. *transgression of divine law.*
   2. *any reprehensible or regrettable action.*
   3. *in archery, to miss the mark.*

A Cuckoo bird repeats its lonesome two-note song on the far bank of the river as a gentle melancholy begins to settle in.

The shadows are getting longer, and the air a bit cooler. My thoughts exhale and return to the ground as Puenta la Reina surrounds and consoles me for such troubles as I have dreamed onto the world, and bids me some peace at least for now. Maybe all roads do lead into one. I head back through town to meet my friends.

We gather as agreed in the lobby of the hotel. After deciding to stay here for dinner, we are astounded to realize that the dining room, bar, and front desk are manned by only one person. Economics have not been good since before the 2008 crisis and unemployment north of 25 percent has created an employer's job market. To make matters worse, much of the employable population left villages behind and flocked to the cities seeking work. Towns like Puenta la Reina now survive mostly because of the Camino's popularity, serving the nearly two hundred thousand pilgrims per year who pass through on their way to Santiago de Compostela. Life, it seems, has been difficult in Spain. I've noticed what I had first thought was indifference, but is more like a certain subdued resignation, a sad world-weariness about many Spanish people. As I slowly fall in love with them, they are beginning to break my heart.

Tomorrow's walk to the small city of Estella promises to be another relatively easy 22 kilometer trek through the deep countryside of Navarre. How the body does adapt. After four days on the Camino, a walk of 22 kilometers, a bit over 13 miles, is now something to be considered relatively easy. I feel strong and healthy and grateful for being so blessed. Though I cannot say what 60-years-old is supposed to feel like, I can say with certainty that I have never felt so new.

CHAPTER 4

I T'S THIS SIMPLE. Wake up, pray, stretch the body, load the pack, walk, and see what happens. I really wondered about this before I came; if there would be some unforeseen daily process revealed at the last minute just to complicate things. But as it turns out, there are only two worldly issues to consider while on the Camino: food and shelter. However as with all needs in the rhythm of the walk, both worldly and spiritual, the Camino, as pilgrims like to say, does provide. I'm reminded of how Greg and I were drawn together by its energy in the harsh winds of the Pyrenees on that first day as we both labored in the climb. I'm also reminded of the direction of the Camino, and that moving forward can often mean letting go.

After our typical pilgrim breakfast of coffee and too many carbohydrates, we pass through town, cross the bridge, and leave Puenta la Reina behind us. Given their aloofness about leaving, I'm led to believe this place resonated with me more than with my companions, though Greg insists on taking a picture of Heinrich and me with the bridge in the background. I comply despite a reflexive resistance to being photographed, which reminds me that Dianne might like to actually see a picture of me in Spain one of these days.

Soon after leaving Puenta la Reina, a light rain begins to fall as we near the village of Maneru, and reading the sky, we decide to stop and put on rain gear. As we round the corner of a building, we come upon a young woman who has the same idea, and introduce ourselves to Enisa, a Muslim pilgrim from the Isle of Wight in the UK. She has an exotic Mid-Eastern appearance, carries a quiet depth about her, and has a light accent I can't quite place. Enisa has a corporate job, and is on the Camino for two weeks, unsure of where she will stop before returning home. This is a common method of pilgrimage for Europeans, often taking several years before eventually walking the entire route.

As we resume our trek, Greg takes the lead as Heinrich and Enisa begin walking together just ahead of me. After a kilometer or so, Enisa moves ahead of Heinrich and eventually catches up to Greg who is now about a hundred meters ahead of us and walking quite briskly. I fall in step with Heinrich as our pace generally tends to match closely.

"Lovely young lady," I say. "I was beginning to wonder if she might be with us for a while."

"No," says Heinrich. "I do not believe so. She seems to be here to think about her life."

And so we walk on. We walk through easy rolling hills where the low parts of the path ahead of us will drop out of view and then reappear on the next crest. We watch as Greg and Enisa gradually pull further ahead, often lost from our sight for a time. I sense a change wind blowing through our little band of pilgrims. This happens. Nothing stays the same. It's the nature of life, and so the nature of the Way.

"It seems the Camino is drawing Greg on," I say.

"Ya, I think that it is. I had a feeling it might," Heinrich replies. "He seemed...how do you say in English...restless to me. Is that the word I want? Restless?"

"Yes," I say. "I believe that *is* the word you want."

Nearing Cirauqui, the rain has stopped and the sky is beginning to clear. We stop here for a *café con leche*. I consider Greg moving on from us and again silently wonder if our separate accommodation last night was in some way connected.

Heinrich seems to be reading my thoughts. "Perhaps we will see Greg again," he offers, "but he thinks he has only a very little time. I hope he does not push too hard and injure himself. I believe those who walk slow and steady will make it to Santiago."

We leave Cirauqui under an improving sky and make our way over the gentle undulations of the Camino toward the town of Lorca and on toward Estella, still some 14 kilometers away. Just before reaching Lorca, we arrive at a medieval bridge used only for the foot traffic of the Camino, and there taking a break on the near side of the bridge we find Enisa. We stop a moment to greet her, and ask if she has seen Greg lately.

"He's moved on ahead. I'm afraid his pace was too quick for me, but he said he would likely end his day in Estella."

Heinrich and I look at each other wordlessly, and both of us bid Enisa a *"Buen Camino."* As we leave her, I reflect on how those words serve well as either a greeting or a goodbye. Today it seems to be leaning on goodbye and as the day wears on, I sense with growing certainty that our season with Greg has passed.

We reach Estella in the mid-afternoon under a warm, bright Spanish sun. Both Heinrich and I are feeling our legs and hope to find an accommodation soon. As we walk the streets both on and off the Camino, our pace slows as we search for an *albergue* or a hostel. Ultimately, we find ourselves at the doorway to a place we have found almost by accident. It is identified only by a small shingle-style sign near the door that says "San Anton." Consulting my guidebook, I find it listed as a pension (usually rooms rented in a home). We enter a parlor area trimmed and furnished in dark woods, the decor suggesting it is a place that time forgot. Following the sound of voices up a stairway to the second floor landing, we find a short, elderly Spanish woman wearing a floral pattern house dress handing a room key to a pilgrim. She greets us with a warm smile and sparkling, laughing eyes that belie her age.

"*Buen dia senora,*" I say. "*Un doble por favor?*"

"*Si, si,*" she replies softly with a nod and slight tilt to her head as she looks away absently, then retreats into another room.

The Spanish do this. They will say yes, but then their gaze trails away as if to avoid eye contact, almost suggesting there could be complications—an unspoken "Well, yes, it is possible. We'll just have to see." She returns in a moment with a key. "*Pasaporte y Credencial?*" We hand over our documents, and again she returns to the other room. Heinrich and I chatter away about how good our showers will feel, wonder about the wifi here, and the like. She returns, hands us our passports and stamped Credencials, and says something in Spanish that I can't understand. I reply by attempting to give her money for the room, but she smiles, almost laughs, and holds up both hands saying, "*Tranquillo, tranquillo.*" I look at Heinrich.

"I think she wants us to look at the room first, then come back down and pay her," he says.

"*Si,*" she smiles, this time not looking away.

We drop our packs in the room on the next floor up, wordlessly claiming our respective beds. Heinrich suggests we wait a few minutes before we go back down to pay.

"Probably a good idea," I say smiling. "We wouldn't want to be too pushy about paying."

I offer Heinrich the use of the shower first, which he readily accepts, thanking me. As he does that, I wander back down to the old woman to pay for the room. While I'm there she insists on giving me a tour of the common areas including the upstairs parlor we are free to use. Like the rest of the home, it is dark but rather ornately decorated. Though I don't know enough about old furniture to adequately describe it, I do find it to be of exceptional quality and well cared for. I compliment her home profusely and she seems genuinely pleased.

For the remainder of the afternoon we post home and nap. I feel almost lazy despite having just walked over 22 kilometers with a pack. As I drift off, my thoughts are on the impermanence of relationships in life, and of course with Greg, our meeting, and the nature of his walk. I only wish I'd had the chance to wish him "*Buen Camino.*"

As late afternoon fades into evening, we find a restaurant on the Plaza de los Fueros. The tables are mostly empty as the locals begin to drift into the bar for tapas and drinks. We order mixed salads and grilled lamb along with a bottle of water. Heinrich stares blankly at the table, twirling an empty drinking glass with his fingertips, then straightens in his seat and clears his throat.

"I have a daughter," he says. "And I am sad because she will not speak to me."

An ice ball seems to burst in my stomach. It appears the Camino has done it again.

"I'm so sorry to hear that, Heinrich. What happened?"

"She disapproves of my choice of wife. At first, I thought perhaps she was…how do you say…influenced by her mother to not like her, but my first wife and I spoke, and she says no, it is our daughter only who does not like my wife."

"How long have you been married?" I ask.

"About four years," he replies. "My daughter thinks she is not the right one for me."

"Have they ever argued?" I ask.

"No, never. And now she has cut off talking to me. 'Go off and walk,' she told me. I sent an email to her several days ago, and as of today, still no answer."

"Heinrich, how old is your daughter?"

"She is 30 years." And waving his hand, "She thinks she knows…"

"I can so easily remember being 30," I say. "I was not doing well then—drinking like a pig, behaving badly with women. But 30 seemed so old to me then. I think I just assumed I had life figured out. Can you believe that was half our lifetimes ago?"

Heinrich smiles at this. "My God," he says.

"Heinrich my friend, it would seem the Camino has worked some magic here with you and me."

"In what way?" he asks.

"I have a daughter. And I'm sad because she won't speak to me."

"What?" Heinrich asks wide-eyed.

"Yes. And it seems the source of her upset centers on my relationship with my girlfriend."

"Oh my," Heinrich says. "You are correct, Stephen. It would seem we could be together for this reason. Thank you, Camino!" he says, now smiling again.

"There is a certain comfort in knowing we're not alone, isn't there?"

"Ya, there is. There is."

"Heinrich, are you angry with her?"

"I am," he says. "I believe she is...how do you say... unrespectful?"

"Disrespectful," I say, gently correcting. "But do you think she intends it that way?"

"No," he says carefully. "But it is how it feels to me. At my age, I believe I have a right to my life as I see it to live, and to be happy. My wife makes me happy," he insists. "Besides," he says as he lightly taps the table, "Even if I am...mistaken, then it is my own matter. Not hers."

"Does your wife know about how she feels?" I ask.

"She does. And it is a hurt to her, and so to me also."

"Women can sometimes be so competitive, Heinrich. It seems as though it's nature's way. If we could only find some way to be okay with it, then maybe we could have some peace about it. I guess like most things, it really is largely beyond our control."

"I have been very good to my daughter. She is my only child," Heinrich says. "I expect more of her. She is doing very well in all the other parts of her life, but I am disappointed with her. It is not good."

"And what did you email to her?" I ask.

"Only that I hope we can find our way through this when I return from Spain."

"Then maybe the time apart will serve you well—allow you both to cool down a little bit. I'd bet she responds to your email. Maybe she's just been busy."

"That would be a relief."

As our salads arrive, Heinrich seems more settled as he says, "My daughter's name is Johanna. And what is your daughter's name?"

"Kathryn," I reply. "She's 32."

"But she is not your only child?"

That question. "No, no she isn't. I had a son, Keith, but we lost him over five years ago," I finally tell him.

"Oh no", Heinrich says. "I am so very sorry. How old was he? What happened to him?"

"Thank you Heinrich. He was 28, and he took his own life."

My friend says nothing, but he has stopped eating and his eyes are riveted on me as I continue.

"He had an awful alcohol and drug addiction for years. He was medicating this, this inner hell that he lived with for so long. It just became so dark for him. He had tried a few times to kill himself in terrible ways, and so we all knew it wouldn't end well. It was overwhelming for him and for us, for his family. Anyway, he was living with his girlfriend at the time, and while she was out, he hung himself in their bedroom closet. She was the one who found him. I just can't imagine what it must have been like for her."

Heinrich is quiet for a moment. I can tell from the movement of his eyes, he is searching like most people do. But he, like them, finds nothing. What can one possibly say? At times like this, I think back to the wake, and the line that was so long, and all the time the people waited, each of them trying with all their might to think of something to say. They would hug me and I would look at their searching, kind faces, and tell them there was nothing they could say besides "I'm here."

"I've been through a lot in this life, Heinrich, but we are not wired to bury our children. It's a pain that lives on."

"How terrible," he says. "It must make these matters with Kathryn even more painful. She is the one who remains."

"In a way it does, yeah. But she had walked away from me and her step family many years before her brother's death. It likely would have continued if that hadn't happened. I've often thought of how hurt she must have been to have left us as she did without saying a word. My calls and emails went unanswered, so in a sense I had lost her before I lost my son. Our relationship has been troubled for some time."

"I see," says Heinrich.

"After Keith died, we came together for a while. A few years later she reached out because she was getting married. Although I had reservations, I decided to take a chance, but we never could get to that conversation I knew we needed to have. I was so willing to listen to her and to make whatever amends was needed, but it just never happened. I suppose in a way our separation was inevitable. If there hadn't been conflict around Dianne, it would have been something else. It seems we have very different views of the world."

"And what now?" Heinrich asks.

"I left it with her that I would contact her after I get home, but I have no expectations. Perhaps it's one of many things to reflect on as I walk the Meseta. I suppose I'll see what comes up then."

"I also have things to think about there," he says. I'm very much looking forward to that time."

The Spanish Meseta is a vast high plain that comprises the middle section of the Camino between the cities of Burgos and Astorga, and is still over a week away. It is relished by some and dreaded by others, breathtakingly monotonous and mostly flat with some rolling hills and notoriously little shade. Many who walk this road seek to face the Meseta alone as a form of meditation, and Heinrich and I both committed to this even before we came here. As this first part of the Camino centers on the body and its surroundings, the Meseta centers on the mind and its thoughts. It is the perfect place to, one might say, sort things out.

After a leisurely stroll around the plaza after dinner, we return to our room and after long calls home, settle in for the night. I happen to be watching in the darkened room as Heinrich checks his email, and in the white glow of his phone screen, I see him smile.

"She was just busy the last few days," he says.

Tomorrow, we walk 22 kilometers to the lonely outpost of Los Arcos, and soon after will pass out of Navarre and into the region of La Rioja.

CHAPTER 5

THOUGH ESTELLA HAD SEEMED almost deserted on Sunday, the feel of the city shifts as we make our way along crowded Monday morning streets seeking the yellow arrows of the Camino that will point us westward. Almost half of today's walking will be uphill to some extent until reaching the town of Villamayor de Monjardin, nearly 10 kilometers into the trek. Curiously, despite the fact we are in a city, there is no place open on the Camino route through town that serves food, so we'll have to delay breakfast and find a cafe along the way. It is a raw, somewhat blustery day, one that could leave us depleted. We hope to find something soon.

The Irache Monastery is about two kilometers west of Estella. Its claim to fame on the Camino is a unique fountain which dispenses both water and wine. As we arrive it occurs to me this may be the most photographed fountain along the Way. But truth be told, the wine comes forth at a trickle and requires more patience than most people have to produce any more than a glassful. As for the monastery, there are renovations underway, and the rumor is it will soon be a luxury hotel. It's a lovely spot, but because of the construction, we're not able to explore the inside of the monastery as we had hoped.

Also lacking here is food of any kind except for a vending machine located near the fountain. We press on hopefully as the Camino meanders through vineyards and fields of early-growth wheat and golden yellow mustard planted across easy sloping hillsides. I have not seen them in the same light as I did near the ruin west of Pamplona. We are becoming ever hungrier as we continue along this upward trending section of the road, but fortunately the beauty of this place with its distant snow-capped mountains distracts us from at least some of our fatigue. As we walk, I check my guidebook, and it lists a "usually closed" café in the village of Azqueta as the only possibility of finding food before reaching Monjardin. As I mention this to Heinrich, he simply replies with a wry smile, "The Camino will provide."

We finally approach Azqueta after about seven kilometers of walking, and ahead we see pilgrims clustered about the bustling, open café. Heinrich smirks just a bit and gives me an "I told you so" look as we lean our packs and sticks against the outside of the building and enter the warmly lit room. The conversation centers on trusting the Camino, and resting in that trust. Had this place been closed, we surely would have been given the energy to continue. We have little doubt of this, but it seems to be our lesson for the day and certainly a lesson of the pilgrimage itself.

The remainder of the walk today is tricky. According to our guidebooks, we will need to fill our water and get sandwiches to pack when we reach Villamayor de Monjardin, because the remaining 13 kilometers from there to Los Arcos, a walk of about four hours, are completely without services. We set off from the warmth of the café feeling hopeful and optimistic about the walk ahead.

The wind lays down as the day wears on, and the skies brighten a bit as the rawness yields to a measure of warmth. The countryside's rugged beauty proves mesmerizing, the full round crunching sound of our footsteps on the path is hypnotic, as we slowly come to realize… we are now at least two kilometers past Villamayor de Monjardin. The town was much smaller than we expected, passage of time became distorted, and we have walked right through without a thought of obtaining food or water for the long stretch ahead. We are incredulous that we have allowed this to happen. It would seem the Camino is having its way, continuing its lesson of trust. We are in the midst of a 13 kilometer stretch without services. Damned if I can see an alternative but to walk and have faith.

Five more kilometers pass as we trudge on toward Los Arcos and we jokingly fantasize about all the food we will eat when we finally arrive. It's interesting how even the perception of being deprived of something will intensify the craving. The road takes a sharp turn to the left, and before us is a rise, obscuring the view beyond the next 15 feet or so. Carried softly on the wind now facing us, and here in the middle of nowhere, we both swear we can hear the sound of really bad 1980s American rock music—the kind associated with big hair and satin jackets with the sleeves pushed up. But how could this be? We stop dead in our tracks as we share this common hallucination, looking at each other in bewilderment. Slowly, we approach the top of the rise, almost afraid of what we'll find on the other side, and there along the road is a towed-in food trailer, tables and chairs, pilgrims eating, and the bad 80s music playing. All we can do is laugh.

We arrive in Los Arcos after a brisk walk in from the oasis, and have some unexpected difficulty finding a place to sleep. We inquire at several different types of accommodations only to be told they are full, but then happen upon a private *albergue* on a small side street that is operated by an Austrian pilgrim confraternity. Heinrich is delighted to find German speaking *hospitaleros* and the atmosphere is warm and inviting.

We spend the rest of the afternoon cleaning up, washing clothes, and posting home, following the usual routine of the pilgrim day. Dinner is on the main plaza of the town in the remaining sunlight of the late afternoon. Also here on the plaza is the Iglesia de Santa Maria de Los Arcos.

The church's interior is dominated by the intricate, luminously ornate retablo behind the main altar, and in the center of it is a statue of Santa Maria. In the ceiling of the church directly above the altar, is a dome that contains several window panels, and it is said that at a certain hour on one day during the summer, the statue is perfectly illuminated by a single shaft of sunlight from the dome. There is something about this cool dark place that quiets me as I slowly walk its creaking wooden floors from the side altars and statues of the nave, up into the choir loft. I don't believe it is reverence or that old mystery of churches that inspires this, but think it has more to do with implications of time and the energies of all who have come through here. Perhaps there is even something more primitive, something I have not yet considered. As I take a seat near the back of the church, my eyes are closed and my thoughts fixed on gratitude for being here, for being on the Camino, for being with Heinrich; my prayers blending with every prayer of every pilgrim ever offered here over the past nine centuries. It feels as though I'm swirling in a vortex with all of it—not merely connected to it, but part of it. I have that odd sense there is more going on here than I'm aware of, that something mystical is happening in an inner place I can't perceive. It's not the first time I've felt this since being on the Camino, another discreet if fleeting call into the thin. Gradually my awareness returns to the surroundings. After a little while I walk over to where my friend is sitting. He is staring toward the altar, but I wonder if he actually sees anything—it's as if he is entranced. As I begin to speak to him, he startles a little and then looks to me. I tell him I'm leaving and that I'll see him back at the *albergue*. He nods absently and says, "I want to stay here for a while." I smile at him as he returns his gaze forward.

Tuesday morning dawns clear and bright after a wonderful night's sleep. We say good-bye to our friendly hosts at the Austrian *albergue*. Before leaving town, we find a café and enjoy our usual breakfast, not wanting to repeat the experience of yesterday, though it is unlikely the Camino would have allowed it. As we eat, I mention to Heinrich how deeply our time in the church last night affected me. In his reserved German way, he will only say he found it "very moving."

We begin the day's 18 kilometer walk to Viana with the still-rising sun casting long shadows before us. The wordless daily dance of finding our rhythm ensues with a random pace to start, and after a while, maybe a kilometer or so, our bodies then offer their opinions. Of course, we each have our own symptoms. If a little too slow, I get an uneasy sense of restlessness and urgency; too fast, and I develop a vague tension in the core and lower back. So the dance then involves making minute adjustments to my own pace and finally to Heinrich's as the distance between us will tend to vary a bit. It is a dance where neither leads. One simply allows. Before long, we are walking more or less together.

The road west of Los Arcos threads between expansive wheat fields and vineyards, and under a nearly cloudless sky, the walk is almost flat and absent of trees as the sun warms us through. Before too long, we find ourselves in view of the small town of Sansol, home to just over 100 people. After passing through, we immediately enter the adjacent town of Torres del Rio, only slightly larger than Sansol, said to have once been an outpost of the Knights Templar.

The landscape begins to change after a while on a long stretch after Torres del Rio. Short, stubby hills covered with scrub brush seem to dominate here, and it strikes me as being rather stark. Soon, we see the hillside town of Viana in the distance. Because our walk was quite easy today, hunger is just now beginning to settle in, so the timing is perfect.

We check in at an *albergue* / hostel and choose a double room for the night. The usual chores and lunch follow, and afterward I head to the *albergue's* common area to do laundry and post home while I wait for the wash to finish.

The internet proves painfully slow, and as I wait for uploads, I notice a young, beautiful married couple who are walking the pilgrimage with their almost one year old child. I remember seeing them once before near Alto de Perdon. The husband carries a huge pack and his wife carries the child in a papoose along with a small day pack. I can overhear their conversation with an older, weathered looking, thickly accented pilgrim from Australia. The couple sounds to be from Holland. They have walked from Saint Jean Pied de Port and the husband has developed terrible blisters—a common condition on the Camino. Two blisters are already open and raw looking, the rest are still closed. Because they are so severe, resembling burns more than blisters, he is at high risk for developing infections.

The Australian knows just what to do. Without hesitation he grabs his pack and motions the couple out into the courtyard of the common area where the light is better, and instructs the young man to have a seat. He opens an outer pocket of the pack and extracts his medical kit, the scope of which I have not seen since my days as a Navy Corpsman. It looks as though it contains enough supplies to perform surgery, and with great authority he lays out exactly what he'll need on a small table. I get the impression he's done this before.

He sits cross-legged before the young man and props a foot up on his knee, then works on the closed blisters first, prepping the skin with alcohol, threading and flaming the needle, then venting the blister. No hesitation—utterly competent, on to the next. With the closed blisters on both feet tended to, he turns his attention to the open blisters. He uses a clear solution first ("Might sting a bit, mate"), then follows with ointments and dressings. As he works so earnestly, the young man tells him how much he truly appreciates the help, that he has no idea how he would have continued.

"Well, you're welcome my friend," the Australian replies. "But it's just how it works out here on the Camino. See, two weeks from now you could find me along the side of the road out in the middle of the Meseta someplace with a rolled up ankle or some such, and I'm thinking you'll probably stop and help me out, right?"

"Of course," says the younger man.

"And even if you never see me again, but you find another broken pilgrim on the road, you'll help him out like I helped you."

"Yes I would."

The last dressing applied, the Australian stands up and smiles broadly. "Well then. *Buen Camino*, mate."

My eyes fill and I swallow hard as I seriously wonder for the very first time how it will ever be possible for me to leave this world behind. Pilgrims talk about returning to "real life" after their Camino ends, but I'm beginning to think this is the most "real" life has ever been. So what now of home?

Heinrich and I decide to spend the late afternoon exploring around Viana before heading to dinner. We find our way to the western side of the town and the ruins of the 13th century Iglesia de San Pedro. There is no roof, and only the crumbling walls have survived time, the rest left to the imagination. High on a wall behind the altar area is the vacant circular frame of what was once a rose window. I'm amazed to see how ravages of time can so closely resemble the effects of a bomb. In contrast, just outside the ruin is a beautiful, manicured park space bordered by the top of the city walls with a view westward toward Logrono. The sky is cloudless and the warmth of the afternoon sun soaks us as we both sit on the lawn, propped against an outer wall of the church. It is impossible not to doze just a little on this perfect spring day, a deep and abiding sense of well-being suffusing me on this, our last full day in the region of Navarre, and our seventh day on the Camino.

The morning sky is mostly cloudy and the day feels somewhat raw as we stop at a café before our walk toward Logrono and on to Navarette, a trek of 22 kilometers. We then follow the yellow arrows through the streets of Viana and out across a plain of vineyards. Looking back after walking a short while, I can see the entire town laid out across the hillside, and topped by the forlorn wall of the ruin of San Pedro containing the empty window—a perfect last image.

My body is adjusting seamlessly, answering the daily call to walk without complaint. I am eating anything I please and have probably lost about seven pounds in this past week. The pack has become such a part of me that it feels strange to be without it, and the sticks have become extensions of my hands. Though I've not necessarily focused on it since first observing Heinrich's graceful strides on the walk to Pamplona, I believe I may even be gliding.

After about seven kilometers of walking, we come upon a lean-to shack, where we find an elderly woman with a deeply etched face, sparkling eyes and an illuminating smile. She sells trinkets and provides water, fruit and stamps. There is a feeling here that is subtle yet profound, most certainly an energy of love, and I notice that pilgrims are lingering—a sure sign. Her *sello* reads *"Higos, Agua Y Amor"* (Figs, Water, and Love), and she places it in each pilgrim passport slowly and deliberately, smiling as she does so. Stamping my Credencial, she offers a discreet *"Buen Camino"* along with a soft yet deeply direct gaze that leaves me feeling as if I'm the only pilgrim she has seen today.

The Basque country of France and Spain is now behind us,

and we have officially entered the region of La Rioja as noted by a sign on an industrial stretch of highway that closely parallels the Camino. Before too long we approach a park along the Rio Ebro, and see a bridge ahead as well as the spires of Catedral de Santa Maria de la Redonda just beyond. We cross the bridge and begin our long walk through the streets of Logrono.

We stop at a bar along the route through the city. As we sip our *café con leche*, we note the almost even distribution of pilgrims and locals in here, and how easy it is to tell the difference. We've noticed how people in the cities tend to avoid eye contact with us, and we both wonder about this. Are they simply weary of us, or do they just think we're all crazy?

Leaving the bar, we wind our way through the stone streets of this old section of town and follow the brass scallop shells attached to the sidewalks and buildings that mark the Camino route through Logrono. Our eyes are used to the yellow arrows of the countryside and small towns and villages, so we must pay particularly close attention. A large city is not the place to get lost.

Directly ahead on a narrow street, we see a group of about 30 older Spanish tourists, men and women, gathered near a corner. Their young tour guide is speaking to them, gesturing as she describes some point of interest neither Heinrich nor I can discern. The group is large enough so that we have to pass them by staying close to the buildings on the right side of the street. Just as we approach, the guide stops speaking, seemingly in mid-sentence, and looks at us directly. Right here, I can sense it coming like a sudden change in the weather. It's gathering itself. I just know it. We both smile at her and say, "*Buenos dias.*" She smiles in return, and then her entire group, speaking in a full, single, richly layered harmonic that echoes off the stone walls, says to us, *"Buen Camino,"* as if they had been queued to do so. Somewhat startled by this, we turn toward them and can see that as they look at each other almost giggling, some of them are surprised as well. I can only think of the singular voice of my friends as we prayed together back home only a few weeks ago.

As we walk on, I say to Heinrich, "I doubt if I will ever forget that."

In a hushed voice, he replies only, "Yes."

We continue through the remainder of busy downtown Logrono, make our way through a lovely park, and leave the city by passing yet another industrial area before finally being released back into the countryside. Throughout the afternoon, our pace is relaxed as we make our way past the red earth of still-bare vineyards toward Navarette.

It is along this stretch that Heinrich and I find ourselves spontaneously discussing the nearly constant duel between goodness and malevolence which takes place within us both and (we hope) within all humans. It seems the Camino and our generally quiet walking habits have somehow brought this to our attention. They go by many names, these two: Jekyll and Hyde, Yin and Yang, and others. My German friend has come to call them Jack and Jones. I think I like these best. Although he can't explain why he gave them American names, he says he has been referring to them this way for quite some time. I tell him my Jack finds this endearing. It seems we have come to some conclusions about them.

Jack is the positive, the kind, the selfless, the loving, and tends to see goodness and the unity of things. His are the ways of gratitude and forgiveness and grace. He is also quiet, speaking only in whispers. To hear him, one must pay very close attention and have good reason to listen.

Jones, on the other hand, is negative, mean-spirited, self-centered, judgmental, quite petty, and believes that all the hurt of life is inflicted and therefore unforgivable. His voice is insistent and quite easy to hear; so easy in fact, that one could even be unconscious and still listen. Jones is an attention seeker and tends to act impulsively and without consult, leading his unwitting host into all forms of difficulty. He can also sound really, really good, appearing to be insightful, even spiritual.

Jack meanwhile, quietly waits to be recognized, knowing his time will come as he gently allows the distractions and chaotic outcomes of Jones's ways to eventually pass. Only then, in the stillness, will he clear his throat and say "Ahem," for there would be no point in speaking any sooner. Heinrich and I agree they are both very important to us. Thing is, it's a Jones kind of world. At least it has been. But this seems to be changing for both of us. The lights are being turned on, revealed in the simplicity of the walk.

I don't mean to sound so disparaging of Jones. I really don't. It's nothing personal with him. He's not out to get me. In fact, he has been my finest teacher in all the forms he's taken over these past 60 years of living. It's his purpose, every bit as divine as Jack's, to show me *this* in relation to *that*, ideas of separation his infallible instrument. He operates in the realm of fear, which works out nicely because humans are pretty well wired that way, even and maybe most especially the courageous ones.

Obviously, I prefer Jack even though they both share my very thoughts. His is the way of love, and in this world things are usually pretty well stacked against him. Long ago, I made it a daily habit of aligning myself with Jack before leaving home, siding with love, compassion, kindness, patience and grace. Yet 20 minutes later, I'll find myself judging the slow-poke in front of me who is trying to rob me of my rightful place a quarter mile further down the road. It seems the game is rigged. I get caught up. I lose my way.

As mentioned before, life is pretty simple for a pilgrim on the Camino de Santiago. There are minimal distractions other than the odd fearful or worrisome observation offered by Jones, and even those have been kindly absorbed into a growing notion that all really is well. As my senses clear, I'm coming to believe Jack may actually have an advantage out here. I recall the days since leaving Saint Jean Pied de Port and can see his lovely influence in everything and in every step.

Before I came here, it almost always had to be pain. Pain in the form of addiction, loss, sadness, worry, rage, or a hundred other means of self-crucifixion that had to be experienced before there could be a resurrection, an awakening, a rising-up from the wreckage of consequence that would eventually allow for light and peace. Now, in the absence of all the clutter and the quieting of the ego, it seems I am being shown another way to this. I am being shown another prayer, and it is a prayer one is most apt to learn in life's later years. It is spoken in a voice now heard more easily on the fragrant breezes of the Camino, rolling across endless fields from distant mountains, and in Grace it is becoming more and more my own. In this new prayer are my hope and my heart's desire to bring this home and keep it with me forever and forever.

And in his own way, Heinrich finds himself in a similar place, fundamentally at peace and in love with life itself. We have been drawn together by something greater. We will keep walking together for a time and maybe speak of things like Jack and Jones. My reserved German friend will sing random lines from not-so-great songs and tell stories about playing the drums with his band. In the meantime, his very presence will speak to my Soul. Soon enough it will be time to walk alone.

For now, it is on to Navarrete.

CHAPTER 6

NAVARRETE IS A CHARMING TOWN arranged in semi-circular fashion around the base of a hill once topped by a castle. As in virtually all Spanish towns regardless of the layout, its center is found at the church. Iglesia de La Asuncion, built during the 16th and 17th centuries, is best known for its implausibly intricate gold Baroque retablo behind the main altar. My guidebook says there is a way to illuminate it for the humble price of one Euro, but we can't seem to find how this works. As we walk through the dimly lit sanctuary, neither Heinrich nor I feel particularly touched as we did two nights ago in Los Arcos. Perhaps a place can be too elaborate to inspire, too mercenary by charging for light.

Our hotel is one of the better places we've stayed, with a spacious double room on the second floor overlooking a quaint narrow street, and fast wifi. Today is not a laundry day, so after a soothing hot shower I'm able to call Dianne as she goes to work, catch up on posting, and take a nap before it's time for dinner. Other than one brief exploration through town in search of an ATM, we decide to stay in for the evening. As we lounge in the room chatting about the day just passed, we develop a general walking strategy for the remainder of our journey together to Burgos, and begin to speak more about what lies beyond. It's good to broach the subject openly at last.

We already know tomorrow's walk of 17 kilometers will be to Najera. Following that, we agree on stops in Santo Domingo de la Calzada, Belorado, Villafranca Montes de Oca, then on to Atapuerca at the edge of the Matagrande Plain. For our final day of walking together, we'll cross the Plain to the city of Burgos, gateway to the vast, open Meseta. We each plan to check into a couple of high end hotels for a well-deserved rest day on our own before we begin to walk in our solitude.

Heinrich strokes the 10 day stubble on his cheek. "I will have a hot shave and it will be so wonderful," he says, drawing out the word *so*. "The towels will be almost too hot, and then will be the warm cream and ah, the long blade...how do you say?"

"A straight razor."

"Yes yes! And then I will have a massage."

"And will that massage be from a woman or a man?" I ask, smiling.

"Oh it must be from a woman, Stephen. A dark, Spanish woman. Ha!"

"So Heinrich, other than indulging in hedonism, are there any other plans for Burgos?"

"I will see the Cathedral, of course. My guidebook says something about a museum of human history. I might look into that. I am not really sure. I may ask at the hotel about the bullfights. I've never seen one. And what of your plans?"

"The Cathedral is the main thing for me, and there is a castle on a hilltop that supposedly has some spectacular views where you can look west to the Meseta."

"Yes. The Meseta. Stephen, I have no idea what I will find there," Heinrich says wistfully.

"Who can know, my friend? If this pilgrimage has shown us anything, we can only trust it will be perfect."

"I am very happy we have walked together."

"Me too," I say. "It seems we both know when to be quiet—when it's okay to let the Camino fill in the spaces."

"Thank God we have some more days on the road together."

"Thank God indeed."

After a restful sleep, we wake somewhat later than usual to a perfect spring day. We take our time preparing and packing, find a cafe for our usual breakfast, and head out onto the Camino for a leisurely day of walking through wine country.

The vineyard's thick red earth holds only a promise of grapes during the early spring in the La Rioja region. In the warmer months, pilgrims passing through will make a habit of picking the vines closest to the path almost clean. The farmers have come to expect it after centuries of summers. It is their long-standing allowance to the Camino and those who walk it, their tacit agreement with this fertile ground. It's this sort of give and take that appeals to me. Everything here has its place. Everything belongs—the rains of spring and the searing heat of the Spanish summer sun, the grapes that find their way to ferment in the casks, and those that feed the hungry, thirsty pilgrims of August. It is in the enduring simplicity of life along the Way that belonging is revealed. And I belong as well.

We walk through the ubiquitous early wheat and mustard fields, through the latent vineyards, and past nameless hamlets, stopping in Ventosa for lunch before continuing on toward Najera. It's mostly a wordless day for us as we march along to the soft crunching of the Camino underfoot and the tapping of our sticks—the rhythms of the walk itself. My body feels aligned with its movement over ground today, and the cool breeze and warm sun comfort me. The clouds are widely spaced this afternoon, and as we look west from the higher ridgelines, we see endless views of valleys and hills mottled by the shadows from the clouds. Sunlight reveals a patchwork of infinite greens and yellows. In shaded light, the red tones in the clay turn to purple.

I suppose it's unavoidable, but towns everywhere seem to present their uglier side first, as industry tends to be on the outskirts. Najera is no exception as it reveals a series of what appear to be stone processing and chemical plants as well as grain elevators. Sometimes, as we approach a smaller town, we will hear the nightmarish sounds of a slaughterhouse, so I'll count my blessings here.

We enter Najera, and after walking only 17 kilometers, we are in no real hurry to check in to our hostel. This is a lovely town, arranged in two sections east and west of the Rio Najerilla, and after walking through the eastern half, we cross a bridge over the fast moving river swollen by spring rains and runoff. From here, we see how the buildings of the western section of town dramatically abut sheer red cliffs that tower over them. This place certainly has the most striking appearance of any of the Camino towns we've seen so far.

This section of Najera is clearly the center of activity. Bars and restaurants are all open, crowds choke the streets, and it's difficult to navigate wearing our bulky packs. I check the time and see it's just past 3:00PM, which causes some confusion. The streets should be deserted, businesses closed—this is peak *siesta* time. Just as we realize this, we hear a marching band, and after rounding a corner we find they are coming straight for us! After ducking into a doorway, I see Heinrich plastered against a building across the street. As the band passes us, we shrug at each other and join the crowd following them as they march to the plaza. My friend loves music, pretty much any kind, and is beside himself that it would seem we have happened upon a festival. I had not yet seen him smile like this.

After spending the better part of an hour finding our hostel which is located back across the river, we shower, post home, and head out for an early, pilgrim-menu dinner. By dusk, the festival on the Plaza de Espagna is in full swing and is officially about a celebration of international music. Despite the chill in the early evening springtime air, we find ourselves eating ice cream cones as we wander through the crowd.

Two sides of the roughly triangular plaza are mostly bordered by shops, bars, and restaurants. The third side is formed by the Monasterio de Santa Maria la Real, built during the 11th century by King Garcia III. It consists of a church and cloister, and contains the tombs of the King and his wife. The church's elegantly lit rugged brown stone walls sharply contrast against the deepening blue of the western sky, its tired light bleeding off behind the cliffs.

The crowds thin as we move away from the plaza and circuitously work our way to the hostel. We pass street vendors, stores, bars, and a human statue who will smile for a one Euro coin. It's dark now and our internal pilgrim clocks are telling us to lie down. We know better than to resist. We've learned well to listen to our bodies. Tomorrow we walk 21 kilometers to Santo Domingo de la Calzada, and a cathedral that houses live chickens.

Heinrich and I both like to sleep with the window cracked, which, when I think about it, is a really important point of compatibility after a week of sharing a room. The early morning of April 29th starts cold. It is chilly. It is bracing. It is crisp. It is brisk. But according to Heinrich, it is...*fresh*. How he came up with this word in English I can't say, but it's *his* word for what it is today. He uses it a lot. It's been fresh most mornings on the Camino so far. I try to correct him by repeating it using a more appropriate term.

"Yes," I say, "it is quite chilly indeed."

"Ya," he says nodding and smiling, "very fresh. We'll need jackets to start today."

After checking out of the hostel, we step out into the street on a sunny and, okay, fresh day, as we find our way across the river and to a café for breakfast. Here we meet a beautiful young Dutch woman whom Heinrich met on the first day in the Pyrenees and has not seen since. She tells us how she became injured, hyper-extending a ligament in her knee while walking between Zubiri and Pamplona. Still in pain and wearing a brace, she is only now able to walk on it to any degree. Her plan is to take another rest day here before attempting to continue. She took a bus from Pamplona to meet her friends, but they've already gone ahead so she'll have to catch up with them gradually.

For so many, it seems the Camino experience involves measures of physical suffering, and to be injured this far from home can be so frightful. But she smiles freely as she speaks to us and talks about feeling thankful for her improvement and her hope that she will resume walking tomorrow. I would not presume to know what the Camino was trying to show her in all this, but I do know how I feel for having met her. I tend to be judgmental of the young. I suppose this can happen as one ages, but her courage and grace have given me pause. Saying goodbye to her, we offer our assurance that, as always, the Camino will provide, especially for one who shows such bravery. As we follow the yellow arrows through Najera, I'm reminded that somewhere along the way today we will pass beyond 200 kilometers of walking. Both of our bodies are completely without pain.

We climb sharply through a high pass in the cliffs and the exertion has us both sweating as we clear through the top. No longer feeling "fresh," we pause to stow our jackets. Looking west from the ridgeline beyond the cliffs, we see the Camino as it threads through the farmland ahead. We descend onto the plains and look to the south, past the lush fields of green wheat and low hillsides of red clay. Beyond, we see snow-capped mountains that will be in sight all the way to Santo Domingo.

The walk today has a lonely, remote, isolated feel and the views are long and wide. Other than the small town of Azofra and the ghost town of Ciruena, there will be no other significant outposts along the way. The mustard plants, though still bright yellow in the sunlight, are slowly fading from their brilliant gold of only a week ago. The bare red soil of the vineyards is empty, the wheat still green. Here, it is the energy of waiting and of change and of new things still to come.

We stop in Azofra, a nondescript little Camino village, for a hearty lunch of *bocadillos* and Cokes, eating outside and feeling warmed in the midday sun. We are enjoying yet another day of spectacular weather, and I've been reluctant to share this with Dianne. It has been Seattle-like in Connecticut for the past two weeks—pretty much solid rain. Here, the locals tell us we're fortunate to be having this beautiful weather now, because during the previous weeks it rained almost every day. Other than a passing shower, the only severe rain I've experienced was on that first day in France.

As we cross the plains, we notice the storks. More and more frequently, we see nests built on high structures, typically church bell towers. We have even been lucky enough to watch these substantial birds gather sticks and fallen branches, then fly in circular patterns upward to place them at the nest. Each spring, some of them return from places like Morocco and Algeria to breed in northern Spain. But others are staying throughout the year though the reasons for this are unclear.

About ten kilometers past Azofra we come upon Ciruena, a ghost town cruelly located adjacent to a thriving, luxurious country club. It has a post-apocalyptic feel with deserted streets, modern yet abandoned shuttered homes and large apartment buildings. Some are completely built, others only partially so. The streets are paved and have light poles installed, even where they pass through empty lots. We look for clues if anyone has lived here, but can find none. Supposedly, this tragic place is an effect of the collapsed housing market some years before. Further on, as we approach the older part of town, some of the buildings are falling-in, essentially in ruins. But there are more buildings that are intact and appear lived-in. We can both feel it in the air—the energy of failed dreams and sadness, disappointment and decay. For both of us there is an urgent need to leave immediately, and stepping up our pace we escape to the plains of LaRioja.

After another five kilometers, Santo Domingo de la Calzada comes into view, a place associated with one of the more colorful Camino tales.

This story dates from the 14th century, almost 200 years after Domingo's death. It strikes me as likely one of the more fantastical tales of the Camino.

A young German named Hugonell was on pilgrimage to Santiago with his mother and father, and passing through Santo Domingo they stayed overnight with a farmer's family. The daughter of the farmer promptly became enamored of the young man, and attempted to seduce him. Apparently Hugonell was a serious and pious pilgrim, and resisted her advances. This did not sit well with the daughter who then plotted her revenge for this grievous rejection. She secretly placed some of her family's silver items in his bag, reported the false larceny to the authorities, and accused the German boy of stealing them. When the items were found in his possession he was convicted of theft, a crime which in 14Th century Spain was punished by hanging. For good measure, the bodies of thieves were left to rot on the gallows as a warning to others. His poor parents, stricken in their grief, continued on their pilgrimage to Santiago de Compostela.

On their return trip, they stopped again in Santo Domingo to visit the remains of their son, but were shocked and delighted…to find him alive! He claimed Saint Dominic had held him up, and so did not die. The parents went immediately to see the magistrate, beseeching him to cut Hugonell down for clearly he must be innocent. The magistrate, who had just sat down to eat a sumptuous dinner of roasted chickens, cried, "He is no more alive than these chickens I'm about to eat!" At this, both chickens stood up, came to life feathers and all, and ran off the table.

In honor of this legend, live chickens, said to be descendants of the resurrected fowl, are kept in the Catedral de Santo Domingo, and a piece of the gallows is displayed above the tomb of Saint Dominic.

I have previously referred to myself as a "cradle" Catholic, meaning I was baptized before the age of consent. I don't want to sound so accusatory about this. I'm presently of the belief that we are spiritually complicit regarding the general path of our life experience prior to showing up here. I also believe this religion was my given compass point on the journey through life, a waymark on the road back home. It has shown me that light is perceived best from shadows, the darker the better. Though I wish we'd parted on better terms, I left the practice of Catholicism at the age of 14. I'd had enough. Enough of the attempted sexual abuses (three I can recall), enough of the perceived hypocrisy, enough of the grammar school years of mental, emotional, and physical cruelties, enough of the insincerities of most of the clergy as they "performed" at Mass (I was an altar boy, privy to views beyond the congregation's). All of this was a bit too much for me to wrap my 14 year old head around. So in my immaturity, I fled though with no real place to go. As long as the mostly vague idea of *God* was connected to this particular idea of *Religion*, there would be confusion and hurt for me, and a lingering deep disappointment for my very devout parents, who thought that passing on their Faith to me was the gift of salvation itself.

This prior experience of Catholicism was almost entirely in the company of the Dominican Order, the Order of Preachers. Though it was founded by another Saint Dominic of Spain, a Castilian priest, it seems the name itself has triggered some memories of the religion that apparently still linger with me. I'm genuinely surprised by this. Having been under the impression I'd long ago resolved such matters in the spirit of *live and let live*, the Camino now begs to differ. As I near this place, resentment is waking up. Time for another, deeper look it would seem.

Our accommodation in town, the place where I, not Heinrich, made an on-line reservation, is operated by an order of nuns. The place is immaculate, in fact, sterile—the picture of perfect order. After checking us in, the nun at the front desk informs us, mostly in Spanish, of the hotel rules and procedures. As I glaze over, I travel back to long ago, to the troubles.

The Catholic nuns of my youth were creatures of mystery. Their very bodies, covered except for faces and hands, inspired great curiosity. What of their arms or necks or hair? Their habits were of a heavy linen material, white in the case of Dominican nuns, ankle length with a thick black leather belt at the waist that held an impossibly large rosary. One particularly stout nun would absent-mindedly swing her rosary like a lasso as she walked the front of the classroom or the recess yard, almost implying it could double as a weapon.

I wondered about life in that convent of theirs. Did they cook and eat like us? Did they do housework? Did they have a doctor? Did they smoke cigarettes like most adults? And how did they not have babies? Was not having a baby an act of God? Was it like Mary, only different? A few of them drove, and one even played basketball with the boys. A couple of them played the piano. But generally, they seemed removed from the rest of society and unto themselves.

The names of Dominican nuns all began with "Mary"; Sister Mary Theresa for example. I never knew of any last names, nor do I recall ever inquiring. During my eight years of grammar school, there were five of them: Sister Mary first grade, Sister Mary second grade (the stout one), Sister Mary fourth grade, Sister Mary seventh grade, and Sister Mary eighth grade. They were partial to corporal punishment (rulers on the hands, yard-sticks on the buttocks, occasional open-handed slaps to the face and one close fisted punch), though Sister Mary eighth grade was old and tired and rarely played that card. Punishments both corporal and psychological were always administered in public, before the entire class. Guilt, shame, humiliation, and fear were the tools of the trade. Complaints at home about such things were pointless for these were women of God, and usually answered with stories of even worse punishment both received and witnessed "back in the old days." Generations of children were indoctrinated to Catholicism and domesticated into life this way. How differently this could have been handled if Jack's voice had been heard, but Jones ruled the day. I'd have to assume things have since changed. Today, these women would either find themselves under arrest, or more hopefully man-dated to some form of treatment. Things gradually do evolve.

Be kind, for everyone you meet is fighting a hard battle...
Ian Maclaren

The nun at the front desk is done with us. The rules and procedures have been explained, and we are dismissed to go up to our room. As we walk away, I ask Heinrich if my glazing-over was obvious. He assures me it was not. Once safely inside the elevator, I ask if he has any idea what the nun said to us. He shakes his head. I suppose we have no choice but to be on our very finest behavior and hope for the best.

Today is a wash day. After cleaning clothes and ourselves, we venture out into town to explore Santo Domingo de la Calzada, check out the chickens in the Cathedral, and at Heinrich's request, splurge on a truly fine dinner. This is a beautiful Camino town, clean and friendly with a wonderful energy. I'm disappointed to find we can't gain access to the Cathedral during its usual open hours this evening because there is a double funeral being conducted. I had hoped to post pictures of the blessed chickens.

As we stroll the streets, Heinrich notices an upscale restaurant, and there we tuck into a lovely dinner of grilled lamb, *paella*, and vegetables. Our bill for everything including dessert is about 50 Euros for both of us, and tipping in excess of 10% in Spain is considered a sign of social ignorance. I could get used to this.

Sleep reluctantly settles over me. I lie in the darkened room at the nun's hotel and consider the day now passing. It's been interesting. Not the most pleasant, but interesting. The

73

Camino has blindsided me with memory. It is its perfect way. I thought it was all behind me, but apparently not. Deep shadows remain, and they belong. They will show me to light and all will be well because the pilgrimage will insist on it. It has a thing to show me. It simply must.

This is how it works here. Early on is the season to become aware. Next is the season to reflect, and then to resolve. And so surely it will be, though further on.

CHAPTER 7

VIGILANT STORKS OCCUPY a few sturdy nests high atop steel poles and bid us a reticent farewell as we leave Santo Domingo de la Calzada. They regard us as we pass beneath them as aristocracy might. Their height is a distinct advantage, their noble profiles quite obvious. If I was gifted enough to speak in the language of storks, I might greet them with a question, maybe something like this: "So what exactly is it that brings you here all the way from the north of Africa?" Were they to reply, I imagine they would say, "We simply follow our bliss."

The sky is nearly cloudless, the air crisp, and the day itself is full of promise and hope as we find our pace on the way to Belorado. Sleep ultimately relented and allowed me in last night, and I have not felt this well rested for days.

About six kilometers after leaving Santo Domingo, the Camino veers a bit south, sliding away from the busy roadway toward Granon. We walk through, observing a simple place, a plain cluster of housing in the midst of expansive farmland. As in so many of the small towns and villages like this we've seen along the path, we find mostly older men and women tending to their backyard gardens, going to the market, or talking in small groups in front of their houses. Always absent are the young, having left these places long ago in the hope of finding something better. After stopping for a *café con leche* near the plaza, we follow the main street out of town and back to the countryside.

Before resuming its proximity to the highway, the Camino zigzags a bit, and contained in my view for a time, I see between one and two kilometers of the path's blond dirt ahead as it courses through the deep green slopes. All along its track are pilgrims, perhaps 30 or so in small clusters or alone, spread-out and moving westward. For just a bare moment, for just the briefest fraction-of-a-footstep-on-a-Morris road of a moment, I see it all differently. No longer do I see pilgrims, I see pilgrimage; a movement toward something, a movement away, a movement of Grace. I realize in this moment I am not apart from them, or they from me. I am in no way living in opposition to them. I *am* them. And in the larger context of life beyond the Camino, all the competing needs and desires, all the conflicting interests, all the wounds inflicted and received, all the differences of body and thought and language and most certainly of religion, are revealed as only mistaken notions of things. Elegies of separation become expressions of compassionate oneness along this thin, magical road to Santiago. Realization loves to dance here, to be glimpsed even if only in the briefest of flashes.

We soon enter the huge autonomous region of Castilla Y Leon, the largest in all of Spain. The Camino will cross this region for 400 kilometers, encompassing roughly half of the entire pilgrimage route and all of the Meseta. For now, the vineyards and the landscape of La Rioja are behind us, and there are fewer trees in this wide open country. There is green wheat here of course, and vast open fields that will yield corn in the summer. It looks much as I imagine the Meseta will be. Low broken clouds mottle the land all around as we pass through the villages of Redecilla and Castildelgado, both quite similar to Granon. Nearly 13 kilometers have passed since Santo Domingo, about four hours of walking on this mostly flat landscape. Though it has been easy, the steps and the pack take a toll, and an extended break will soon be welcome.

Within a kilometer of leaving Castildelgado, the Camino again leans away toward the south from the N-120 and we approach the small, nondescript town of Viloria de la Rioja. We look carefully, but can find nothing here to indicate that this is the birthplace of Domingo de la Calzada. His home was demolished, and all that remains of his life here is the font where he was baptized early in the 11th century. There are no signs proclaiming him, no Iglesia de Santo Domingo. Were it not for my guidebook, I'd never have known.

Viloria de la Rioja ultimately redeems itself in the form of a devoted older Spanish woman who cooks and provides beds for the simple love of pilgrims. She operates a café on the ground floor of her rustic *albergue*. She works steadily but not quickly, and with a thin smile that expresses mostly in her eyes. The woman seems to be in a state of peace and muted joy; in quiet service to the pilgrims she meets. As she hands us our plates, she smiles more broadly, and when I ask how much, she gestures toward a small box labeled "donativo." She charges in the same way for her beds upstairs. As we eat with a group of Australians, laughing and trading our stories of the road, I notice her as she cleans up in the open kitchen area, often looking our way and softly regarding us all.

For the rest of today's walk to Belorado, a distance of about 10 kilometers, we remain directly alongside the constant hissing chant of tires-on-pavement that is the N-120. The road is heavily traveled and we had been warned of this. The highway is always on our right, with endless expanses of wheat and bare earth to the left. Occasional relief from the nearly incessant noise from the road is offered by the tapping of the sticks, and that old faithful round crunching sound of our shoes on the path.

After leaving Villamayor del Rio, we have five monotonously straight kilometers before arriving in Belorado. I see a pilgrim about a hundred meters ahead. His gait is chaotic and quite unlike anything I've ever seen. Though he is still distant, I can tell he is probably an older man who seems to be somewhat heavyset, and is wearing a pack a bit larger than most. He swings his hips wildly as if both are in equal need of replacement surgery. The momentum of his swinging hips forces his upper body to rock from side to side in a jerking movement, with the appearance of all this likely exaggerated by his pack. The difference in our pace allows us to close quickly on him. Now I can see the movement of his sticks, which seem to be flailing in some sort of frantic effort by him to remain upright. He appears to be on the verge of toppling over.

My steps bring me closer still and then I can see the finer details of his walk. He is mesmerizing. The movements of his body are one thing, but his use of the sticks is something else entirely. He is not flailing away by any means. His economy of movement allows them to be used both for balance and for drive. The placement of each stick is purposeful and precise, unique to right and left, exactly the same for every step. He is an absolute master of his walk. As I draw to him I notice his pack is old and worn, as are his clothes and wide brimmed hat. Even the scallop shell attached with a leather strand wears the grime of the road. He's been here before, and I wonder how many times he's walked to Santiago. I anticipate that as I pass by, I will see a face contorted by all the pain I've assigned him. Just off his right shoulder now, he hears my footsteps and begins to turn his head toward me.

"*Hola!*" I say. "*Buenos dias. Buen Camino!*"

Now I can see his face fully, weathered and old and olive toned with deep creases and surprisingly, pale blue eyes that shimmer and dance as he grins at me.

"*Buen Camino!*" he says almost laughing.

"How are you today my friend?" I ask in English to see if more conversation is possible, desperately wanting to know more about him. "Where are you walking?"

He only smiles and nods in return, so I'm left to wonder as I walk ahead.

> "*Isn't it interesting how it looked to be nothing other than chaos and pain, and yet all the while there was only the perfection of his walk?*"
> "*Yes. Yes it is. When will I ever learn?*"

We are relieved to finally arrive in Belorado. More storks nesting on the various levels of a church tower welcome us to town as we make our way to the main plaza for a planned rendezvous. Three nights ago while in Navarette, I had mistakenly booked a room on-line in a hotel *rustica* which on closer inspection was located *near* Belorado but off the Camino. I called right away to cancel and spoke to Alma, who operates the small hotel with her mother. Her English was about as good as my Spanish, but somehow we managed a conversation. She told me to call her from the plaza when we arrive. She'd come pick us up and then return us to the same spot after we check out the following morning. I had misgivings about the arrangement, but in the worst case there would likely be *albergue* beds available in Belorado.

With some apprehension I call, and 10 minutes later she is driving us to her hotel about six kilometers away. Alma, pretty and earthy in her early 30s, shows us around the warm, inviting dining area and living room of stone walls and wooden beams and floors. The aromas of dinner cooking waft through the air. We meet her mother who comes out of the kitchen to greet us. As Alma hands us the room key, she suggests we get go freshen-up for now, and check in later.

Heinrich walks into the rustic, wood paneled room first, goes to the window, and quietly says, "Stephen, you must come and look at this."

I drop my pack on a chair and join him at the window. In the immediate foreground, I see the tiny hamlet and lush pastures we just came through from the main road, and beyond are some low-lying wooded hills slowly coming into a spring bloom. In the distance, perhaps five or six kilometers away, are tall, jagged mountains, still snow covered now in late April, their very tops just lost into a low overcast sky.

"I do not believe," says Heinrich, "that you made any mistake by booking this room for us."

There are four other guests in the hotel tonight, two French gentlemen as well as a married couple from Seattle, and everyone is a pilgrim. We're all staying in for dinner and agree it was the aroma that sold us. We are eating essentially peasant food, but it is beyond delicious— a lightly spiced potato soup for starters, beautifully seasoned baked chicken with vegetables, and for dessert, *flan* (think *crème brule*). Because there are only six of us, seconds are offered.

After a stroll around the hamlet after dinner, Heinrich and I decide to read and post home as we settle into the warm, snug living room where a fire burns, suppressing an evening chill. The tempered glow of the fire sets the earthy tones of the room, the family photos in wooden frames, the objects so carefully gathered and placed, into my memory forever. There is a feeling here that summons a sense of belonging and familiarity. I think of Dianne so far away and how enchanted she would be with this place. It will likely be difficult to leave in the morning.

After breakfast Alma checks her other guests out, then returns us to the main plaza in Belorado. She hugs us both warmly, wishes us *"Buen Camino,"* and is on her way. Heinrich and I agree that her small hotel *rustica* in the hamlet of Quintanilla del Monte en Rioja has been our most comfortable and memorable accommodation on the Camino so far. It was good to be home for a night.

Today we are walking only 12 kilometers to the small town of Villafranca Montes de Oca on another perfect day that is warming nicely and with just the right amount of fair weather clouds above. We needed to do a short leg before Burgos to avoid a walk of over 30 kilometers, and felt today, Sunday, would be best for an easy walk because it's the one day of the week when services can be spotty.

The Camino first brings us through Tosantos, a 10th century village with a population of less than 60. Its name is derived from the phrase *todos los santos* (all of the saints). As we leave, we see cliffs just to the north that contain numerous caves carved impossibly high into the rock, clearly visible from the path. Supposedly they were once occupied by saintly hermits. One cave, an *ermita* (hermitage), actually has the façade of a typical church, and was constructed to honor a legend of this cave. In the eighth century it was used to hide an image of the child Jesus from invading Muslims. The image still exists today. It is kept in the *ermita* during the winter months and at San Esteban in summer.

We continue through the familiar terrain of gentle hills, green wheat and still-empty fields that roll off to the horizon, walking easily as seasoned pilgrims would on this, our 12th day on the Camino de Santiago. The path again drifts to the south and away from its proximity to the roadway, alerting us to our arrival in Villambistia. In the center of the village there is a fountain with a story that reminds us how easily a legend can develop here in Spain. My guide book states that immersing our heads in this fountain will cure us of tiredness, and suggests we try! I think we can take it on "faith" that dunking our warm heads in cold water would be a stimulating experience.

After leaving the next hamlet of Espinosa, and with Villafranca in sight a kilometer to our south, we come upon a ruin directly next to the Camino at the edge of a large wheat field. At first glance, it looks like a pile of rocks topped by grass. But as we walk around the remains of the place we find an arched, gated entranceway. The entire structure has a footprint of perhaps 30 by 30 feet and is no more than 20 feet high. It is all that remains of a 9th century Mozarabic monastery, a relic of Christianity under Moorish rule, and only the corner section of a much larger complex of buildings. I listen closely as the wind blows through this isolated ruin that continues to bear witness to the passing of four hundred thousand days. There is a lonesome ancient song that echoes here as I contemplate its age, and the countless footsteps that have passed it on the road to Santiago. Time again joins me to that thin, delicate energy that ambles through this land of very old things, and consigns me to a deepening sense of humility.

Our accommodation in Villafranca Montes de Oca is the latest incarnation of a storied place in Camino history. Its origins date back to the 13th century as a place of rest and healing for pilgrims. It has been modified and enlarged several times, most recently in the past few years. Now known as San Antonio Abad Hotel and Albergue, it is decidedly upscale which surprises us both.

We enter the crowded lobby and make our way to the desk.

"*Buenos dias*," I say to the smartly dressed, attractive middle aged woman.

"*Buenos dias. Tu nombre, por favor.*" I give her my name as she consults the computer screen.

She looks at Heinrich, then at me, and seems puzzled. "You are together?" she asks in serviceable English.

"We are. Is there a problem?"

Her gaze fades from me in that Spanish way as she says looking back to the screen, "Yes, it is possible."

I look over at Heinrich.

"It appears," she says tentatively, "that the room we have for you has one bed only, a double."

"Is there another room?"

"No. *Completo* today. The hotel is full."

"Are there beds in the *albergue?*"

"*Completo*," she says.

"Is a cot available?"

"We have none," she replies.

I turn to Heinrich. "Do you want to look around for other beds in town?"

Before he can answer, the woman tells us if we leave, she can't hold our bed because of the demand for rooms today.

"We'll take it," I say.

Heinrich clears his throat. "Ah, Stephen?" He looks concerned. Gravely.

The woman and I continue our transaction as she takes my passport and payment. I'm trying not to laugh.

"Heinrich, my friend. All is well. I've become very fond of you, but I have no intention of sharing a bed with you. You're simply not my type. I have an idea."

We finish our business at the desk and leave with our key.

"I propose we strip the bed of blankets and pillows, make a bed on the floor for me. You can have the mattress and use your sleeping bag."

He looks at me blankly. "I cannot let you do that," he says.

"Sure you can. It's a gift for me to do this, and don't forget I made the call on taking the room. My pleasure, really."

The following morning, I require more than the usual stretching to work out the kinks after attempting to sleep on the floor. There was little to be had. Breakfast proves to be our best yet, an American style buffet of eggs, bacon, sausage, and pastries. I load up my plate as I trade lost sleep for calories.

Today, our penultimate day together, Heinrich and I will walk just over 18 kilometers through the once dreaded Oca hills to the outpost of Atapuerca at the edge of the Matagrande plain. Again, we are enjoying perfect weather under a warm sun with gentle breezes and the bluest cloudless sky to round-out the atmosphere for a wonderful day of walking. We leave the San Antonio Abad through the courtyard and directly onto the Camino which immediately launches into the steepest climb we have seen in days.

Our climb continues for about five kilometers, and though the ascent does flatten somewhat, we need frequent water breaks. Walking the Oca hills was a terrifying prospect for medieval pilgrims. The geography here supported ambush, and thievery was commonplace. During the late 1930s, the hills served as a dumping ground for the bodies of Franco supporters who were killed in the area. The Camino leads us through seemingly enchanted pine forests with a whimsical patchy undergrowth of wild lavender. After about 12 kilometers of walking, we descend from the hills into the hamlet of San Juan de Ortega which consists of a church, an *albergue*, and a café that all border a plaza.

After eating, we explore the Iglesia de San Juan de Ortega where the saint's tomb is located. As a young man, Juan Velaquez became a disciple of Domingo de la Calzada. Together they constructed several bridges along the Camino. After the death of Domingo, Juan went on pilgrimage to the Holy Land and as he returned, became shipwrecked. He was spared, and in gratitude he gave the remainder of his life in service to the Camino, developing the route through the dangerous Oca hills from Villafranca to Burgos. He was also responsible for the opening of a pilgrim hospice where the hamlet is located today, and is considered the patron saint of innkeepers.

Feeling rejuvenated after a long stop and lunch, Heinrich and I continue along the Camino through more forest before it opens into a beautiful countryside of wheat and fading mustard fields. We pass through the village of Ages, then towards our last overnight stop together in the small town of Atapuerca. We check into a *casa rural* near the top of a rise at the northern edge of town, just across from the Iglesia de San Martin Obispo. Tomorrow, it is Burgos at last.

And once again the change winds blow. Feeling restless after dinner, I go for a walk past the church and toward the crest of the rise. I sit against a stone wall looking to the plains north and west. The shadows draw long, and the light shifts to the brick red of evening just before the sun sets as a sweet melancholy settles in. The familiar themes are with me: The Camino goes forward. It teaches the high station of letting go. It brings together. It separates. It advises a purposeful movement to the west always, never to the east. Soon it will be time again to add another pearl to a 60 year string of goodbyes, at least this time with no hard feelings. More than anything else, walking beside Heinrich has been about a brotherhood of companionship, little need for words, and the simple, shared experience of learning to walk this road and to make our way. Tomorrow we will part, and alone go deeper into the interior of things.

The room is dark, lit only with the light from the cracked bathroom door.

"Goodnight, Stephen."

"Goodnight, Heinrich."

Our final day together, a Tuesday, dawns cold and breezy under another perfect azure sky. We wake up early as Heinrich pokes his head out of the small window and declares the air to be...fresh. Feeling the excitement of another beautiful day of walking, we leave the hotel early and backtrack through town for a half kilometer or so to a café we noticed on the way in yesterday. After two full weeks of walking from Saint Jean Pied de Port, we are looking forward to a full day of rest tomorrow. Heinrich has been fixated on a hot shave for days now, and I'm looking forward to visiting the Cathedral in Burgos. But before us are 20 kilometers and our final experience of walking together.

After breakfast, we leave along the main street and begin one last difficult climb together, a steep and rocky haul of about two kilometers to the top before it finally plateaus. At the western side of the summit, we view the remainder of the day's trek. Laid out before us is the entire expanse of the Matagrande Plain, with the villages of Villaval and Cardenuela Riopico tucked into the foreground. Beyond is the city of Burgos still 15 kilometers away. We step down the hill and through sweeping green fields under a warming sun and a gentle, offsetting breeze. At Cardenuela Riopico, we settle in for coffee at a bustling café, joining in some idle conversation with pilgrims nearby.

We swing on our packs, and before too long we turn off the Camino onto the first part of an alternate way into Burgos known as the "river route." It allows us to avoid an eight kilometer walk through an industrial area and takes us through open fields that border the airport. It's poorly marked, but Heinrich is so sure of his way that I can't help but trust him absolutely. In little more than an hour, we find ourselves walking beside the Rio Arlanzon through a pristine park-like area on a path that is gradually revealing the beautiful city of Burgos, the gateway to the Meseta.

It's early afternoon as the spires of the cathedral slowly come into view across the river that transects the city, and nearby is Heinrich's hotel. We find a place for lunch, one last *bocadillo* together.

"So Heinrich, my friend," I say smiling, "I hope you enjoy that shave."

Stroking his bristled chin, he replies, "I will certainly enjoy my shave. Have a wonderful Meseta, a wonderful Camino. We walk in a similar pace. Perhaps we meet again soon. Who knows?"

"I hope we will, and if we can meet in Santiago, I'll buy you a dinner for your birthday."

"Yes! I would like that very much indeed. I'll be…how do you say…keeping an eye for you."

Heinrich's hotel is on this side of the river; mine across, about a block from the Cathedral. On the street near a bridge, we hug each other, though with our packs on it feels clumsy. In deference to his reserved German sensibilities I lean heavily toward restraint. But truthfully, I could have kissed him.

On this perfect spring day in Burgos, warmer now and sunny, surrounded by the traffic and the crowds and the paler greens of spring in the trees, I cross the bridge over the Rio Arlanzon and realize that I am now alone for the first time since climbing the high pass in the French Pyrenees through driving rain and wind and a measure of fear. Over 290 kilometers have now passed and it just seems so long ago. Seasons do change. Curiously, my eyes are filling and I'm smiling.

CHAPTER 8

OTHER THAN A DAY OF REST, there is another purpose at the root of my stay in Burgos. I've made a promise.

Nearly four years ago, I had the experience of being called, and as previously mentioned, a concern that perhaps I'd lost my mind. It's times like these when one reaches for someone who may know best. So like any good Catholic boy, I went running to a priest hoping a fellow like that might know a thing or two about being called. And not just any priest.

We first met many years ago under rather interesting circumstances. I was attending a Twelve Step meeting that gathers weekly in the chapel of the beautiful old Catholic retreat house near my home. The property has great religious significance to the local community, and is what I and others have always considered to be a thin-place. We heard that a newly assigned Spiritual Director had arrived, but none of the meeting regulars had yet met him. On this particular night, a member came in who was obviously rather stewed. Our tradition is that if the intoxicated person does not disturb the meeting, he is welcome to stay. Unfortunately, our friend became boisterous and thought it would be okay to walk the halls on the ground floor of the house bellowing obscenities. Two of the younger men escorted him out, and the meeting continued. Soon, State Police cars were outside, and our drunken friend was in handcuffs. It seems that he decided he was going to drive home, refused the offer of a ride, and left the two young men no other choice than to call the police. It was, in short, a fiasco.

After the meeting ended, I went outside and saw an older gentleman in a windbreaker with khaki pants walking around and looking concerned. Somebody advised me he was the new Director. Being an established member of the group, I felt it would be wise to make earnest apologies for the disturbance lest we get the boot. By all appearances we were not off to a good start with him.

"Father," I said. "I'm beyond sorry for all of this trouble. We've never had this sort of thing happen before. We so love meeting here and..."

He looked at me in my obvious upset, put a hand up and interrupted me. "Hey hey hey! Relax! It's okay! Shit happens!"

Thus was the beginning of my lovely friendship with Father John, Montfort missionary, and one of the most beautiful souls I have known.

When I had the experience of the mystical step along the road near home that day, it was natural for me to seek him out. We spoke during a late summer afternoon on the veranda of the house which overlooks a large sloping lawn from a hilltop, and several miles beyond across a mostly wooded landscape.

He listened intently to my experience. John was careful not to interpret what was subjectively mine, but he suggested something of significance had occurred, and how beautiful it would be if I were actually able to complete a pilgrimage to Santiago de Compostela. I left him feeling my sanity was intact, and that perhaps I really had been blessed with something wonderful.

Years passed and the day for me to leave was growing closer. John had graciously allowed the retreat house to be used for my Camino send-off gathering, and had led us all through *The Pilgrims Prayer*. While I accepted this as a blessing, I wanted something more personal. A few days before I left, we met alone in the chapel. At the end he asked a favor of me.

"Stephen, when you're in Burgos, if you could visit the cathedral there and just think of me, I'd really appreciate that. It would mean a lot."

"I most certainly will. You have my word."

The Catedral de Santa Maria de Burgos in all its gothic magnificence, the result of several centuries of construction, is today mostly a museum, albeit a remarkable one. Though Mass is celebrated in the main sanctuary on special occasions, the church must accommodate huge daily crowds who come to experience the grandeur of the place, making worship impossible. Because of this, a quiet chapel, or *capilla*, located in a front corner of the cathedral is set aside for prayer, meditation, and daily Mass. No photography is allowed here in honor of its holy purpose and silence is expected.

The Capilla de Santo Cristo de Burgos contains the sculpture of the Black Christ on the cross, a source of much fervor by the faithful. It is located in the customary spot above the altar. Legend holds that the hair and skin (bovine) are real. It is one of the most haunting images of the crucifixion I have ever seen, issuing forth both unfathomable suffering, yet utter surrender and peace. Though mesmerizing, I must look away; a response to something in me, dusty and old, but still having the power to break my heart.

The Chapel is silent and dark, lit mostly by candles and a bit of sunlight and the air is cool. I enter into the place of no place, of no here and no there, no yet and no before. I go where hopefully is only the holiest, the deepest, the It in the midst. With me now are thoughts of John. I return to an autumn of grief and despair as he invites me to stay at the house for a few days to hopefully collect myself after the death of my son. On the heels of that, I remember how he patiently listens to me coming to terms with the guilt and sadness of yet another divorce. Now, I can see him sitting with my father who seems so lost and confused at his grandson's wake. And next, I'm on a retreat as he speaks with me in the kitchen about how those nuns may have been so very wounded, showing me a kitchen Catholicism of the finest kind—kitchen forgiveness and kitchen peace. Love is always found in the kitchen, rarely in the parlor. That's just what Mom would always say. I think of John celebrating Mass, his gaze transfixed upon the host and the chalice during consecration, a man consumed by the miracle, transported, absent of the rote. I think of him delivering a sermon laced with non-duality and speaking of a Christ so very close. I think of him as he has asked, and I am here as I was called.

"I can only hope the irony has not escaped you."
"It has not."

Burgos, like all the Spanish cities I've seen so far, is immaculate; the park spaces are manicured and perfect with sculpted topiary and lush gardens, the plazas all full of life. I have today and all of tomorrow, more perfect weather to enjoy, and a sense of freedom that rivals any I have known before. There is more culture here than I could experience over a week's time, so I'm focusing on the Cathedral, the castle atop the highest point, and the crowded, vibrant streets. But for now I want an ice cream cone and a hot shower after a long walk.

The hotel is delightfully bourgeois, a decadent treat, a somewhat guilty indulgence. What kind of pilgrim would stay in a joint like this? How things have changed from a time when an indoor accommodation was a kindness offered by a family seeking good favor from Saint James, a time when the pilgrim walked to Santiago *and then walked home.* But a rest day is a rest day, I rationalize. Gotta sleep someplace. In my spacious room, the king size bed is directly across from French doors which open onto a tiny second floor balcony that affords a view overlooking a small plaza. Beyond, a perfect row of trees separates a street from a promenade that traces along the Rio Arlanzon.

After cleaning up, I put on fresh clothes and venture out into the late afternoon of Burgos. I walk the block to the plaza that borders the right side of the Cathedral, and climb the stairs to another plaza that faces the front entrance. One more set of stairs rises from there to the level of the street that runs along the left side, and from here I can shoot pictures that capture the church's façade and spires. I'm told the only vantage point where the entire roofline of the Cathedral can be seen is from a place close to the castle on the nearby hill overlooking the city, so up I go.

Climbing, I'm suddenly aware that my body has changed quite a bit during the two weeks on the Camino. I've probably lost more than ten pounds now, a remarkable thing when I consider the carbs I'm eating every day. More than that is a feeling of fitness unknown to me in decades. I feel like I could do anything within reason, nearly invincible. The walk to the castle is not long, but very steep. Yet, without the pack on, I can almost bound up the walkways and steps, and when I reach the top I recover from the exertion nearly instantly.

The castle is closed this afternoon, but a sign tells me tomorrow I'll find it open. It is situated in another beautiful park, and I follow along below the imposing perimeter walls with embattlements spaced along the top. I try to imagine this place before the park, before admission fees and times. Just below the very top of the hill, I come across Mirador del Castillo (Castle Lookout). It is a large circular area rimmed by a stone railing, and along the top of the rail is an inlay of the same panoramic view before me but from an earlier time. The lookout faces to the east and southeast such that I can see back across the Matagrande Plain to the hills I descended this morning with Heinrich. Just before me I can take in the whole roofline of the Cathedral and most of Burgos. It is a moment that begs a frequent question: Am I really here?

The evening chill arrives early; the city's taller buildings make deep, cool shadows that are swept by late afternoon breezes. I'd like to eat at an outdoor table, but the coolness drives me indoors. Because I am a pilgrim, dinner on most days comes much earlier than for the rest of Spain, so I have the restaurant to myself. My table is at a front window and across the plaza I can see the ground level of the Cathedral. The waitress asks if I'd care for a pilgrim menu or regular, and I opt for the former, best to keep it simple. I'm hungry and growing tired as my body follows the daily walking rhythms. She is friendlier than most and seems to nearly pity my being alone. Her affect is almost motherly. It's lovely to feel so cared-for, even as I celebrate aloneness.

After dinner I walk past the Cathedral, down a few side streets, and purchase desert, a large vanilla ice cream on a tall, slender Spanish cone, my second of the day. Within a block I come face to face with Heinrich who predictably, is also eating an ice cream cone. After we embrace, I compliment him on his clean-shaven face.

"You look years younger, my friend."

He runs the palm of his hand along his cheek, still enjoying the novelty of it. "Ya ya, it was so good—the hot towels, the blade. I feel clean again. The next one will be in Santiago!"

"I can see we still have our ice cream addiction," I say.

"And even when it is so fresh outside," he replies, laughing again.

We wish each other a good night's rest in our sumptuous beds. It's been good to see my friend. Back at the hotel I make a long, sweet call to Dianne and the day is over.

A bright slit of sunlight knifes between two curtain panels as the muffled sounds of early morning Burgos begin to seep in. I reach for my phone to find it is just after 8:00 and realize I've slept for nine hours. In the fog of waking, I need to remind myself that there will be no walk beyond Burgos today. After tending to the soul, I head downstairs to the dining room and find an American-style breakfast buffet.

As I eat, I decide to run an errand before exploring. Though I've only had to use it a few times, my rain poncho is sorely lacking, made of the flimsiest plastic. It works adequately in a light shower, but any wind renders it useless, and the forecast for tomorrow is calling for rain to the west. A big box European outdoor gear store has an outlet in Burgos, so I'm going to upgrade the poncho. After breakfast, the desk clerk calls a taxi for me, and while waiting I practice my Spanish. I think we'll be okay as long as the discussion doesn't stray to politics. A friendly enough driver who is about my age pulls up. I give him the address and ask if he will wait just a few minutes for me when we arrive. He readily agrees and then starts having a conversation with me, about what I have no idea. Success! He thinks I know Spanish! As my head begins to swell, I have to tell him that I'm sorry, but I know very little Spanish (this too I can say really well). He says, "Okay" which is apparently the extent of his English, and our ride continues in a comfortable silence. I run into the store, and ten minutes later come out with a beast of a poncho made of heavier gauge plastic, a hood and sleeves that cinch, stows in a bag that is less than one third the size of a football, *and* will cover a 75 liter pack (mine is 48). Let it rain.

> *"Come, let us build ourselves a city, and a tower whose top is in the heavens; let us make a name for ourselves..."*
> Genesis 11:4, (*Tower of Babel*)

The very first stone of the Catedral de Santa Maria de Burgos was laid in the year 1221, almost three hundred years before Columbus set off to accidentally discover a new world. I can barely fathom this. Yet coming upon things approaching 800 years old is becoming more of a routine occurrence. Some 20 generations of craftsmen and laborers built this place; a process of addition and adornment that continued for about 500 years. Incredibly, the ceiling vaults were closed in 1243, a span of only 22 years. Over the centuries, the goal was consistent—to inspire wonder and awe and to create a structure with tapering spires that from the plains of Burgos reached to the clouds and to heaven beyond. Though primarily Gothic in its design, Renaissance influence is present because of such passage of time.

I enter as I'm directed through the ground floor of the south side, present my Credencial, and am afforded a half-price admission and a Cathedral stamp. I'm given a hand-held listening device that will guide me through the building at my own pace. It will tell me of construction milestones and techniques, inform me about the purpose and dedication of each of the chapels, the identity of the human remains in every tomb and sepulcher, the location of the burial place of El Cid and his wife. It will speak to me of art in the forms of paintings and sculptures and objects that span the centuries and the techniques by which they were created and preserved, the gravity defying and heavenly designs of the domes, and the comments of royalty. It will describe the minutiae of each of the more than 20 retablos located in the chapels surrounding the central nave and of the main sanctuary itself. It will tell me the details of the choir space which contains the tomb of a bishop placed under a structure of polished copper and wood and precious stones, and of the horizontally and vertically mounted organ pipes. It will, in short, overwhelm me and not speak to my soul, and so I will turn it off and walk through the all of it slowly and I will feel. It's my way.

Beneath the elegance, beneath the exquisite art, beneath the grandeur and grandiosity and utter magnificence of the spaces, beneath the influences of politics and religion colliding, beneath the sheer wealth of it all, I can feel something primitive that comes from the depths of the human heart, something pure and holy and timeless. It is what speaks to me every day, what energizes me, what inspires me, and what brought me here. It is an Essence, an unspeakable Love, a great devotion and yearning, the holiest desire to reach to the Creator and express allegiance to It—five centuries of building and expressing what is as close as breath here and now under the spires of the Soul, held in the sacred irony of our Source.

When I'm done, I turn in my device and exit through the gift shop. Standing in the brilliant sunlight of yet another flawless day in the north of Spain, I feel compelled to attend to something, to settle something. I go to the front of the Cathedral and into the Capilla de Santo Cristo, a more authentic sanctuary, once again. And I sit in the cool dark quiet to listen—to simply listen. Will I hear the still, small voice?

Listen: Verb—
 1. *attend closely for the purpose of hearing.*
 2. *pay attention; heed; obey.*
 3. *to wait attentively for a sound.*

Looking forward to an exploration of Castilla de Burgos, I light up the hill stopping briefly at the lookout and arrive well after the stated opening time. Other pilgrims are gathered at the locked gate. There is nothing to suggest when it may actually open and no one is around to ask. I shoot multiple photos of the castle's exterior, and as I'm walking around I run into a local who tells me I'm not really missing much other than perhaps some more panoramic views than the lookout allows.

I find a place on this highest point in Burgos to look west. Pilgrims will often do this. Beyond the outskirts of the city I can see the very first of the Meseta, my splendid place of walking for the next 230 kilometers. A mostly flat high plateau, it is still capable of presenting elevations of 400 meters or more. Though known for the desolation of the landscape, its perfect secret is the endless sky, big as all Montana where storms are seen from hours away and the clouds can come in so low as to be almost within reach.

My pilgrim soul, restless after a day of rest, longs to walk the soul of Spain.

CHAPTER 9

To walk right through the soul of Spain, the soul of Spain,
And contemplate perhaps
In the echo-less wide open,
A pain not my own.

IT IS JUST PAST SEVEN ON A COOL and lightly overcast morning as I tap through the quiet, early streets of Burgos. The bag feels good on my back, the sticks are in my hands once again, and I return to the Camino de Santiago. Just over 31 kilometers away is the town of Hontanas, an ambitious eight or nine hour day of walking after 40 hours of rest. Though rain has been forecasted, I do not yet feel it in the air. Still, the pack cover is on and I've put the new poncho in the top compartment should there be a sudden need. There is much urban walking yet before the beautiful crunchy dirt of the Camino.

After almost nine kilometers under now-cleared skies, the path ducks under the N-120 and finally at least some of the typical Meseta landscape begins to surround me. Only about two hours have passed, but the walk has been quite flat. Just ahead now is Tardajos.

The air is sun-warmed and dry and clean as I sip on a *café con leche*. I must slow this walk down a little, I think. Instead of standing up and shouldering the pack, I stretch out in the flimsy red plastic chair as best I can, lean back, close my eyes, and pitch my baseball cap far back on my head. The sun's warmth touches my face and the backs of my hands resting in my lap. I hear the pilgrims at the tables around me chatting away in Spanish, French, and Russian.

After 20 more minutes and another *café con leche*, it's time to walk again. Leaving Tardajos behind, I soon pass through the village of Rabe de las Calzadas, then finally the big sky and endless wheat unfold. My pace is relaxed and perfect as I'm brought into the lonely and empty Meseta I have dreamt of since I first read of it. Gently and with great discretion, it begins to insinuate its magic on me like the swinging watch of a hypnotist.

There are many who I carry with me on this walk, hold close in my heart. I think of them often. Some, especially Dianne, have shared the living of a life with me, and some, their troubles and joys. All have shared their souls. But these days, I'm haunted by the echoes of other footsteps. They have followed me for some time now, and likely always will.

* * * * *

He was beautiful. Yet when I first saw him I was terrified, for him and for me. Would I ever measure up? Could I possibly do this? I've seen what can happen. His body rotated as it mercifully expelled seemingly spring-loaded from his mother in a torrent of fluids and relief. He came into the world as a still, porcelain little god, ashen colored, unanimated. There was palpable concern in the room and I wanted to look away for fear he was dead. In an instant came a thought, and as I now recall, it was remarkably similar to the thought that called me to the Camino. It told me with absolute clarity to look, because there was something I *must* see, something I must not miss, something beyond a mere heartbeat. So I continued to look, and then I saw the form become possessed of life with a subtle little twitch, then color, then movement, then his sound. The gravitas in the room gave way to joy and they handed him to me, my reluctant little passenger. Thus we began—my son Keith and me. But then again, who knows when these things really do begin?

In those days, cameras held film. Our new obsession was at hand and it was all about exposure; the quest for the perfect exposure of the perfect subject. There was no instant gratification then; film had to be processed. In retrospect, those were days of patience and anticipation. The result was his image on paper that we could hold and regard and then place in a frame or a box or an envelope. The boxes and envelopes could be opened as the years passed, and the images touched by hands, fingertips lightly passing over his face on paper, most recently in dimly lit rooms, floods of recall, rivers of smiles, oceans of tears. The images would outlive him, forever young and beautiful and perfectly exposed.

Lately, in a slow and deliberate dance, a ritual, I open the boxes and envelopes as my holy devices of acceptance. Images of a still-bloody newborn, a perfect infant wrapped in a towel, a toddler with his mouth agape in joy and running around with his arms in the air, a kindergarten graduate, a cub scout wearing his first uniform with an understated pride, a ten year old playing with his younger sister near a waterfall. Who could have possibly known what would follow? Open, hold, touch, grieve, accept his absolute gone-ness. Time has passed and so I go there less frequently, but still I do this. Because I need to. Because he killed himself. Sometimes I will look at his eyes, and depending on my mood, see them pleading with me. "Will you remember me as I was here? Will you remember me forever and forever? Will you please, in God's name, just remember the times before it got so dark?" And there are other times I see something else. "How could you?"

Echoes of footsteps…

As an older child he saved two lives. He was about 11 when he prevented a baby from drowning in a swimming pool at the home of his after-school caregiver. At age 13, he saved his three-year-old step sister from being killed by a car. We were walking together in the city, my second wife-to-be Sharon, her three and my two. The youngest one, Alicia, was just in front of me and with Keith as she always preferred to be. As we approached a corner, she impulsively ran toward the street, toward the very edge of the curb. Keith reached out, grabbed her by the collar, gave a yank and said, "Whoa little one," as a car sped past just in front of her. He never made a big deal of either circumstance, but I often think of all the anguish spared by his acts.

*   *   *   *   *

The Camino carves its way through the deep green wheat fields, exquisite and lush. On rare occasions a lone tree stands against the horizon in the midst of it all, maybe an ancient seed delivered on the wind and left unattended to grow. I stop for a long moment and realize the silence. There is not even a soft breeze to be heard, but there is one winsome exception. Though I cannot see them, two Cuckoo birds are singing to me, their call coming from either side of the path. Cuckoos have been with me since walking in the Pyrenees, my companions, my lovely amusement. The song never varies, just two notes. Are they trying to tell me something? Sometimes I whistle back, but they don't buy it ever and reply with their silence.

I top a plateau around mid-day and at a distance of about two kilometers can see the Camino before me as it traces directly into the village of Hornillos del Camino, sitting nestled in a shallow valley. As I enter the town I spot a café. Though I will sometimes continue on to see if there is a better looking offering, I'm famished now. This will do just fine. Walking toward the back of the outdoor seating area, I see a pilgrim swinging his pack on to leave. Below his sunglasses is a broad smile and he seems to be looking in my direction. Robert, one of my lunch companions from Saint Jean Pied de Port greets me warmly. We chat for a few moments, and Sarah comes out from inside the café. We wish each other *"Buen Camino"* as they head out. "Lovely to see you both again," I say.

I take off my pack and untie my shoes. I think of Heinrich and wonder where he might be today. It's odd to be on the Camino without him, ordering my first solo *boccadillo*. Oh yes... *the high station of letting go. It brings together. It separates. And always to the west* it dreamily moves. I eat slowly and allow the fatigue of 21 kilometers of walking to evaporate. It's remarkable how the body and mind do recover. Just 10 kilometers of open Meseta remain between here and Hontanas. After an hour of rest, I leave Hornillos del Camino behind.

*   *   *   *   *

Sit beside me while I drive,
And ask me questions I've never heard before.
Why are the planets always round?

We'd lost him just over a decade before he ended his life. All the usual questions arose. What could I have done differently? Could I have made a difference? Could I have eased his pain? Could I have made his darkness turn to light? Could I have been more compassionate? Could I have been more kind? Could I have somehow saved his goddamn life?

A couple of years before he began to fade from us, we took a trip, just him and me; 50 miles in a canoe down the Delaware River, camping with his Boy Scout troop. We'd switch front and rear positions after rest and food stops. That boy could really handle a canoe. It was a magical trip as we shot rapids, watched bald eagles build nests in trees along the river banks, fished Muskies, and in general had a beautiful time together. I always promised myself that if he had ever found a true, sustained recovery, the kind that lifts you up to celebrate every single day, we'd do that same trip again. We all need a dream I suppose, or at least some lovely memory.

It was a long, arduous path for him and all of us who loved and cared for him. His mother, his step-mother, his sister and step-sisters, his grandparents and I all wondered why. Why would this beautiful, blond, tow-headed boy, once so full of light and happiness, become so hopelessly addicted, so absolutely beyond reason and human assistance? What could have driven him to this? But to understand, it's important to look back from the answer to the question.

The answer is a moment of bliss and peace and loving connection. It's a warm blanket by a fire on the coldest day, the sweetest hug from mom. It's the body gone all beautifully numb and quiet. It's a feeling of heaven itself, a paradise that cannot be known here, not even on rivers where eagles build nests. Nothing of this world can touch the answer, at least once it takes a hold, and to lose it is to lose air and food and water and so life itself. To even think of losing it is absurd and ridiculous and quite impossible. The answer has never been about a party.

The question is always reducible to pain. Always. In all ways. He'd want this known.

*   *   *   *   *

Along the road to Hontanas is a place, barely a hamlet, called San Bol, just 300 meters south of the Camino and marked by a hand-painted sign with an arrow. At the end of the short road is a rustic *albergue* and a fountain. Local legend says that if I had pain in my feet, I would have only to soak them in the fountain pool at San Bol and they would be cured. This place contains more touchstones of a thousand years' time passed in the form of the ruins of an 11th century monastery scattered nearby. Though it's a pretty and alluring spot, I don't rest. I want to keep walking.

Returning to the Camino I head toward Hontanas, still about five kilometers away. The Castilian Meseta now holds sway over me. I love this place more than I could have imagined. I feel as though I could just walk here forever and allow it to take me, falling, deeper and deeper and deeper still. For the first time, I spontaneously and unexpectedly burst into tears, yet for the life of me I don't know why. Though I've had these thoughts of Keith, I can't seem to attach this feeling to any single thing. And these are not *tears that gently well and fall, quietly absent of overt drama.* I sob; great, chest heaving sobs. Brief but unrestrained cries of loaded anguish roll out of me and absorb into the wheat, a primal voice perhaps expelling something very old and corrosive. Because it is so vague, I suspect the magical energy of the Camino, its ways, its wonders, its mysteries. As this passes I look behind me to find I'm alone here. There are no witnesses.

"Am I dreaming all of this?"
"What do you mean?"
"Please."
"Well, some would say yes, some no."
"Okay. What would you say?"
"I'd say you've been dreaming for 60 years."

The road is so flat and it seems to never end. Just when I begin to wonder if it ever will, I see sprouting from the ground ahead, the very top of a church tower. Coming closer, the roof-tops of Hontanas, tucked into a river valley, abruptly reveal themselves. The Camino flows down into the main street, and I easily find my accommodation directly across from the church, the 14th century Iglesia de la Immaculada Concepcion.

I should feel more fatigue than I do. I've walked over 31 kilometers with 17 pounds on my back. I could have walked more. Nothing hurts, nothing at all. I'm compelled to take this as a symptom of some kind of unburdening or lifting, something to be exceedingly grateful for.

In the late afternoon I venture out for a look around Hontanas. Some high overcast has moved in and cooled the day down a bit. I enter the church and am struck by its simple beauty, almost odd after the ostentatious atmosphere of the cathedral yesterday. Come to think of it, I feel a million miles removed from there, the glittering and bejeweled high temple. This is more for me: a quiet, simple, thick-walled place of echoing creaky wood floors, a plain stone baptismal, an altar, a reasonable retablo. Here I can pray. Here I can just be—undistracted and un-bedazzled.

Walking along the main street, I join a gathering of pilgrims in front of an *albergue*. They are singing along to some pretty decent guitar playing. There is a familiar face here, and we recognize each other straight away. Bill, one of my dinner companions in Roncevalles on the first night, comes right over.

"Stephen! How the hell are you? How is your Camino?" he asks with a grin.

"Doing well, Bill. Good to see you, brother. It's been amazing. You remember Heinrich? The tall German guy? Walked with him from just outside of Zubiri to Burgos. Now we're both flying solo for the Meseta. It's been more than I could have hoped for."

"Know what you mean, yeah. How about Greg? You two were together, right?"

"Yeah we met in the Pyrenees during the climb. Heinrich and I lost him after Puenta la Reina. I think he needed to push a bit more. Have you seen him at all?"

"No, can't say I have. But I had a couple of days off the Camino," he says with a wry smile.

"Oh?"

"Yeah. Got a weird pain in my leg before Santo Domingo and took a bus to Burgos. So I'm on the bus and I meet this mother and daughter who live just outside Burgos in this little place, Cortes."

"You're kidding, right?" I ask, laughing.

"God as my witness and I don't know which one was hotter looking."

"I remember you saying something about maybe getting laid. Thoughts create, eh?"

"I was hoping they'd put me up, but no such luck. They showed me around Burgos though, took me to the bullfights, had me over for dinner—just a great time. Nothing much happened."

"Much?" I ask.

"Much," he says, smiling.

I ask him if he'd like to grab dinner, but he just ate. I give him a quick hug, and we exchange "Buen Camino's." I've a good feeling I'll be seeing him down the road, provided he doesn't get distracted again.

I finish wandering about Hontanas with a pilgrim meal at an *albergue* near the center of town. Finally, I'm starting to feel the day in my body.

As I lay down, the day passes by in thoughts. I would love to find some deeper understanding as I sleep, though I seldom remember dreams. In some way or another, I suspect the Camino will provide. But in the darkened room my mind wanders. The faces I walk with dreamily pass before me. I miss my girl. I miss my son, my mother, and father. I wonder about my daughter. I love this place so. I love the crunching sound of my steps and Cuckoo birds and *bocadillos* and the big, big sky. I'm a pilgrim on the Camino. I feel so thankful. And sleep gently falls in over me.

I hear rain falling. Well, it's about time I think as wakefulness slowly creeps in. I pray, stretch and exercise, wash-up and pack. The rain is fairly light, so the poncho is on standby for now. I check the weather radar on my phone and see the green blotches all around, but moving swiftly as they pass above. It's still early, before 7:00, when I go downstairs to the vestibule.

The lady who checked me in yesterday explained that no one shows up before 7:30 or so, and the front door is locked from the inside with a key. She showed me a basket on a wall shelf, told me I will find the front door key here, and to leave my room key in the same basket. Though she spoke to me in Spanish, I somehow understood.

In the vestibule I find two other pilgrims, men only a little younger than I. They're also packed and ready to go, expectantly looking out the front window and obviously perplexed. I know that I'm about to come to their rescue.

"*Hola, buenos dias,*" I say.

"*Buenos dias,*" they reply together.

One of them is a Frenchman named Jean who doesn't speak any English, the other is a Filipino-American from San Francisco by the name of Romeo ("call me Romy"). After our brief introductions, I go to the secret basket, drop my room key, and pluck out the front door key.

"Here's what you want," I say, unlocking the door.

"Oh!" says Romy, laughing. "*That's* what she was trying to tell me. Thank you, my friend! I thought for sure we'd have to wait until God knows when."

"You're very welcome. Enjoy your pilgrimage today. *Buen Camino!*"

They walk briskly down the street, immediately heading out of town to the west. I walk back to the *albergue* for breakfast. Eating alone, I peruse the guidebook for a look at today's walk, the stage profile, and historical information about what lies ahead. It looks to be flat as a board with the exception of Alto de Mosteltares not quite halfway through the trek. A steadier rain is falling now as I emerge from the café, so my new poncho is on and I'm feeling invincible. Far from torrential, the rain is an atmosphere, a music for the day as I set out for the almost 29 kilometer walk to Boadilla del Camino.

Immediately west of Hontanas, the Camino traces a flat course through a river valley with low lying hills to either side. The wheat is jade under the light of gray skies, and there is a smattering of trees. The path is narrow along here, and pilgrims are spread-out, pacing their walk so as not to overtake their fellow travelers. After a few kilometers, the dirt path joins a small paved road.

Before long, the famed ruins of Convento de San Anton come into view. The buildings here date back to the 14th and 15th centuries and are the remains of a monastery and hospital of the Order of San Anton. The hospital specialized in the treatment of a bizarre disease that resembled leprosy known as Saint Anthony's Fire. Somehow, it was traced to a fungus that had infected barley. The treatment prescribed included an increased intake of red wine (to dilate the blood vessels), elimination of barley bread, and vigorous exercise...such as pilgrimage! The Order developed a reputation for dealing with this and other socially troublesome diseases, earning the favor and generous funding of royalty.

After another few kilometers of road walking, the Camino veers off and enters Castrojeriz. The town is arranged around the base of a mesa with the ruins of a pre-Roman castle perched on its flat top. I'm more than ready for a break and stop at the first café, which is quite crowded. As I wait to place my order at the counter, I see Bill in a seemingly intense conversation with a younger woman. He glances toward me, sees me smiling at him, and after a few minutes, comes over.

"Mornin', Bill. Getting an early start?" I ask with a grin, not feeling the need to clarify further.

"Yeah. Guess so," he says ruefully. "Rain give you any trouble yet?"

"Not at all. Been a breeze. Why? You get caught in something?"

"I'll say. About a half hour ago—got drenched. I'm here to dry my shit out."

"I guess I just missed it. Nice girl," I say gesturing toward his friend. "Just met?"

"Not really. She was in Hontanas last night with the others singing along out on the street. Nice kid."

"Uh huh. So where are you heading today?"

"I might just take the day here and hang out 'till the *albergue* opens later. My leg still isn't right, man."

"Well I really hope you feel better, my friend. The Energy will take care of you," I say, wondering how much the leg really has to do with it. Immediately, I realize the implied judgement of that last thought. Perhaps I've just been given a glimpse of myself in another time.

It's still raining steadily as I leave the café, and at the outer gate of the patio I meet Heinrich, just coming in from the road. After exchanging big smiles and an ungainly pack-wearing hug, I ask how he is. He is giddy, almost starry-eyed as he tells me he has no idea how far he will walk today or where he will sleep. Such is the whimsical character of his Meseta. I tell him Bill from our dinner in Roncevalles is here at the cafe, and wish him a "*Buen Camino.*"

I follow the road through the main part of the town that hugs the waist of the mesa. Walking the wet stone streets, I briefly consider a strenuous climb to the castle for a look but decide instead to save my energy for the hard ascent ahead, still a few kilometers from here. This place feels ancient, made more so by the gray light and rain. I stop frequently to take a closer look at the 13th and 14th century churches spaced throughout the town. Soon the Camino leads me away and into open space.

The path meanders across a plain containing an intricate medieval irrigation system of bridges and aqueducts that looks as though it could still work well today. The rain has stopped and the sky has brightened just a bit. I pause to stow the poncho and look ahead. About a kilometer away, I see the Camino trace up the side of the next mesa, the imposing Alto de Mosteltares. As I reach the base of the hill, a sign advises this steep climb will involve a 12 percent grade. I gulp some water and set off.

I'm somehow reminded of the first day of walking back in France. I choose a slow but deliberate pace, and in about 20 minutes find myself at the top—considerably less time than the hours spent climbing in the Pyrenees. There is a shelter here with an overlook facing back toward Castrojeriz. I can see the town and the castle in the distant east, pinpoints in the vastness of this place. Across the seemingly endless emerald expanse I can more easily perceive what my guidebook has told me; that the mesas were the original landscape and the plains around them were carved out by the merciless erosion of wind and flooding water over the millennia. In this moment it all seems so still, yet I know it can't be. Forces are always working if only to move a pebble. Always, always and always, forever it changes. Nothing remains as it was. In three months' time, this lush green place will turn dusty pale blond clear to the horizons.

I walk the table-flat top of the hill for half a kilometer and come to the edge of the descent on the western side. I stop here to linger for a moment. The Camino threads its way across the classic lonesome patchwork of the vast Meseta, westward toward the great cities of Leon and Astorga, Ponferrada and Santiago de Compostela, perhaps even toward some mystical infinite place known only in dreams. It could end in some other world, maybe in a room of heaven where illumined mustard fields radiate the warmest golden yellow in front of old stone ruins. Maybe there.

*　*　*　*　*

"Why do I feel like I could burst into tears again today?"
"Why do you need to ask me why you feel?"
"I don't know."

It simply said, "Please call home." That's all, nothing more. It's amazing to me how three words can set off such a visceral reaction, an ice ball in the stomach, a flush of the face, a throbbing pulse in the neck. At once I regretted checking my email, yet clamored to find my phone, to turn it on, to get to the contact list, to push *Home*. Home was about a nine hour drive away. I'd come to Virginia Beach alone as I was want to do in those days, and my wife Sharon was always accommodating. Separate vacations had become our way over 17 years together. It wasn't that I was especially happy to leave home or sad to return. Were someone to ask how I felt about such things then, I'd likely just say, "I don't know."

But I was here to spend some time with my best friend Hugh, a Navy buddy whom I've known since I was 21. It's rare that men can cultivate a relationship of such long standing, but we'd managed nicely and came to have a history together. I had hoped that we'd be able to get in a good sail on the Chesapeake aboard a friend's boat, but a nasty low pressure system left dismal weather overhead the whole time. I was on a schedule of sorts. The day the email came was Friday. I'd planned to return to Connecticut on Sunday and go back to work on Tuesday morning.

I called Sharon. Her voice was at once troubled and flat. She told me that Alicia, the youngest, recently graduated from high school as her class president, had experienced a mental break at home in her room earlier that morning and had been admitted to the hospital. We'd known for a while something was wrong but had suspected drug use. Sharon told me I didn't need to come home but just wanted me to know. When I protested, saying I'd leave as soon as I could pack, she said in a reticent, almost innocent way, "I was hoping you could go sailing." I told her I'd be there by early evening.

When Sharon and I started seeing each other at the end of her first marriage, first started falling in love, Alicia was nearing the end of her diaper days. Her other two daughters were five and seven respectively, pretty tough ages all to have parents divorcing. Such began the tightrope walk of step-parenting, the impossible dance of substitution absent of replacement.

I walked into the house, dropped my bag and sat next to her on the couch. I asked her what had transpired since we spoke on the phone and she filled me in. There would be a week or so of evaluation, meds would be given, observations made. She described in greater detail what she had seen that morning in Alicia's room. I listened and I asked questions.

With great hesitation I asked one more. "Did you really want me to come home, but didn't want to ask?" She nodded yes as if she was acknowledging something secret and wrong.

Saturday, Sunday and Monday we visited Alicia. After an elevator ride to the locally infamous "eighth Floor", we'd sit with her in a sterile looking room containing no loose objects and pass the time in silences interrupted by superficial exchanges. Something had happened within her that created a very different reality, one unique to her and not shared. Optimistically, we hoped it would prove to be something that would eventually resolve itself. It's good to have hope. For now, there were far more questions than answers, and in these moments she was lost to us.

On Tuesday at one in the morning, the house phone rang. Sharon answered, told me it was Susan (my first wife) and that something was very wrong. Of course I knew. I picked up the phone. All she could get out was that Keith was dead, and gave me the phone number for the state police. Any hope of misunderstanding or miscommunication bled from me when I identified myself and heard the trooper say, "Sir, I'm so very sorry."

His girlfriend had come home from work and found him in their bedroom closet. He had left a trail of boxes leading from the front door of the apartment to where he was. She found him hanging there on Monday, October 4th, 2010, at 11:30pm. It's when everything changed.

I got off the phone, turned to Sharon who was quietly crying now, and said, "Well, thank God he's finally at peace."

It had actually come to that. Just less than 29 years had passed since I saw life twitch into his body.

CHAPTER 10

I'VE LONG PASSED SAN NICOLAS CHAPEL, a medieval, rustic *albergue* that still practices the beautiful ritual of washing pilgrims' feet. The clouds are low, slate gray and threatening, and there are about five more kilometers between me and Boadilla del Camino. In the distance I see a storm cell creeping across the Camino from the south, moving north. Much further south, another larger cell lumbers along and looks to be taking exactly the same path. I maintain a brisk pace to see if I can slide behind the first cell, but stay in front of the second. The endless horizons of the Meseta allow for this sort of play with nature. It's just so big out here.

The streets of Boadilla are wet from the storm that passed just before my arrival, but I remain dry. Following the Camino arrows through town, I'm walking quickly under rumbling skies. My hotel now in sight, I wonder if I'll make it. The air feels loaded with the coming rain. As the lobby door closes behind me, I feel the sharp snap of the thunder and turn to see the clouds open in a torrential downpour. The man behind the desk is helping another pilgrim, but smiles and speaks to me in Spanish. I imagine it translating into something like this: "Pilgrim, you must be so very blessed to have come in here at the moment you did. I hope you understand that you walk in Grace."

As I stare out at the rain for several minutes, two more pilgrims arrive. They are completely soaked and their boots squish as they step across the stone floor. We are all given room keys and a suggestion to shower, change clothes, relax, and come back later to check-in. Climbing the stairs, I consider how impossible such casual hospitality would be back in the States.

The accommodation is a combined *albergue* and basic hotel, and tonight's dinner is being served family-style in a common dining area. I'm looking forward to this after a day alone in thoughts. Pilgrims are happiest when eating. Well-being pervades, and any tendency toward guardedness around others evaporates. We are seated at long tables by order of our arrival, but given the noise levels, it allows for conversation only with those nearby. Diagonally across from me is Jean the Frenchman from the hotel earlier this morning. He smiles and waves at me, apparently still grateful for being set free to walk. He gestures toward me while speaking to a friend, who smiles at me and nods. On my right is Percy, a fit 60-something from the Seattle area, and to my left a heavily accented German woman whose name I just can't understand. Directly across are a couple of younger women from Italy who keep to themselves. Looks like it's Percy and me for chatting. Before long Romy, my other friend from this morning comes by the table. It seems he knows just about everyone here, even the Italian girls. He shakes hands all around, telling the people immediately around me about being locked inside the hotel in Hontanas. In fact he tells it so well, I almost forget about having been part of the story.

After Romy leaves us for another section of the table, Percy comments to me, "What a great guy. It seems like just about everybody knows him."

"I think he should run for mayor of the Camino," I reply smiling. "He has wonderful energy about him."

"He really does. I first met him in Burgos and saw him on the road a few times. He's done the Camino Portugues route before, but this is his first time on the Frances."

"Your first Camino?" I ask.

"It is. I'd been meaning to do this walk for a few years now since I saw the movie, but I kept putting it off. Lately, the pull got stronger and it was all I could think about. I'd watch Camino videos and start getting emotional. I finally spoke to my wife about it and she didn't really seem to mind. It just came together a couple of months ago. I recently retired, so it's nice to be able to do this."

"Did she seem like she wanted to join you?"

Percy laughed while shaking his head a little. "Not the adventurous type, I'm afraid. There isn't much we do together these days. What brought you here?"

Given the surroundings, I answer with an abridged version of being called to the walk. He is very attentive though, and I find myself hoping the Camino will bring us together again further on for something a bit deeper. For now, we share stories of the road and our impressions of pilgrimage and the beautiful north of Spain.

The sun rises to clearing weather after rain during the night. I wander into the dining room and sit alone with my guidebook, checking today's 25 kilometer route to Carrion de los Condes. Food is served as people arrive, not in a single seating like dinner. Soon I'm eating the usual *albergue* breakfast of thick toast with butter, coffee, and a piece of cake topped with powdered sugar. Guess I'll have to find some protein on the road.

Leaving the wet, still-puddled stone streets of Boadilla del Camino, the road changes to a gravel and mud mixture as it moves into the countryside. It's easy to find a walkable path that will keep my shoes dry though, as I make my way past farm fields and neatly planted rows of new growth trees. The sky is full of countless shades of textured gray with impossibly deep blue breaks between the clouds, as the rising sun lights the earth in warm tones leaving long shadows. There is something new about the air after it rains, as new as springtime, as peaceful as the fall. The colors seem deeper, the contrasts sharper, any dull finish on the world made bright again, all scrubbed and perfect. My pace settles in quickly this morning, my core muscles are relaxed and I barely notice the weight of the pack. Soon the Camino parallels the Canal de Castilla as it will for the remainder of the idyllic six kilometer walk into Fromista.

*   *   *   *   *

Once the autumns were of warm colors and deep relief,
The gentle exhale of summer
into something more clear and crisp,
A long sleeve shirt,

a jacket collar turned up against breezes
that carry flights of leaves,
aromas of warm sweet tasting things
and wood smoke…but now?
Now, it seems I just don't know.

I tried to sleep the night he left us. I really did. But of course there were only tears. My wife and I laid there in our grief, so sadly unavailable to each other's comfort. Finally I got up, got dressed, and left to drive the empty two-in-the-morning streets with no idea where I was going; a meditation behind the wheel, good for the broken soul. At that hour there is always a risk of being pulled over. I imagined it could go something like this:

"Do you know why I stopped you?"

"I don't."

"You crossed the line a couple of times."

"I really try not to do that these days."

"Have you been drinking? Your eyes are a little red."

"No drinking. Been crying. My son just hung himself."

"Maybe you shouldn't be out driving."

I drove until 4:00AM, until I could sleep, until I had emptied the tank of tears at least for now. In the midst of this, I had decided on some fundamental things: I was not going to make this about me. I was going to focus on our wounded family. I was going to feel absolutely all of this and in that would be found blessings. It was a start.

First, to my father's house. I had called to tell him Sharon and I would be over and he instinctively knew it was bad news, likely having to do with Keith. How very different this visit would have been if my mother was still alive, though I really have no way of knowing how. I've become so used to a world without her.

He sat at the dining room table and lit a cigarette."I have a feeling I'm not going to like this," he said.

"You're not. Keith passed last night."

I watched as my words slowly soaked in.

"How?"

"He killed himself."

"How?"

"By hanging."

Staring at the table, hands folded right over left, cigarette perched between his right index and middle fingers, he shook his head ever so slightly and took a deep pull. As he exhaled smoke through his nostrils, I looked carefully but saw no tears.

"What a wasted life," he said. Meaning well and not knowing what else to say, he asked, "How are you feeling?"

Fatigue and raw grief conspired as I answered harshly, "I don't know, Dad. My kid is dead." Immediately I regretted my words and my tone and how easily I had forgotten my earlier decision. "I'm sorry," I said. "Been a rough morning."

We had to leave him because there was so much to do. We had to leave him to smoke his cigarettes and remember and be quiet and alone as he preferred; to wait patiently until noon to open his first beer. I knew he missed my mother terribly these past nine years, though he rarely said so. I wondered if he'd speak to her after we left. I think he did that sometimes.

Death has a way of forcing reluctant participants together. Kathryn answered the door of her mother's house—Kathryn who had felt so deeply wounded, that she left me and her step-family without a word some six years before. Despite all attempts to contact her, she'd remained away ever since. Though I'd never been given the opportunity to know the cause of her upset, my prayer before we arrived was that our presence would be tolerable for her in the midst of all she was feeling, that she'd be okay. Thankfully, Sharon and I entered to a warm greeting. She hugged me and told me she was so sorry, though I really wasn't sure which matter she was referring to. We sat together at the kitchen table, my former wife, my daughter, and wife to plan the funeral of our son, our brother. Isn't it always the kitchen table for this sort of thing?

After the reminiscing one would expect, after the guarded sharing of our most profound grief, we got down to the matter of how to bury Keith's remains and honor his troubled life. His mother wanted a wake with an open casket if possible, and though I personally feel these are an ordeal for all involved, I went along as a sort of living amends to her for our deeply troubled past. Sharon was so kind to agree, though I knew she felt as I did about these things because her father had passed only months before. When it came time to decide on burial, we discussed the more obvious options. Then came a loaded pause, one of those pregnant moments that happen before inspired things come through. Susan and Kathryn and I all looked at each other and then virtually together expressed a shared thought—that his body should be buried with his grandmother's.

To know the depth of their love for each other, how it transcended the usual grandparent and grandchild relationship, is to know just how perfect this really was. The lasting image I will never forget is how they would stand next to each other at the kitchen counter while she made dinner for us. He'd look up to her with his beautiful, blue, clear eight year old eyes, and she would sing to him.

Later on, at the funeral home, we worked out the details. If my father would agree, we could bury Keith's cremated remains with my mother's body. I called him right away to ask, and without any hesitation he gave his permission as I knew he would. It was his way to be generous when it mattered most. Kathryn essentially wrote the obituary which by consensus contained nothing of suicide or addiction, something that left me uneasy then and still does. Keeping these secrets seemed to endorse the idea that his death was shameful. Sharon had a work colleague who was a minister and offered to arrange for the graveside prayers. I would see to the new stone for my mother and my son. The wake would be in three days, on Friday, hopefully enough time to at least collect ourselves. In the face of such a grief as ours, it seemed Grace allowed for an ease among us, and sorrow itself provided a gentle sort of exhaustion that rendered resistance nearly impossible.

Sharon had phoned the staff at the Eighth Floor earlier to advise them that Alicia's step brother had killed himself. There had already been a tentative plan to discharge her Friday. We agreed to a meeting with her caregivers later in the afternoon to discuss this and how we might go about telling her what happened. As for me, I prayed. I prayed for patience and grace with the staff. I prayed the best way would be found. Mostly, I prayed for love to prevail.

Before meeting with Alicia, we gathered with about five or six of them. There was a psychiatrist, a psychiatric nurse practitioner, a social worker, her nurse for the day, some sort of supervisor and maybe a student something-or-other. I'm not sure we were capable of hearing them, but it seemed important to them that they have their say. When they were done I exchanged a look with Sharon and then had mine. I said something about being grateful that Alicia was in such a supportive environment, and followed with a suggestion that Sharon and I speak to her alone. If she reacted in some unforeseen way, we'd rest in the assurance that clinical assistance was right outside the door. Their egos assuaged, they looked at each other, gave a collective shrug and said that seemed like a good idea. It also let them off the hook.

She knew something was so wrong and her anxiety was palpable. This was not visiting time and this room was not where we usually sat. She looked at us and we at her. We told her and then held on tightly as her grief rose up against the effects of the medications she'd been given. Grief prevailed. Her brother. The one she felt so close to. The one who had saved her life even before she could reliably remember. Look at almost any photograph of the children over time and there she would be next to him. Now? Gone. Just like that. Now, of all the times.

*   *   *   *   *

A steel bridge carries the Camino across the canal locks in Fromista. A perfect breeze plays lightly on the air as I enter the town and walk down the street. Breakfast has worn-off and it's time to eat again. I find an empty café and the owner makes a fresh bacon *bocadillo* for me. Sitting there, I consider the remainder of the walk for today across a 25 kilometer swath of the great Meseta, flat and open as the infinite can seem on earth. I'm hoping the sky does not change its character today with low chunky clouds all the way to the horizons and spaced so perfectly. Several small Camino towns and villages lie ahead and the track of the path is quite straight.

It's a dreamy sort of day. I'm walking easily, unconcerned about time or distance, absorbing and noticing as best I can. There is a large golden field of mustard with a lone tree at its center and even under the overcast sky, its beauty stops me cold. I have not seen a mustard field since before Burgos, and the memory of that first one near Pamplona fills my mind. I stop to photograph a snail as it crosses the Camino and looking at the shot I can see it will also remind me of the typical fine stone and dirt finish of the path that allows for that beautiful crunch under foot I love so much.

Passing through Villamentero, population 11, I notice an *albergue* and café with an inviting looking yard that has tables and chairs scattered throughout. Sitting at the edge of the yard with a Coke in hand, I watch a donkey wander in and go from table to table. Pilgrims pet it on the snout until the owner shoos the animal away, admonishing harshly for begging. A rough looking dog arrives to assist and herds the donkey out of the yard. Finishing my drink, I leave here and continue through the flat, endless emerald wheat and grasses, the clouds cruising low and deep. I could just touch them, I swear.

The Camino parallels a roadway for the final long stretch of the day. A man and a woman walk together ahead, and I am gaining on them slowly. As I get closer I can tell they are both laughing and talking loudly. Their mood is contagious, and as I approach to pass I tell them, "Hey you two, you're having way too much fun out here. Don't you know we are supposed to be suffering?" They both laugh, and as I pass I recognize the man as Romy. Looks as though he's made yet another friend and now behind me, I hear him begin to tell her his story of how I rescued him from the hotel lobby in Hontanas.

Further on, I turn left across the roadway and follow the yellow arrows into Carrion de los Condes. Immediately I come upon the 13th century Monasterio de Santa Clara, which is said to have housed Saint Francis while he was on this pilgrimage. I remove the pack and sit on a bench, my walk for the day nearly over. I contemplate his life of simplicity, his gentle insistence on forgiveness, and his suggestion that in dying, we awaken to our eternal nature.

"So, dying to awaken? Is that how it goes?"
"Something like that. Well, sort of."
"What do you mean?"
"Well, what if we were never born, so we never die?"

I'm lost; hopelessly, utterly lost. I have walked Carrion de los Condes from end to end twice and cannot find my accommodation for the night. I am out of options. I surrender. *Suficiente.* It is late afternoon and the plaza before me is mobbed. I'm looking over the tops of heads trying to get my bearings, when out of the crowd an older couple materializes and the woman addresses me. *"Peregrino!"* Then, by her body language I can tell she is asking me what I'm looking for.

"Gracias," I say. *"Donde esta Hotel Santiago?"*

The man nods and motions for me to come with him. I look at his wife and she too nods, points to her husband and gestures for me to follow. He leads me to a paint-chipped, unmarked door between two shops, reaches into his pocket, and extracts a key ring the size of his fist. There must be 50 keys, but he selects one and immediately unlocks the door. He enters, takes a step, and turns to make sure I'm following. The room is long and dark, some kind of storage area. At the other end is an open doorway leading to an alley. Potential headlines start to flash through my mind, but he somehow seems safe to me like any gruff angel would, so I follow. He leads me through the room, through a maze of alleys, another storage area, and finally to a side entrance of the Hotel Santiago.

"*Muchas Gracias senor,*" I say.

"*Nada,*" he says as he vanishes back into the shadows of his urban maze.

There is a tradition among those who live along the various routes of the Camino de Santiago, especially those who are older. When a pilgrim needs assistance, it presents an opportunity to improve one's standing with the Lord by providing for them. The Camino will always provide.

The hotel is dingy, but a shower and a bed are my only requirements these days. My efforts for this evening center on preparation for an unusual walk tomorrow. After leaving Carrion de los Condes, the Camino will maintain a straight path through 17 very flat kilometers of Meseta to the isolated outpost of Calzadilla de la Cueza. No services are listed for this stretch, so carrying food and plenty of water will be essential.

After a shower and change of clothes, I venture out the front entrance of the hotel in search of a market, now surer of my surroundings. There is an information booth I somehow missed before that is set up near a large exhibition of farm equipment. In broken Spanish I make an inquiry. My answer comes from a pleasant young man. By paying close attention and noting his gestures, I'm able to find a large market near the outskirts of town.

My eyes open to see rivulets of raindrops coursing down the window pane. After my usual routine of tending to the body, the spirit and the pack, I flip on the tablet to look at the local radar. Green and yellow returns are all about, blobs of precipitation moving quickly across the entirety of the walk to Calzadilla. Today will be challenging—a day of wind and rain. I dare not complain, for the usually wet springtime of Spain has thus far been so kind.

Poncho on, I leave the hotel in search of breakfast and ultimately I find a café. As I sit under an awning to eat, I can't deny a sense of dread setting in. Suffering is an option, I remind myself. Embrace this now and all will be well. The Camino comes to us in many ways and there is perfection in all of them. Soon, I set off.

For the first kilometer of the path just beyond Carrion de los Condes, the increasing wind is generally at my back. Already, my pant legs are soaked below the poncho's bottom edge. But now the winds shift abruptly and blow directly from the west, driving a much heavier rain into my face. The character of the walk today is no longer uncertain or ambiguous. The trek along this straight, flat, open place will be outwardly focused on the five feet of space before me. I have put my head down and opened my stride into the wind and water so I may close the distance between me and Calzadilla de la Cueza. The rain will force out my surroundings and drive me inward. This is the Camino's way for me today.

*   *   *   *   *

Hang in there. Hang tight. Hang loose. Hang around. Hang ten.
Hang out. Hang on. Hang up. Hang about. Hang until...

They drove a long way to be there for us. The funeral home was in central Connecticut, a place appropriately called Middletown. Our friends drove through Friday night traffic from the northwest corner of the state. All of them lined-up to visit with our family and see the body of our dead son lying in a casket we would soon burn. They stood in front of me wanting to be anywhere else and searched for something meaningful to say, and I looked at each of them and told them it's okay because there is nothing they could say that will ever make this right or better or make any sense. They stood there with us and sent a very clear message that we were not alone. They were our perfect angels. One lady, a distinguished woman who commands some serious respect in our circle, looked me in the eye and said, "This. Just. Sucks."

Other than the sight of my son's body in a casket, there were a few lasting images of the wake that will stay with me always.

There were two lost souls with us that night. My father and Alicia sat alone in the same row of family chairs, separated by three empty seats, delivered to their present condition by very different circumstances. Yet somehow they joined in an odd fellowship of the wrecked and devastated.

Dad was hard of hearing, nearly deaf, which isolated him. He also possessed a personality averse to interaction with others, isolating him even more. Sitting within a veneer of observation, a blank look on his face, he appeared insulated from any real emotion. Although he had always been an enigma to me, he seemed especially frail and feeble as he sat in a now over-sized suit that draped over his body ravaged by the effects of pulmonary disease. He was within the last three years of his life, hopelessly addicted to smoking, committed to his own form of suicide. But that night there was the added layer of the inevitable memories, the hidden sorrow, the sealed-in grief. As he sat there, his field of vision was filled by the casket and its contents, and his son warmly greeting and hugging a stream of anonymous people he did not know. The aloneness seemed too much even for him. When Father John offered me his condolences, I asked him if he would sit with Dad for a while and advised him to speak loudly. A few minutes later I noticed them together, but could not tell if John's visit was having any effect. To me, my father looked small and diminished and defeated, a vision of failed self-sufficiency sitting absolutely alone in an ocean of love and support.

Alicia sat in her own reality, one that I simply did not have the capacity to imagine or to join. Her grief was not occult. It was in her eyes, in how she stared into space, vacant and medicated yet laden with sorrow. It was in her slumped posture, her body language that screamed for love and help and to be left the fuck alone. She was conflicted in every domain of her humanity. Occasionally her mother or one of her sisters would try to have a word, but they'd end up walking away. I questioned the wisdom of her being there, yet could not think of any place else she could possibly have been. Despite the uniqueness of her reality, she was likely the one of us most present in overwhelming loss. In the strangest way, she may well have been the most authentic person in the room. Above all, what has stayed with me about her that night was her great courage as she confronted such an overwhelming loss.

My most intimate memory of my son's wake, the memory which only added to a quiet and complete sense of loss, came at the very beginning. We were gathered together in the foyer of the funeral home, confronted at last with that which all of us had dreaded for so many years. I looked to my former wife and my wife and said, "Let's go in now." Susan approached our dead son's body, between Sharon and me. We stared for an eternal moment before Susan lowered herself onto the kneeler and began to softly sob. My wife and I stood to either side of her, each of us with an arm around her, connected to her yet not at all to each other. An odd and overwhelming sense of the events of almost 30 years began to swirl about in a vortex of thought, as I realized the closing of one circle and the breaking apart of another.

"Never born? Never die?"
"Never mind."
"Cute. I suppose next I'll be told to just keep walking."
"That would be good. You still have so very far to go."

* * * * *

The rain is relentless, falling heavily and wind-driven for nine kilometers now. The water has wicked up my pant legs and I'm wet to the waist under the poncho. My shoes are soaked through. Though my eyes have remained fixed on those five feet in front of me, I somehow notice a seasonal food stand just off the road, a trailer reminiscent of the one Heinrich and I found in that other middle-of-nowhere. I walk over, but there is no shelter here and few places to even stand that aren't deep puddles. I can't really take the poncho and pack cover off to get my snacks, so I buy a bottle of water, a bag of chips and a pastry. That'll have to keep me going for the next eight kilometers to Calzadilla. I've long since surrendered to the rain, the wind, and my thoughts. Around two more hours of walking remain, maybe less with some focus.

Finally, Calzadilla looms ahead, first announced by a lonely church just north of the Camino. I slog through town and enter the warmth of the hotel and café as the young woman at the front desk holds me in kind regard. She checks me in and tells me to bring my dirty and wet clothing to her as soon as possible. It's almost the cut-off time for laundry service. For five Euros, she will wash and dry my clothes. I try hard to resist kissing her.

Underneath the poncho and pack cover, all my worldly possessions inside the bag have remained bone-dry. I dig out the flatly stowed newspaper, something I've been carrying for just such an occasion. I stuff my walking shoes with it and place them on the radiator. One cannot imagine the absolute necessity of dry shoes. With almost 400 kilometers of the walk behind me, I haven't had a hint of a blister. But after the soaking of today's walk, I check my feet carefully and find nothing brewing. Showered and changed into dry clothing, my laundry being tended to, I go down to the café just off the lobby for a late lunch. Ensconced now in these warm, cozy environs, a hearty *bocadillo* before me, I look outside at the pouring rain, immersed in gratitude for feeling clean and dry. Some pilgrims approach and enter the lobby. As I imagine the relief they must feel, my eyes begin to fill. I recognize this as compassion.

After eating, I bring the empty plate to the counter and ask for a *café con leche*. From my side I hear, "Hey man, feeling good to be dry?" I turn to see Romy grinning and nodding.

"Just can't tell you. That was quite a haul today. I came from Carrion de los Condes…you must have as well?"

"Yeah. Gotta feed now. Gotta feed. Mind if I sit with you?"

"I'd really like that…been looking forward to chatting with you since the other day."

We sit together and rehash our walking day. I've already looked at the weather forecast which is calling for clearing overnight and share the good news. He tells me he was reluctant to look.

"This Camino energy is really crazy sometimes," he says. "It didn't happen today, but sometimes I'll be walking along and everything seems fine, no worries, just into what's around me, and all of a sudden I burst into tears. Thank God it only happens when I'm alone. Ever happen to you?"

"Um…yeah. That's happened. Thought I might be going crazy. I'm really glad you said that."

"What do you think it is?" he asks.

"I think it must be different for each person, but for me it feels like something being purged, pushed out. I also get the feeling of being overwhelmingly grateful. I swear to God, though, there is intention and intelligence behind it. I'm convinced of that."

"Yeah, exactly! I know what you mean. I did the Portoguese route two years ago and never had it happen. Either it's the energy of the Frances route or something is different with me this time."

"Romy, I really think whatever brings us here is personal for each of us, but the Camino may be showing us this stuff just knowing we're gonna talk to each other about it. Maybe one thing it's trying to show us is that we've got a lot more in common than we ever thought; that there is some connection between all of us who ever walked this road or ever will. I can tell you that idea has occurred to me a few times. But what do I know? I'm thinking maybe we just need to let it be and let it teach us and not try to figure it out or push it along. It's a whole lot bigger and smarter than we are. Just need to let it be."

He looks blankly at me for a moment. "What?" I ask.

"The other day after I met you in Hontanas, I kind of separated from the French guy. So I'm walking alone and I start to pray and I'm talking out loud. I find myself getting forceful, you know? I'm like, 'Hey, it's the Meseta here. Shouldn't there be some insights going on? I'm ready for my message! Let's go!' Nothing is happening and I'm actually getting pissed. I get into Castrojeriz and hit that first café, and as soon as I walk into the place a song comes on the radio in there...*Let It Be*. It all came together for me. Don't force it. You can't force it. Just let it be. Now you use the same words. That's not an accident, man."

Romy's met a lot of people. It's the nature of his personality that informs his Camino. He loves to tell stories about the people who have shared the experience of the road with him, just as he has told others of our first meeting. His stories have some common threads. It seems he's been placed here to bring together, to remind, to validate, to allow for something, to create belonging for those so far from home.

Once, he saved two other pilgrim's Camino.

"I was taking a rest in that small village on the hillside after Pamplona. Can't remember the name," he said.

"Zariquegui?"

"Yeah, that's the one. So a Guardia Civil guy came in and I could hear him asking at the desk about a Canadian named Jeanette. Turns out her passport was found and turned over to the authorities, so they were looking to get it back to her. I asked the guy if I could see her photo in case I ran across her anywhere. You know how it is here. You can't get around without a passport. He showed it to me and said all she needs to do is call the Guardia and they'd get it right back to her."

"I just know where this is going."

"Right?" he says. "Next day I'm in Puenta la Reina and I meet these two Canadian women in a café who are trying to figure out how to get to the Canadian Consulate in Madrid to replace a lost passport. I recognized the one lady from her photo. Said, 'I got some news for you.' Couple of happy pilgrims right there, man."

Miracles happen on the Camino de Santiago and angels do exist. I've a hunch this particular angel is not quite done with me.

*   *   *   *   *

In the sweat of thy face shalt thou eat bread,
Till thou return unto the ground,
For dust thou art,
And unto dust shalt thou return... Genesis 3:19

For two days after the wake, I had intrusive thoughts about his body burning in cremation. Curiously, they were not terribly disturbing. I had considered keeping a small quantity of ash, but for what good purpose? It was only carbon. It was all that remained of his form. Better to let all of it eventually return to the good earth.

The service at the cemetery was mercifully simple and brief. The minister did a reading based on Christian beliefs, and her way was gentle and compassionate. Keith's mother then spoke from a pain rivaling that of his birth. Lastly it fell to me. Grief had its way. It always does. It erupted. I sobbed, I choked, I vomited-up the words from a sorrow I had never known before nor likely would again. It was not so much his death I grieved; more than that it was the hopelessness and suffering that was the second half of his life. But despite the method he chose, underneath its appearance of violence and desperation, I saw his death as soul's gentle release, a quiet choice, a peaceful lifting of burden. I saw it as his chance to breathe again, to see a light he seemed to long for all the time he was here, to find his own perfect place, and there heal his pain at last.

I still see his smiling blue eyes looking toward me so long ago from the rear of our canoe, and I wonder. I will wonder forever, I think.

He was beautiful.

CHAPTER 11

THE DAWN INSINUATES its earliest light discreetly, giving no real hint of what will follow. The streets are dusky and I watch my step until I finally clear the buildings of Calzadilla de la Cueza, looking to the eastern sky. Soon the sun breaks over the horizon, and in an instant the scattered clouds are brilliantly backlit in orange, yellow, pink, and purple as the light of day sears through. High-up and flimsy, they are no match for such a sunrise as this. Today the light prevails and I'm thankful for the clouds and their good service to morning. Today the light prevails indeed.

My dear old friend, the N-120 roadway, has swung back toward the Camino for one last appearance, though its hum and rumble are much less obtrusive now. It tracks along beside the Camino all the way into the first village of Ledigos, and will continue to do so past the small Meseta towns of Terradillos de los Templarios, Moratinos, and San Nicolas del Real Camino.

It will end just southwest of Sahagun, but other roads will replace it I suppose. There will always be another road.

Today the great sky is the star of my walk. It changes character every time I take notice of it. There are times when the clouds are diffused and high like when the sun rose, yet within mere steps a solid, low overcast holds sway. Next, a mixture of high and low clouds with large streaks of clear sky paints a patchwork of color across the contours of the land. It stops me cold as a hundred shades of green from deep emerald to almost yellow lay out before me. In the next moment, to the north and barely distant, I see a rainstorm as it pulls away toward the far mountains and beyond to the Bay of Biscay.

There are no pilgrims near me and good thing too. Another burst of tears arrives, divorced from any specific thought, to purge and cleanse—an emotional evisceration passing as quickly and cleanly as the changing sky.

The Camino de Santiago is having its way with me, and I surrender as completely as I have surrendered to anything before. Resistance has only proven futile. Awash in gratitude for my holy pain, in a resigned acceptance of its mysterious methods, I walk on. And as I march along, I do so in time, in a remembrance of the sum of events that brought me to this strange road, crossing the north of Spain. What an odd idea this really has been; to fly across the Atlantic Ocean to the Pyrenees Mountains and walk west toward the bones of a saint, following a route taken for a thousand years. Mystical energies charge the ground and swirl through the air of this thin place. The silence of it all is so powerful, maybe the loudest thing I've ever heard. In the dead quiet of the day, it rises up from the ground through my feet, at once ominous yet benevolent, then straight to my heart. It knows just how to hit the mark, to follow the path of no resistance. I have come to trust in the Camino's ways absolutely, and this is the very biggest thing there is because my heart doesn't open that freely. It simply cannot be broken apart again. I won't have it.

*   *   *   *   *

In times now past,
Remembered best for simple sweetness,
We would sit in the deep shade of the backyard tree,
Cooled in the hot stitch of summer,
And talk idly of anything that came to mind,
As he'd sip on warm beer in quiet Sunday rest.
When the time came to say goodbye,
We had learned well to speak with our eyes in the silences
of our deepest love.

Above all else, my father-in-law loved his time with the family. Pop also loved the simplicity of an inexpensive (okay, cheap) beer served at room temperature (okay, warm). When the heart doctor told him to cut down, he did, setting aside French-Canadian-raised-in-Maine stubbornness. Some things just made good sense. Some things didn't make good sense. Things like walking a few city blocks to the hospital while having a heart attack because he liked to walk and might not be able to do so for a while.

He called the house phone one night and I answered.

"Hey mista!" (He called me that). "If Sharon's with you, don't say anything. I'm at the hospital a few days now and..."

Intuitively, she was already directly in front of me.

"Sorry Pop, it's already too late. She's right here and she knows."

"Aw gawddammit."

A short, bald guy out of the north woods, he worked hard all his life and provided well for his family by laboring in the grimy industrial jungle of Bridgeport, Connecticut. He escaped Maine by way of a hitch in the Navy as a 16 year old during World War II, which he managed by fudging the birthdate and a signature on his enlistment papers. A tough guy in his youth and middle-age, he'd always throw the first punch in a bar fight and then buy the guy a beer afterward. This was in a time before the police would be called or lawsuits filed over such things. He was possessed of dancing blue eyes that could pull anyone in and make them feel at home, and to be in his favor was a good thing indeed. For me, being well regarded by him was the closest I had ever known of a father's approval, and it was pretty okay with him that I'd also been in the Navy. There was a quiet, reflective side to him as well. Deeply Catholic, he walked a few miles to Mass and back every day when his health allowed. Though he never talked much about his faith, it seemed something big happened for him there. His other church was Long Island Sound; his other prayer was fishing.

But to consider Pop, as it turned out, was to consider Grace itself. It was a lesson I walk with still today, and something to remind me that gratitude has nothing to do with outer circumstances.

In the early spring of 2010 while he was in the shower, Pop noticed an electrical wire poking out of the skin of his chest. Only he could see something like this and not be terribly alarmed. It would, he thought, be a good idea to make sure the site of the poking was extra clean, so he soaped it up, rinsed well, placed a Band-Aid over it and went on with his day. He had an appointment with his cardiologist in the not too distant future and didn't want to bother him with it until then. The wire, which had been attached to a pacemaker, somehow disconnected and worked its way through his skin. As it turned out, the situation was not an easy one to remedy, and apparently far beyond making a small incision and plugging it back in.

This was the first in a chain of events that led to a 56 day hospital stay while in varying degrees of heart failure. This was a man who would rather be walking, working in his garden, fishing, and well…anywhere else. He was taken there by ambulance this time, too weak to make the walk. I'm sure it was a tough call for him.

There was a sense from the outset that this might just be it. His stay was a roller coaster of medical status from "stable" to "guarded" to "serious" to "critical" and then back again as they tried to tweak his tired heart, maybe even to fool it. But hearts are quite wise, especially the older ones. They have a way of knowing when the jig is up.

While all this tweaking and life-saving was going on, there was Pop in the center of it, an island of peace and gratitude and tacit cooperation—even though he knew better, maybe even *because* he knew better. One day, I went to visit when he was in the Telemetry Unit, a place he and I referred to as the fishbowl. Floor to ceiling glass constituted the front wall of the room, and there were curtains available to provide an illusion of privacy. The door was cracked open. Laying there gray and motionless, his half-open lifeless eyes were fixed somewhere past the ceiling. I thought he was dead and no one had noticed. I turned away to look at the wall behind the nurses station that held the bank of monitors and found his. There was a tracing, a picture of his heart beating happily along. This did not make sense. Then from inside his room, I heard the familiar "Hey mista!" and turned back to find my clear-eyed, rosy cheeked father-in-law smiling at me.

"Sorry Pop. I didn't mean to wake you."

"I guess I musta dozed-off. Good to see ya. How you doin'?"

How am *I* doing?

I have a theory. I think he may have been exploring—the Soul out looking about at what might be next, maybe getting over a vague apprehension about leaving town. I could not help but recall that day many years before when I saw life take up my baby's body, that presence beyond a heartbeat. Life has its odd ways of reminding us about important things.

I kept it to myself for the most part, but I visited so often because our time together was drawing close, because each goodbye held the distinct possibility of it being the last. I don't think I was alone in that. So I watched him intently. I watched how every person who came into the room, whether to empty the trash can or stick yet another needle into his deeply bruised arms would always, *always* be greeted with a smile and a "thank you." I watched the absolute absence of sarcasm or frustration of any kind. I watched a man who could acknowledge his pain yet refuse to suffer. This was the Master's Class of grace and gratitude and acceptance.

And on the 56th day they let him go home. Hooked to a central intravenous line that infused a drug called Dobutamine, the big equation was reduced to this: Stopping the medicine meant the end. Home infusion requires skilled care, and Sharon, an RN, would provide this exclusively. She took a leave of absence from her work to do this for her father and to walk with him through the answer to the most important question: When is it okay?

He had faced this many years before when his wife had passed on. Then, he'd left it up to Sharon to know when. This time, he'd need to answer for himself. I knew what he'd do. I just knew.

I sat in his living room late one night on the recliner and started dozing. Pop was to my right on the couch, depleted and exhausted, looking so unnaturally small. Sharon sat to my left and faced her father. My head rolled to the right toward Pop as I tried to stay awake but fell off for just a few moments. As my eyes opened again, I saw him looking across to her. He did not see me looking at him. Slowly I shifted to see Sharon gazing toward him, her eyes locked on his. In loaded silence, they spoke of when. Their dialogue was left to my imagination.

I don't want this anymore.

I know.

Am I doing the right thing? Can you let me go?

You've always done the right thing. And yes I can. I just want you to be happy.

I know.

It remained as it should, between them.

The next day, they stopped the Dobutamine and a few days later he left us as he slept.

It was important to Keith that he join us for both the funeral and the family gathering afterward in Pop's backyard under the big tree. I remember how he fretted the details of getting a ride;

double and triple checking the arrangements. Keith said it mattered to him that he honor the old man, and I know he meant that because he loved Pop. But there was more to it. On that day with us he was bright and funny and warm. He was completely present and unimpaired which was not easy for him. He came through for his family when it really mattered. It was also *his* goodbye, for most would not see him again. As always, when he left he was sure to tell everyone he loved them. It was his way.

Pop was one of those people who could never really leave. Not completely. There will always be the things that have stayed with me. My consolation then and now has rested in what he taught me. Whenever I'm struck by a moment of Grace, or blessed with such gratitude that it wets my eyes, I think of his 56 days and all he showed me without saying a word; how he lived fully and then died with peace and dignity. I miss him terribly, but much remains.

On a mid-summer day, warm and clear and lovely, we who so loved him motored from the dock through the pungent aroma of tides and scattered Pop's ashes on the same glistening waters he loved to fish, while herring gulls circled and called out their plaintive welcome.

Release: Verb

　　1. to free from confinement, bondage, obligation,
　　　pain, let go.
　　2. to free from anything that restrains.
　　3. to allow to be known, issued, done.
　　4. to give up, relinquish, or surrender.

*   *   *   *   *

There is a curious yet sublime tension between the beauty that surrounds me on the path and the thoughts that inform these moments. How I wish I could give my fullest attention to each at the same time, but of course that would be impossible, wouldn't it? One colors the other I suppose.

In the village of San Nicolas del Real Camino, I come across Percy sitting alone on a bench in a small plaza. He stares at the ground in front of him, briefly looks toward me, but returns his gaze downward. I don't plan to disturb him, but as I walk past he asks if I will take a picture of him as he hands me his phone. I notice he is not smiling as I shoot the photo. I ask how far he is walking today, and he tells me he'll finish the day in Sahagun.

"Perhaps we'll meet," I say. He answers only with a nod.

After leaving San Nicolas, the Camino returns to follow the N-120 for most of the remaining seven kilometers of today's trek. I cross the road, and after a short while pass over a small stone bridge that brings me to Ermita Virgen del Puente. This represents the halfway point between Roncevalles and Santiago de Compostela. With the buildings of Sahagun now in sight, I take a moment at the simple stone chapel of the Ermita to give thanks for the untroubled passing of over 400 kilometers, a body intact and absent of pain, a mind at peace and a heart quite full. There have been about a half-million steps since leaving Saint Jean Pied de Port, and I maintain more than ever that I'm being carried through every one.

It's early in the afternoon when I check into the hotel. It occurs to me that I'm quite hungry having passed several opportunities to eat along the way, preoccupied with thoughts.

There is a café in the hotel that serves tapas until dinner time. After showering and posting home, I tuck in to several small plates of bar food. My friend Percy strolls in and looks around. Spotting me across the room, he smiles broadly and comes over to join me. His mood has apparently lifted from earlier. Of all the accommodations in this town, we find ourselves sharing this one, and now know the comfort of finding company so far from home. Sometimes, a pilgrim just needs a break from feeling alone, even on the Meseta.

Percy is a quiet, slender man in his early sixties with a shock of silvery gray hair. His wire rimmed glasses give him the appearance of being intellectual though they age him somewhat. He has a quiet voice but enunciates clearly and is well-spoken.

I'm in the mood to listen to anyone other than myself. He seems to be in the mood to be heard, yet I have the feeling this is rare for him. I sense he wants to take advantage of speaking to someone far removed from his life in Seattle—easy to find in the heart of Spain.

He speaks reticently of home and admits to a measure of guilt about leaving his wife alone. Other than some road trips with friends on his motorcycle, he has not been away for this long.

"I guess I owe her some travel after this," he says. "It's just that all she likes to do is go for long drives in the car. I'd rather take her on the motorcycle, but she won't go near it, and the car just bores me, miles and miles of nothing. I drive, she looks out the window. It's just one more thing that seems to remind me how little there really is to talk about."

"Not much to say these days?" I ask. "I'd think you walking the Camino might make for some conversation."

"You'd think."

"How long have you been together?"

He sighs a long, loaded sigh. "Married thirty-four years, together for thirty-seven."

"Long enough to run out of things to say?"

"Yeah. Long enough."

"You here to figure out what you want to do?"

"I'm hoping for some answers, that's for sure."

He fidgets a little, just enough to signal he's uncomfortable. I begin to wonder if maybe I asked one question too many. We stay quiet a moment.

"I've been walking on and off with someone since Pamplona," he finally says.

"Oh?"

He straightens in his seat, his eyes soften and his face relaxes.

"Yeah. Last saw her in Hontanas. Said she wanted a few days alone on the Meseta, but we've been keeping in touch by phone. There's nothing physical going on or anything like that, we just seem to have a whole lot in common and she's really easy to talk to. We laugh a lot and look at things much the same way. When we're walking, 20 kilometers goes by like five. Her name's Dani. Ever run into her?"

"No, can't say I've met anyone by that name."

"We'll probably meet up in the next few days, for sure by Leon."

"You think about her a lot?"

"I do, yeah."

"There's something about Dani, eh?"

"Yeah, but I have to be realistic about this, ya know? Other than being on the Camino, our lives are very different. She's an artist from the Sedona area; has obligations and family there."

"Married? Significant other?"

"No. She got divorced about a year ago. It's one of those things she came here to work through."

"And now here she is, thick into your Camino. So did she come to show you something or distract you or break your heart or maybe all of that?"

"I just don't know, but..."

"But there's something about Dani."

Another loaded sigh. "Yeah."

"I know what you mean, my friend. Sometimes the heart and the head can seem a million miles apart. Next thing you know they're like the jaws of a vice."

"I'll say," he says staring, lost into the space between us.

"Percy," I think to myself, "you're looking a little confused… and maybe a little familiar."

"You know, there are times when I wonder about the possibility of something beginning to make sense out here. That would be nice."

"Things rarely do make sense 'out here'. Besides, you've only come halfway. Why so impatient? And why the sarcasm?"

"I've been told that's my way…on both counts."

"Maybe it's time to change that. By the way, you could just let it be."

Halfway to Santiago and time is compressing. It seems as though my friends at home sent me off so long ago, yet leaving Saint Jean seems like yesterday despite the distance I've walked. The reality of life at home has very definitely transitioned into another one here, worlds apart in every sense. There are influences moving about this place that color things quite differently. "Just walk," I was told, "and watch what comes up." Sounds simple enough. But to pick out any single thing inevitably leads me down a labyrinth with a thousand passages that weave through the decades of my life. Thank God this pilgrimage has a million steps. I may need more.

*   *   *   *   *

I've always fallen into relationships easily—relationships of all kinds really, but I speak here of the more intimate ones. I tend to idealize, to try and see the best in others and in circumstances. I also tend to see myself more clearly in reflection.

But in the before-life of drinking, this was terrible and dangerous because my view outward was always distorted. Hostages were taken. Hearts were broken. Disappointment and uncertainty ruled the days for anyone who came too close. Darkness would envelop all my attempts to be decent and kind, and hope would be swallowed up whole. Relationships are always the most fertile ground for the carnage of our addictions. At my good and decent core, I could not stand the thought of doing harm. And so neither could I stand to look into the mirror. Conflict like this can only be drowned, alone in darkened rooms, head in hand. Drowned until the pain becomes too great, and the required storms gather. The choice of drinking or dying arises, grace intercedes, the white flag is finally run up, and the drowning ends.

The fog of war lifted, and my personality settled down. There were periods of genuine insight as brain and mind came-to. It had certainly felt cathartic to me. Time had passed. People told me I seemed "much better." But in truth I had been troubled and compromised still. Turns out, simply not drinking was not sufficient for a case like mine. I hadn't listened carefully enough in the church basements. I'm sure they'd warned me. Take away the almighty answer? Now we really have problems. Better have a plan B, my friend. But instead, all of the usual delusions of early abstinence took root. The concept that, "as long as I'm not drinking, all is well," partnered-up with, "all my troubles were caused by drinking. Thank God that's all over now." The basement people would have suggested I reconsider. Almost three years into my marriage with Sharon I finally did. Because I had become insufferable. Because I had failed at living. I returned with a high and singular purpose to a recovering life, ironically delivered on the wings of an angel who had asked for my help. But the truest, deepest changes happen slowly. It can be excruciating. The remnants of addictive thinking linger everywhere and inform everything. I could not simply flip a switch to dissolve it all at once.

Once upon a time and long ago, Sharon and I would speak with our eyes. Entire exchanges. Just like I'd seen her do with Pop. We would do this alone or in the presence of others, across a table for two or a crowded room. We would look to each other and something so certain and fine would resonate within us, within our tissues. I would first feel it in my chest, and then it would swell and spread all over. It was remarkable—this playful knowing and oneness of spiritual intimacy, a confidence, a security, a well-being. Easy, warm, full brown eyes of infinite depth and expression, they would pull me in and tell me a secret thing. When it begins this way, how could there be a doubt? How could that ever change? How could it not last forever?

Magical times breed magical thinking, I suppose. But of all the things between us that passed into never again, I know I have missed this one most. I can't remember the last time we spoke that way. I asked myself how this could have happened. I guess it began with the incremental ending of sweet things. Wordless volumes passing across a late night kitchen table became something else less lovely and then vanished. Hope for a family life at last became misdirected and distracted by the mundane, the business of running a home, and then a house. We ran for cover to our rooms, and wished we could have just said something that would allow for magic's return. Long-silenced wounds woke from their denial and begged to be considered more carefully, as the sure promise of change didn't arrive quite soon enough. What once looked good on paper just didn't hold up to a sharper scrutiny. Finally, under the weight of nearly unbearable grief, we became unavailable to each other's gently offered kindnesses and gestures of support as we fled in full retreat, believing we had come to not matter. Even the spaces of anger went vacant, bled of all desire. The only potential that remained in such entrenched circumstances as these was for a passive contempt to seep-in. And this would never do. This was not who we were.

And so finally, after such an extraordinary year of loss and heartache and pain, as the winter settled in, we faced our final pain together. At last, a conversation. With words. Words spoken without interruption, and listened to with kindness and compassion. These things we still held dear. I remember speaking of a hope that our hurts would heal and soften to something more kind to each—that in the end, only the love would remain. Lofty maybe, but I certainly meant it. It was a talk that made for an ache in the heart and a sigh of relief. Those who fear simply give up, whereas those who love accept what is. I once heard someone speak of the mistaken idea of failed marriages. Marriages are not failed, they said, marriages are completed. Now that's a lovely thought indeed.

*   *   *   *   *

Whether you turn to the right or to the left, your ears will hear a voice behind you, saying, "This is the way; walk in it." Isaiah 30:21

Leaving Sahagun under another richly textured sky, I cross an ancient Roman bridge that spans the rain swollen torrent of the muddy Rio Cea. Soon I'm back into the open flatness I hope will never end. Not only am I in the second half of the Camino de Frances, but in the middle of the Meseta as well. I want to slow myself to a crawl and have it last for the longest time. What I really want is to find a lonesome hamlet and a modest room with a window that looks toward the mountains in the distant north, where I can write forever as I gaze across the plains. This is my dreamy longing on my walk alone through the gently waving green of the Meseta. This is my heaven. Should I ever go missing, I'll likely be found here.

The road forks ahead where one branch of the Camino leans to the north, the other south. There are advantages to each, and I've considered them carefully. Forks in the road are interesting even if a bit shop-worn as metaphors. I come to a fork, choose a road and everything changes. But either way, I travel neither alone nor unguided. This is the great promise. Today I go north.

It is less of a choice than I'm making of it. Both roads rejoin in Reliegos where I will be tomorrow. I chose the northern route because it is the original one; the southern spur is an alternate. This way includes some of the finest examples of Roman roads in Spain. My feet will walk on material that was originally laid by workers of the Roman Empire during and before the time of Jesus. The road is so old that the original stone surface has worn away. The stone and dirt mixture is the substrate that provided support to the road's top layer. I am walking where Roman soldiers marched, where caravans of wagons bearing gold from the Galician mines traveled east across the Iberian Peninsula to the Pyrenees Mountains and ultimately to Rome.

Today's walk is one of absolute solitude, yet in an evident Presence. I am acutely awake to a shifting sky and a gentle breeze, to my shoes meeting the ancient roads, to a pack that carries well, to the endless horizons west and south. Far off to the north are the snow-capped Cantabrica Mountains. There are almost no other pilgrims here. I can only surmise they've taken the alternate route.

After a mere 14 kilometers, Calzadilla de los Hermanillos begins to show on the horizon. I sit in the grass on the side of the road. No one is around me, and I feel microscopic. It's just so big. I lose all perspective for a moment, but for some reason looking at my hands seems to help, then at a walking stick, then my pack. A sense of scale returns. I walk slowly into town in the early afternoon of the day, still a little early to check in to the *casa rural* where I'm staying for the night.

I'm compelled to wonder how people come to be in the midst of such a desolate, lonely place. The streets are deserted, and buildings are shuttered. It occurs to me that to live here must require an extraordinary love of place, though I wonder how the souls who populate the town might feel about this. I take a seat in the shade of a welcoming café, drink a Coke quickly, then another less so. I want to learn more about this stranded outpost. There was nothing for eight kilometers before it to the east. There will be nothing for 17 kilometers heading west.

After much wandering about, I find the *casa rural* which is lovely and inviting. A dining area with a vaulted ceiling occupies much of the ground floor, and there is a cozy living room off that. The bedrooms are arranged along a balcony above the dining room, accessed from a central staircase. The use of dark, roughly finished wood on the stairs, railings and beams creates a rustic feel, yet the place is immaculate and well maintained. I am soon greeted by a younger middle-aged woman.

"*Bienvenido,*" she says, smiling warmly. Somehow guessing my language before I have the chance to respond, she follows with, "It's good to have you here with us." Her English is only lightly accented.

After checking me in and stamping my Credencial, she leads me up the creaking stairs to the balcony, telling me, "You are the first one here today, so you can choose your room."

She shows me a few, and I select one at the end of the hall. Though any room would have been fine, this one has a view of the distant mountains.

"If you are hungry, come down after you freshen up and my husband will make something for you. Dinner is not until 7:00. You won't be disappointed. He is a wonderful cook."

I notice a menu on a table for two, take a seat, and begin reading although I know what I want. I can taste it. A smiling man wearing an apron bounds out of the kitchen and comes right toward me as if he's been expecting me.

"Hola!" he bellows from halfway across the room.

"Hola," I reply.

He arrives next to me, snatches the menu from my hand and turns it face down, slapping it onto the table with great flourish.

"What would you like me to make for you, my friend?" he asks in a thick accent.

"What I would really like is a *bocadillo* with fresh bacon and a Coke, *por favor*."

"*Muy bien*," he says smiling broadly. Tapping me smartly on my shoulder, he returns to his kitchen.

It's remarkable how something so simple can be made to taste so heavenly, but what he has prepared with his hands is delicious. Thick slabs of bacon are still sizzling and cooked soft as is the custom in Spain. The *bocadillo* bread has the usual tension between the hard crust and soft dough, but he has also warmed it for me, a beautiful touch. After eating, I climb the stairs to my room and allow myself the luxury of an afternoon nap. It seems I'm still the only guest in the house.

As I wake, I can hear two women laughing. They are in the room next to mine. Though they are giggling like teenagers, I can tell from the timbre of their voices they are older. I can't help but laugh myself as their silliness extends through the stucco walls between us.

As I make my way along the balcony, another pilgrim is being shown to his room. We smile as we make eye contact. He is my age, perhaps older, distinguished as one can look coming in from a day of walking the Camino. For some reason, his features conspire to inform me he is Spanish.

"*Hola, buenos dias. Bienvenido,*" I say.

"*Hola,*" he replies quietly as we pass.

In the living room, I sit and read and post for a while before dinner. A fire burns in the wood stove to ward off a late afternoon chill (I've noticed the Spanish have a very low tolerance for anything close to cold). Family photos adorn the walls, an odd mix of comfortable furniture is casually arranged about, and as with that small hotel near Belorado, I feel as though I am a guest in someone's home.

With almost an hour to go before dinner, I take a walk through the streets for a more intimate experience of this small, dusty Camino town. In waning daylight, a place will often seem more vulnerable to me, more willing to reveal itself, the details easier to see in a kinder light. Many of the buildings are made from mudbrick and as I look more closely, I see strands of straw mixed in with the hardened, dry mud. I place my thumb against the surface and press, easily leaving an indentation. Though it yields, there is a great strength, a sturdiness to it. I continue walking through the deserted streets to the very edge of the town, facing south where the immense plain goes on and on.

The tops of the wheat sweep languidly under a gentle breeze, soft and barely heard. I am a witness to the utter absence of any other sound than this. It is a place at the brink of everything else in the world. And where is everyone? How can I possibly be so alone in this town? A vague discomfort encroaches. Part of me wants to flee, but I stay until it just begins to break my heart with an ancient melancholy, until it almost hurts. There. *There* is the feeling of Calzadilla de los Hermanillos. Now I know. I know this place better.

Entering the front door of the hotel, I see two ladies sitting beside each other at a table for four. The gentleman I saw before is coming down the stairs. He and I arrive at the table at the same time.

"May we join you?" I ask, smiling.

"It would be foolish not to," one of them says with a smirk. "I'm Allison, and this is Jeannette. We're from British Columbia."

"A pleasure. I'm Stephen from Connecticut in the States and I'm so glad you folks got that pesky passport matter cleared up."

They both look at me dumbfounded until I tell them I've met Romy and then they both laugh out loud.

"I think everybody on the Camino has met Romy," Jeannette says. "But what an angel."

"I'm Peter from Holland and if you're talking about the Filipino gentleman from America, I've met him as well."

We're all still laughing as the woman innkeeper brings the wine and water bottles to the table.

Turns out I wasn't all that far off with Peter's nationality. He is married to a woman from Barcelona, and happens to be fluent in Spanish and English as well as his native Dutch.

Carlos comes out from the kitchen and introduces himself and his wife Isabella. He seems to fancy himself a comedian as he informs us we are the only guests and so has taken the liberty of pairing up Jeannette with Peter and Allison with me. He would like us to begin carrying on now. After he leaves for the kitchen, I tell Allison I'm beyond honored. She laughs. Peter may be embarrassed.

The Canadian Girls (as I dub them) are lovely and celebrate a lack of concern with appearances which is one of the many freedoms of pilgrimage. Jeannette is sporting a solid inch of grayish white roots under relatively short chestnut colored hair. She self-effacingly says, "When I get to Santiago, people who met me in Saint Jean Pied de Port will probably say, 'Oh, we thought you were a much younger woman.' By that time, it should be about half and half." Allison has short, spikey, sandy colored hair and dark rimmed glasses. Both women have an athletic appearance and are similar in age to Peter and me.

Isabella was correct about Carlos' cooking. His main course for us is prawns in a delicious sauce served over *paella*. He presents himself at the table several times to entertain and conspicuously seek praise for the food. As his comments become progressively more risqué, we see this as an opportunity to practice the ways of the road. On the Camino, one can expect to find eccentric characters, and it's easy to imagine how the isolation of a place like this could affect some.

Our conversation for the rest of the evening is of the typical pilgrim variety—shared experiences of the Camino and others, and of course each of us has had our own memorable involvements with Romy. We speak easily of how we came to be here. The Canadian Girls were inspired by seeing *The Way* and by their longstanding friendship. Peter, being from Holland, has known of the Camino since childhood. He is walking as Europeans usually do, for one or two weeks a year until the pilgrimage is complete, but he wishes circumstances would have allowed him a continuous journey. This is his second trip, beginning almost a week ago in Burgos.

There are advantages to both ways I suppose. Now in the second half of this walk, I'm more aware that even if only because it is so far from home, ending the Camino will likely be forever, the experience of it reluctantly consigned to memory. Of course I could always walk again, walk perhaps on another route, but then whatever would become of the wonder?

The 21st day of walking the road to Santiago begins shortly after dawn. There are predictions of rain later in the day, and with over 17 kilometers of open Meseta without services or shelter until reaching the first town of Reliegos, an early start makes sense. Last night, my fellow pilgrims and I beseeched our hosts to feed us breakfast before the usual time. They readily and cheerfully agreed even though it has required them to wake up before sunrise. This is typical of those who work along the pilgrim routes.

We all share the destination of Mansilla de las Mulas, though we will not walk together. This morning we speak about the opportunity for reflection before us, the lonesome beauty we will pass through, and this commitment we each have made to worthy effort. But mostly, we each have a very clear eye to the steps in which we follow, when this walk was so gravely arduous. Once again, pilgrims rise to walk the road.

The sky is clear, the air cool and crisp, as the early morning sun lights the world in warm and soothing tones. I walk through the streets of the town, past the yellow Camino arrows, and onto the great open plain. My shoes find the dirt and stone of the Roman road once again. My stride is broad and relaxed and the sticks are driving me smoothly on as I follow my long shadow into the open west.

CHAPTER 12

THE CANTABRICA MOUNTAINS, reassuring from their sturdy place to the north, a steadfast reminder of ascension yet to come, are with me again today. It's good to know they are there, for the Meseta in all its barren beauty and glory, its occasional eviscerations, has been a rough go. Some difficult memories are being exhumed out here, and the escape routes have all been sealed. I'm most certainly not complaining. This has been the agreement since long before I came to the pilgrimage. It's also been the point of the exercise. But the distant snow-capped granite that has rarely strayed from my sight now holds a promise of redemption and a healthy measure of hope. "Child, child," it says, "Walk on and you will be lifted to places you have not yet even dreamed."

I'm trying my best to stay more outwardly present in these 17 unbroken kilometers to Reliegos, to allow the senses their day. It's not easy. The mind wants to wander from the long flat of the walk, from the feel of my steps under the pack, the sun's warmth. It wants again and again to drift into the thin places where my attention is drawn away from the dirt and stone of the path, away from the luscious, gently waving green of the wheat and grasses, away from the nostalgic song of the Cuckoos, from the ever changing sky. It wants again to fold inward and show me new old things. The Meseta is sweeping past me. I am almost to Leon. Time, be my friend and slow this down.

"There's a difference between being easily distracted and being avoidant."

"Are you seriously accusing me of being avoidant?"

"I don't accuse. I observe. I make a statement. To say you're being snippy would be an accusation."

"Sorry. But I just want to soak this place into my soul. I want to keep it forever."

"I understand. How could you not?"

"I'll try to keep an open mind."

"Yes. Keep that."

Since the year when so much happened and everything changed, it could have gone any number of ways. I could have destroyed myself, for I surely know how to do that. Instead it seems I've been kindly regarded by the ways of grace and now carried along to Spain; here to contemplate not just the wounds of times past, but their direct connection to a deeper blessing today. I've been following this thread for some time, for years now. When I float that thought back home, I get some odd looks, yet most here readily nod in agreement. Their reactions are not surprising given the view of life that will deliver someone to walk an eight hundred kilometer pilgrimage. These are my kin. We have come to find such things.

Light encroaches. I can feel it. Though this walk was meant to acknowledge darkness, it will be transformed. It's nature's way. Crucifixion, reflection, resurrection. I remember my childhood nightmares would end as the lights magically came on, and fear dissolved in my mother's smile. Was it merely the lights or my mother's loving hand that removed the dark? These days, many loving hands conspire to help light the way.

*　　*　　*　　*　　*

"My name is Stephen. I'm alcoholic."
(All together now) "Hi Stephen."
Jesus Christ, it's come to this.

All I wanted back then during the early summer of 1991, was for one of them to disagree with me. Just one.

"Actually," one of them could have said, "You're most likely not alcoholic at all. You strike me as a possible problem drinker who's just going through a rough spell. We're real drunks here. This place is not for you. Go home and cut the shit. You'll be fine."

But no. They just said "hi."

I believed alcohol to be the problem. It simply had to be only that. For nine long years it went on before life finally delivered a message: Get to the real problem and into the solution or lose everything. I had become irritable and angry and discontented. Nothing seemed right and everything seemed wrong. My answer had been removed and nothing had replaced it. Even worse, others were involved and we were going down fast.

A call came asking for my help. A call from Keith. Darkness yields.

Angels can appear in unlikely ways. But this one had a pedigree, had saved lives before. It came out of the blue as good things often will. His request was simple enough: "Could you take me to a meeting? I don't think I can do this anymore." There really are no rules in Twelve Step land, but there are strong suggestions. Not becoming involved in the recovery of a family member is one. It just never works out. I'm aware that 'never' is an absolute. But go to a meeting? Sure thing. I hadn't darkened the doors there in quite some time. It would be good to see if anything had changed.

A church basement, metal folding chairs, cheap coffee, florescent lights, slogan signs on the walls. Only things missing were the ashtrays. Times do change. Crusty characters mostly, but generally younger than I recall. That's too bad. Waiting for the meeting to start and looking around, I couldn't help laughing.

"What?" he asked.

"We used to go to Cub Scout meetings together. Now this?"

"Thanks for bringing me."

He was 19 years old.

I still can't exactly explain what happened that night, but it felt like this: It was as though nine years had been compressed into two or three days. It was as though I knew every soul in the room. It was as though I'd never been away. It was as though I belonged like I'd never belonged before. I just knew this would last. The lights had magically come on. How I wish he could have felt these things too, but it was not his way to go.

In the very early times of AA, there was a quaint custom that took root. In those days, people looking to sober-up would go to a meeting intoxicated, and one or two members would take them to the hospital for detoxification since alcohol withdrawal is potentially fatal. Most of the time, the drunks were broke, so one of the members would sign the patient in, or "sponsor" him into treatment. Upon discharge, the sponsor would show up with new clothing, usually a suit, and then take his fresh prospect to a meeting. In the process, he would share all he knew about staying away from the deadly first drink, thus insuring the continued sobriety of both. Of course it was rarely quite that tidy, but generally it worked well. Members have been "passing it on" for over 80 years and though having a sponsor is not required, it's strongly suggested. Going it alone in such endeavors is risky at best. The logic of it is breathtakingly simple: If you want what I have, then do what I did.

Enter Bob V., another French Canadian guy, a short bull of a man with very little hair and a pencil thin mustache, the kind you wouldn't even notice until after it's been shaved. He was 18 years my senior, recently retired after 40 years as a city policeman, and possessed of piercing cop's eyes. Bob was a family man with a drinking history that made sense to me. Many in AA have descriptive nicknames distinguishing them—his was Parking Lot Bob. If he cornered you after the meeting in the parking lot to talk sobriety, you'd be in for a long night. With newcomers, his strategy was to keep them busy until the bars closed.

Bob was placed before me as an example of how a sober man lives. When he spoke in meetings and afterward, I heard confidence and competence. Something suggested I pay close attention. Most important to me was that the life he spoke of matched the life he lived. I asked if he would share his way with me, if he would be my sponsor. He didn't say yes, he didn't say no. He said we'll talk about it. This is how it started with us.

Thus began the shift to a spiritually directed life, a commitment to living in the principles of humility, acceptance, surrender, self-examination and disclosure; a life offered in submission to the power of change, righted relationships in the world and with the divine. Though I have been far from perfect with these things, they are what have sustained me ever since. It is the most salient, most fundamental thing there is or ever was. Bobby showed me the way to it, firmly, consistently, and with infinite patience. He neither pushed nor pulled. He simply opened a door to new things, to unlimited possibility, and said, "This way, please."

During the early spring of 2010, he began telling me I'd outgrown him. I remember feeling that ice ball in the gut at just the thought of no longer having him there. I also wondered what he was really trying to say. He was dancing around something, being vague, being unlike himself. For people in recovery, radical shifts like this never bode well.

It was the first of the storms that year—before Pop, before Alicia, before Keith, before the end of my marriage to Sharon. A call came from Bob's wife. All she said was, "You need to come over and see this." Her shaking voice dripped with sorrow and disgust. I went.

He would not admit to being drunk. He insisted it was a reaction to medication. His wife looked on wordlessly, her eyes speaking of a nightmare returned, a terror, a curse, an unfathomable disappointment, and a betrayal just as surely as if there had been another woman.

"Do what you need to do," she finally said to me. "I won't have this here."

I felt it best to stay out of his battle, to follow some path that would hopefully break his denial from within. I told him that whatever had happened seemed to be very serious, and we should go to the hospital together to have this medication issue ironed-out. It took surprisingly little convincing. I helped him to my truck and slid him into the front seat. I found it odd that I could not smell alcohol, forgetting that for some reason I've always had trouble with that. As I drove, I began to entertain the idea that perhaps it was a medication problem after all, that my sponsor was not really intoxicated.

The medications were fine. His blood alcohol level was .239%.

One does not simply "decide" to do this after a long period of abstinence. Relapse is always a process, the end of which is a return to active drinking. Some things had started to happen that supported drinking, and some things had stopped that supported sobriety. But alcohol was not the real problem here. Alcohol had become, once again, the answer. What could have been his question?

We spoke the next day after he slept. He had talked with his wife and decided to check into a nearby rehab known locally as "the farm." His motives were unclear, but I suspected he was doing this so that life at home could become normal, which of course it never would. He asked if I would bring him. I told him I'd be honored. He was talkative on the ride up and this surprised me. Most who find themselves in this situation are usually very quiet. Perhaps he was trying to prevent me from asking questions he would not answer. He told me to find another sponsor. I responded emphatically that he would always be my sponsor. Nothing could ever change what he had already given me. I was very clear with him that I wanted a relationship, that I wasn't going anywhere and hoped the same was true for him. But our roles were reversing too quickly, and I just wasn't ready for this. Changes like this come hard for me. I found myself taking a shortcut and driving a little faster.

The following week I went to the open Saturday night AA meeting at the farm where speakers from the recovering community share their stories and offer those who are in treatment some experience, strength and hope. As I drove in, I saw him sitting in a rocking chair on the porch of the barn-like meeting space. He seemed so out of place here, a normal character in some bizarre dream. Though he greeted me exactly as he did through so many years of weekly breakfast talks, the light about him had dimmed. As we spoke, I'd hoped he would say something, anything of what he felt had happened, but nothing came. He spoke ambiguously, around the edges of things, never approaching the center. Clearly he was concealing something. I was accustomed to his insight and depth. Yet to press now would only have hardened the walls around him. Tonight, I'd be left to wonder some more. I listened with the frustration and compassion that only a fellow sufferer can know, wanting at once to shake him and then hold him close. A bell rang for the meeting to start and we went inside.

> *Constant elegies of time now passed,*
> *Nothing ever remains,*
> *Nothing can.*

Bobby was living in a disinterested, faint reflection of the sobriety he had once known. Treatment ended and he left the farm. For him, meetings were something to do, a place to go to get out of the house and away from the aloneness that had filled the place. He had no interest in sharing anything of substance. He had no interest in anything that I could see. I continued to meet with him and listen as he had always listened to me, and I would drive away from being with him feeling depleted. All through the summer and early fall my friend was leaving me in wistful little degrees, every day a little further away. And still, he had nothing to say about what had led him to drink.

When I called him on the day after Keith killed himself, he cried with me. It was all I could have wanted from him. On that day there was little else. Yet something that had been engrained in him awakened. I heard it through the phone. The best ideas are the simplest. Helping others helps us. An empire of recovery was built on this. Being there for me lifted him to higher purpose. Bob returned to me outright as my sponsor that day. I could not have dreamed of a kinder, more present friend. Strange as I know this may sound, it was one of the first tangible blessings around my son's death.

The week after the burial, Sharon and I had invited some Twelve Step friends over to the house under the guise of making use of all the food we'd been given. Truth is we wanted them with us so we could say thank you and maybe, just maybe have a few laughs. God knows we needed them. Bobby was with us that night and it was like old times. Completely in his element, he was animated and funny and sharp. One of his personal trademarks was an almost total inability to leave a place once he said he needed to go home. He had us in hysterics with about ten trips to the door handle. It was quintessentially Bob all the way. He finally did leave.

It's called *the last hurrah*. I don't like the term, yet I've used it. It seems flippant and disrespectful of its holy purpose. I've seen it before, many of us have; those last beautiful human expressions of the soul on earth as it collects itself to depart for kinder realms, one more spark of the personality as it prepares to end, one last chance to say, "this was a good thing we did here, my friends." The purity of this is virtually assured by its spontaneity, an inside job of the highest and deepest order. I will hold this memory of him for as long as I live because I believe that is why it was given to us all.

In early November, about a month after Keith passed, Bob and I spoke briefly on the phone. He had called to cancel a breakfast date because he was feeling terribly. I asked if he needed my help, and he refused. It was the last time we talked. Turned out he was loaded with cancer, and it was his secret to the end. He had told no one. This is all I actually know. It was the question he had answered with alcohol. He was gone in less than a month.

I sponsor men, but in that role I will never hold a candle to him. Not ever. He was indefatigable and felt understanding both problem and solution was well worth painstaking, meticulous effort. It was not unusual for our discussions to last two or three hours. He would have gone to any length to pass it on and did so—many times. Bob's ways were not for the faint of heart. Neither is recovery from alcoholism. To be sponsored by him required patience and diligence, but I was rewarded beyond any reasonable measure. Anyone I may have somehow managed to help along the way has Bob to thank, and it is my mission for them to know this.

At the wake, his wife gave me his copy of the Big Book, the text of Alcoholics Anonymous. She said he'd want me to have it. His beginners copy, it's full of brackets, asterisks, and underlined passages. It contains his presence and is the book I use today. There is a lovely innocence in those carefully read, annotated pages—an innocence that is the truth of us, the core of who we are. The Great Innocence, the ego at least momentarily diminished, willing to go to any lengths to save its holy Self. His final lesson to me? Stay innocent.

*   *   *   *   *

The Camino turns and descends a gentle hill into Reliegos, where the alternate spur from outside Sahagun rejoins the traditional road. I pass small *bodegas*, cellars dug into the hillside that serve mostly as storage spaces, sometimes as homes. The town is carved into a hollow near the edge of a large plain, a sleepy place where most of those walking about are pilgrims.

After five hours of continuous walking, I find a café with the familiar red plastic tables and chairs outside, drop my pack, and take a seat. It seems that every piece of outdoor café furniture on the Camino is colored red. I can spot these as easily as the yellow arrows, though from a greater distance. I eat and relax for an entire hour before restlessness calls once again.

The path leaves Reliegos, then parallels a long, straight roadway for six kilometers into Mansilla de las Mulas. I find my accommodation easily, a combined hotel and *albergue* with a well-manicured lawn where tables and chairs are scattered about. Some other early arrivals are getting a head start on pilgrim social hour. After checking in, showering, and posting home, I decide to get social as well. With dinner still more than an hour away, I head for the lawn. The soothing, burnt orange of a settling sun casts its dwindling light on a day now in retreat and welcome rest is in the air.

The Canadian Girls are among those gathered, and it's good to see people I know. After greeting everyone, I tell the girls this would be just the kind of place where one could reasonably expect Romy to appear. Allison tells me that Radio Camino (rumor mill) has him past Leon and suddenly walking 40-plus kilometer legs. Although we can't imagine why he would do this, we have little doubt our mystical friend has some kind of higher purpose driving him that way.

We share road stories and some laughs. The conversation turns to tomorrow's walk to Leon, a magnificent Camino city where I'll stop for two days to rest. The guidebooks describe the trek from here to Leon as dingy and industrial. My book goes so far as to suggest that if one was inclined to skip a day of walking, this would undoubtedly be it. I listen carefully to my fellow pilgrims, but say little. They present some compelling arguments for using the bus instead of our tired feet. Adding to the dilemma is a prediction of steady rain for the morning. All of them seem to be decided on taking the bus. Social hour breaks up and I take a stroll through Mansilla de las Mulas to consider the options.

There really are none. I came to walk. I came to carry my pack, my burden, my longing, every day through every step of the Camino from Saint Jean Pied de Port in France to Santiago de Compostela in the northwest of Spain. I came to walk in the breathtaking beauty of the Pyrenees, the hilly wine country of La Rioja, the heartbreak of the Meseta, then ascend into the hills and mountains of Galicia. I came, as did those before me, to do this in rain and in wind and whatever pain or discomfort may come my way, for to make this pilgrimage is unconditional. And at the end, when I look at my Credencial and documents, and kneel before the relics of Santiago, I will know I did what I promised to myself and others. This has never been an act to gain favor with some God beyond me. But it is all I can do to honor the everyday miracles that brought me here and those who walk with me, who are joined in my soul. The surroundings do not matter. Like life itself, sometimes they will be lovely and sometimes not. I most certainly will walk into Leon.

The rain drives against the window as I wake. I pray. I call on grace and patience. There are two full rest days just beyond the walk today. The memory of the long, drenching slog after Carrion de los Condes is with me, but I know I can do this. I will be wet and probably cold, but then I will dry and become warm. It is simply the way for me today. I take my time packing, go to breakfast, and look out the window as a soft, easy rain falls. I want to get to it. The leisurely pace of the morning has been my friend as the worst of the rain seems to have passed. I check-out of the *albergue* and take to the road.

The walk to Leon is 18 kilometers; the first six mostly wet, breezy, and raw. Entering the town of Villarente, I cross the Rio Porma, swollen to the banks by rain. A small restaurant beckons, and I stop for a couple *of grande café con leche's* and the comfort of the ubiquitous chocolate croissant. There is no push today. I'm more than glad I took my time and left later than usual. The steadier, heavier rain had fled north as I procrastinated leaving. I have no regrets about walking today. The worst I can say is the surroundings have been unremarkable.

Approaching Arcahueja near the outskirts of Leon, a burst of wind and rain slows the walk and soaks me. But by the time I first see the spires of Catedral de Santa Maria de Leon in the distance, the last of the rain is done and the wind lies down. An hour's trek along the sidewalks awaits me before I reach the Old City walls, so I collapse the sticks. The timing is perfect for me to call Dianne during the remainder of my walk through the busy streets.

My Camino has been difficult for her. We don't live together, so thankfully there is not the half empty bed to consider, but we are partners of the soul. Still, we are elsewhere and it makes for a hurt in the heart that will last for nearly two months. For the first time, we have very different agendas an ocean apart and this has been challenging to reconcile. Phone calls, though surely a blessing, magnify the challenge. On my end, I try to balance sharing the given day on the Camino, and making genuinely interested inquiry into her day at home. But I know her intuitively and can sense her natural suspicion of the latter. I find myself hoping we are doing well; that somehow we are coming to learn a deeper, more subtle language. Her presence is with me in every step. She shares in my act of pilgrimage. Yet how can I ever convey this? For today though, I talk with her most of the way to the walls of Old City Leon, and our conversation is lovely and lighthearted. It's time for her to start working and we have to end our call, but it's so good she is there for me to miss.

I've gone bourgeois again. Having recently turned 60, maybe I'm just feeling a bit entitled. As in Burgos, another posh hotel is my home for the next two days. It takes a little while to locate, because like many buildings behind the walls of old Leon, it is unmarked. I finally find it about a block from the cathedral on Plaza Mayor de Leon. After 18 kilometers of walking through varying degrees of wind and rain and wearing a backpack, I'm not sure I fit in all too well in the hotel's lobby. But with a swipe of my credit card, appearances are apparently forgiven. After a shower and change of clothing, I consider a nap, but decide instead to stroll around for a while and begin to take in the beautiful city of Leon.

I walk up a narrow street from the hotel onto the Plaza de Regla and stand before the magnificent Catedral de Santa Maria de Leon. Its construction began during the 13th century and took between 50 and 100 years to complete. A system of interlacing arches in the ceiling provides most of the support, taking the load away from the walls. The design allowed for huge windows, making use of the spiritual element of light filtered through over 1800 square meters of stained glass. My hope is to walk through at various times over the next two days and experience the interplay of light and glass under various skies. I resist the urge to go inside until I'm more rested.

It is late afternoon, *siesta* time. The plaza is almost completely deserted except for a few tourists and pilgrims. Out of this relative quiet I hear a woman begin singing. She is a busker, a street singer, standing near a corner of the Cathedral in an area that allows her voice to reverberate against the buildings. Her tone is flawless. I don't know what she is singing, but it sounds like a song of worship. Sitting on a bench now and closing my eyes, I'm transported by her voice in a swirl of echoes. Images from along the Camino come to mind like a slideshow, though in no particular order. It seems beyond my control. I have little idea how long this has lasted, but after a time she stops singing, and I open my eyes to see her walking away. I'm left wondering what brought her here when there were so few to listen.

I return to the plaza after dinner, hoping to see her again but I don't. More people are walking about now that siesta has passed. From a side street leading to the plaza, out of sight, I hear the sound of a single drum beat punctuated by wooden sticks tapping the stones of the street. Two taps for every beat of the drum. I follow the sound and see the front of a procession. It moves at a crawl along the street toward the plaza under a light gray sky in an early evening chill. Three middle-aged women hold an ornate, gold fringed banner aloft, depicting the Sacred Heart. Following them is the drummer, a young girl. Behind her is a large statue surrounded by flowers on a wooden platform being carried on the shoulders of fifteen or twenty women, also middle-aged. Six of these women carry long, thick black sticks, tapping in perfect unison. The procession moves for perhaps twenty feet, then stops. A few moments pass and it moves again. As the statue gets closer, I recognize it as an image of Mary sitting with her crucified son, reminiscent of the *Pieta*. The crowd, a mixture of locals, tourists, and pilgrims are absolutely silent as the statue passes on its way to the plaza. I follow, and as we approach the front gate of the Cathedral, several priests wearing vestments wait for the procession to arrive. Slowly turning through the gate, it stops to receive a blessing from the priests before it disappears into the sanctuary, the crowd folding in behind.

I cannot know what motivates these women in their faith, but there is something beautiful and deep expressing itself on this chilly evening in Leon, Spain. I have a growing sense that there may be more here for me to consider. Though still vague and amorphous, I may be at a beginning of something.

After an uninterrupted night of sound sleep, I wake to a clear and sunny Friday morning. My first thought is of how the sun must be pouring through the stained glass at the Cathedral. I want to run there.

An hour later I enter and as is my practice, first look to the ceiling. The placement of the rectangular stones defies gravity and I cannot comprehend how it holds. Everything I see tells me I should be in a shower of stone, that there must be a mystical force holding it all in place. Adding to this are the pointed windows that intersect the ceiling and create the illusion of the stained glass supporting the roof. The sun is still low in the east, behind the surrounding buildings, but the colors of the glass inform the light, and the very air of the room takes on a subtle rosy hue. The contrast between here and the Cathedral in Burgos is striking. I am immediately, almost involuntarily led to consider my own interior space, my interior life. This, it would seem, is the high purpose of church. Though certainly ornate in its own right, there is simplicity and humility expressed here. The chapels surrounding the main sanctuary are more subdued, more discreet; their artistry more easily seen absent of the glare of shiny gold and silver things. There is an understated power in this church that I have seen in the smaller, simpler places of worship along the Meseta. Here I can more easily see the plain beauty of stone carved by hands. As I walk around, I shoot pictures, but atmosphere can't be photographed, it can only be felt and remembered. The light is changing now.

Walking in the cloisters, I notice a cover of high clouds has moved in. Having now seen the light of indirect sun and overcast through the stained glass, I resolve to return when direct sun will shine through. The cloisters' passageways lead me to a chapel located next to the main sanctuary, but sealed-off from it by heavy doors. I take a seat in the rear pew and allow myself to sink in, to relax my body and feel its full weight against the wood. I close my eyes and fall into my breath. There is no sound here. There is absolute silence. It is remarkable. I have no prayers, I desire no thoughts. I want to be still. There is always noise. But not here. How can this be?

Leon represents a break from the road. More important to me is a break from the mind, the incessant thoughts and memories. The city's beauty, the crowds of people, the comfort of the bourgeois hotel and the food, are a relieving dip back into carnality, a rejoining with the good world of earth. I have no grievance with endless horizons, distant mountains, waving oceans of emerald green, or small, heartbreaking villages. There are simply shifting seasons. It's nearing a time on the Camino to slip into something finer, more discreet. But for now, I'll be content to move about the city, to live in it for a while.

Later in the afternoon, I follow the yellow Camino arrows through the labyrinth of narrow streets in Old Leon, through the city walls, and into the bustling, modern downtown. Eventually I'm led to Plaza San Marcos where I find one of the famous Parador Hotels. There are many of these in cities across Spain and all are located in historical buildings. This one is no exception, dating back to the 15th century and once used as a pilgrim hospital and *albergue*. Today, it represents the pinnacle of luxury, the finest of accommodations complete with silk sheets, and was used as a location for the movie *The Way*.

Facing the Parador San Marcos on the plaza is a bronze statue. It is of a medieval pilgrim seated on a stone step, his sandals off and placed beside his feet. He wears the cloak and tattered stockings of his times. His head is tilted back and his eyes are closed, hands in his lap with the right hand holding the left wrist. He bears a countenance of deepest prayer and utter exhaustion. I want to sit and have a word with him, to find out where he is from, to hear him tell me of how his village sent him off, and if they prayed with him as mine did. I want to know of all his hardships, how the kindness of strangers has carried him to this place, and where he might sleep tonight. I want to hear how much he misses his family and what he longs for most right now. Is he in pain? And what of his purpose? Is it forgiveness? Is it redemption? Is it to know the presence of God? I wonder if he is traveling to Santiago or on his way home as he maintains his station, placed here in an irony of the highest order before the silk sheets and room service of the luxurious Parador. He is at once inspiring and heartbreaking— yet another quiet statement of the Great Innocence, dressed in rags, going to any lengths as it seeks to save its holy Self. In him, I see us all.

Spain lives at night. Pilgrims go to bed early to rise at first light and walk. Consequently, I have not seen any nightlife since I've been in this country. Saturday morning holds no agenda, and tonight I will take in Spanish life after sunset. Leon is the place to do this.

Barrio Humedo (wet neighborhood) is not far from Plaza Mayor where the hotel is located, and it is something to behold. The only businesses here are bars, absolutely nothing else. It is an alcoholic paradise where tapas, small plates with a variety of foods, are served free with the drinks. Attractive to me is the drinks apparently do not need to contain alcohol to get the free tapas. A Coke for 2 euros has earned me a plate of *chorizo* and cheese with a piece of crusty toast topped by a slice of tomato.

I stroll through crowded Old Leon beyond the Barrio Humedo as the last traces of light fade in the western sky. Silhouettes of clouds are now barely visible. Before long it is fully dark, and I can more appreciate the multicolored lighting of buildings and fountains. This nocturnal culture has an artful means of lighting their way. But even in this busy place there is peace encroaching, a time when the city says, "enough." Some will protest; others like me will take heed. I walk through Plaza de Regla and stand in front of the Cathedral, otherworldly and illumined against the night as if from within the stones themselves. It is now as it has stood for over two hundred thousand nights before and begs to be the last thing I see tonight. I turn into a dark street and return to the hotel.

Saturday morning begins raw and overcast. It is market day, and I have never seen so much produce in one place. This is unlike the typical farmers market back home where often the goods extend beyond what is grown from the land. Here, the abundance of fruits, vegetables, cheeses, and meats is remarkable; especially considering it is only the middle of May.

I walk to the Cathedral Plaza to pick up the Camino arrows. Yesterday, when I explored Plaza San Marcos, I passed by the beautiful Basilica de San Isidoro, an 11th century Romanesque church commissioned by Fernando I. As the maze of narrow streets and alleyways delivers me there, I consider my purpose. I'd like to visit there to pray and collect today's *sello* for my Credencial.

The Basilica's design is quite unlike the Cathedral. Short, thick walls support the structure and allow for few windows. There is a retablo behind the main altar containing 24 panels depicting a variety of scenes from scripture. The light brown stone sanctuary is subdued, in its original state with the exception of modern pews that seem out of place. The minimal natural lighting is discreet as well, shafts of gray streaming through the small windows.

I'm directed through a side door to the church's sacristy where the *sello* is obtained. On the way I find a small chapel, quiet and comforting. Strangely, behind the altar is an ornate, shimmering gold retablo. As I sit here, I remove my pocket notebook and write the prayer I will offer at Cruz de Ferro just four days from now, where I will leave the stones I've been carrying. My prayer is for release, for forgiveness, for grace, a surrender of burdens. I've been considering it for some time and the words come quickly. Leaving the sacristy chapel, I find the *sello* on a small table and stamp my Credencial.

The overcast sky breaks up around mid-day and I sit on a bench in the crowded, bustling plaza in front of the Cathedral. I've decided to attempt an exercise of sorts in the lost art of being present, but absent of sight. I close my eyes. My posture is perfect, hands in my lap, palms up. A light breeze touches me. The sun warms my face and it cools again as a cloud moves over. I hear the voices around me, the conversations coming in and out of range as they pass by. I notice the variety of languages.

Sometimes, I hear a voice whose quality begs me to open my eyes, but I resist. In the distance I hear a familiar voice, faint and much smaller in the noise of the plaza today, but distinct and beautiful—the voice of the busker I heard the day I arrived. Still I keep my eyes closed. Some of her notes incise me, but most are lost into the crowd. Footsteps surround me, the soft click of hard soles and heels on the stone. A wisp of aromas, mostly of coffee and fresh pastries, waft over from the café behind me. I am here in an ocean of voices, faint singing, footsteps, the murmur of the crowds, a sweet, cool breeze, and sun kissed air. Finally it feels right to open my eyes. Just feels right.

Looking directly in front of me across the plaza, I see a pilgrim. Wearing his pack and still carrying his sticks, he obviously just arrived. He is limping as he walks toward me. Now I can see a broad smile, though his face is shaded under a floppy, wide brimmed hat. As he comes closer, I recognize Bill, whom I first met in Roncevalles, then again in Hontanas and Castrojeriz. Amazed, I stand to hug him.

"Stephen! Good to see you, my man. I saw you from across the plaza. What were you doing, meditating or something?"

"Something like that I guess. Good to see you as well. I saw you limping, brother. Leg still acting up?"

"I'll say. I'm taking a rest day here. Boy, what an ugly walk into town, huh?" he says with a grin.

"Not one of my favorites. You weren't tempted by the bus?"

"Nah. Here to walk, man. How long have you been here?"

"Two days now. I'm leaving in the morning for Villar de Mazarife."

He pulls out a map of Leon from a side pocket of his pants, and points to a spot.

"Can you show me how to get here? There's an *albergue* and I booked a bed."

I take a look and have to chuckle at the coincidence. "I was just there. It's right near Basilica de San Isidoro. Let's walk."

"Yes yes," he says. "That's the place. Thanks!"

Through the many turns of the Camino, we get caught up on our pilgrimage and who we've seen. As we walk together, I realize I'm having a different experience of him. He is more considered, more thoughtful, softer than before, the effect of having his life presented to him even though he had not been consciously seeking it. He has been lulled into the quiet way on the Meseta. The more life one lives before arriving here, the more things fold in. This is why the young tend to eschew it. There is usually less for them here, or maybe their thoughts just lie more in the uncertainty of the future. And what can one ever find there?

"Somebody was asking about you," he says.

"Oh? Who was that?"

"Can't remember now. Jeez, who was that?"

"Man or woman?"

"Don't know. I'm trying to remember."

"Thanks for mentioning it, Bill. That was helpful," I say laughing.

"Sorry, man."

"Have you seen Heinrich at all?" I ask.

"Not since the last time I saw you in Castrojeriz."

"Do you know Romy? Seen him?"

"I do. I think everybody knows that dude. Saw him just a little while ago. He was planning on longer stages—said he was meeting someone further on and had to push."

"No kidding. I heard he was doing 40s, so it makes sense. I wonder what that's all about."

We pass the Basilica and find the *albergue*.

"Thanks for guiding me in, Stephen. Damn good to see you again."

"You're welcome. Glad to help of course. I hope to see you along the way, my friend. *Buen Camino.*"

"*Buen Camino,*" he says softly, hugging me again.

As I leave him, I reflect again on how we once were and now are. Pilgrims change on the Camino de Santiago. We change indeed.

The sun shines through broken clouds when I return to the Plaza de Regla and enter the Cathedral. But almost immediately, overcast fills the sky, so I won't get to see the sunlight through the stained glass as I'd hoped. After walking through, I console myself with one more visit to the muted chapel in the cloister as I pray my goodbye to this beautiful church. In a silence so quiet I swear I can hear the energy of the world humming an endless single note, I realize more fully that I'm in the waning days of walking the Meseta. It is an idea that sits better with me now because I accept that my Camino must move forward to Compostela.

After two days, my old restlessness is stirring again. It's time to shoulder the pack, pick up the sticks, and walk the road west. The coming days hold the promise of change as the Meseta will shift into my past. The outer landscape will lift into rolling foothills and then to more dramatic ascents through the mountains of Galicia. But the pilgrim's challenge is to always stay in the present step.

CHAPTER 13

THE HOTEL BREAKFAST BUFFET BEGINS AT 7:00, which I really appreciate. I've not been off the Camino for this long and uneasiness has me in its grip this morning. I'm sitting here eating with the outward appearance of being calm, but truthfully, I'm tense. I feel coiled, loaded as a cat would be with his prey in sight; all of this potential energy confined to a table in the dining room. The remedy is to get up and walk, but eating is important so I keep packing in the carbs and proteins and *café con leches*.

Finally, I leave the hotel onto a deserted Plaza Mayor. The sky is a perfect cloudless blue, the temperature in the sixties with little if any breeze. I swing on the bag and step off. I'm walking again; the pack is snug, settling into my shoulders and hips as restlessness quiets. The side streets are nearly empty as I make my way to the Plaza de Regla. I stop to look at the Cathedral one last time. Slowly, I take the first few steps backwards before finally peeling my gaze away, turning to walk past the yellow Camino arrows and into the shadows of an alleyway. Before too long, I'm approaching the plaza adjacent to Basilica de San Isidoro where I left Bill yesterday. Just beyond are the walls of the Old City, where I will pass into modern Leon for about seven more kilometers of city walking before rejoining the open Meseta once again.

As I woke this morning, an idea occurred to me that almost took me by surprise given my commitment to walking the Meseta alone. I'm open to some company today. I don't know why, I just am. Maybe I've had too much time in my own head. But as I walk down the avenue leading to Plaza San Marcos on this Sunday morning, I can count those in my sight on one hand. I'll just leave it to the Camino. I walk past the Parador Hotel and pause for a moment at the pilgrim statue. I touch him on the knee as I say goodbye and wish him a "*Buen Camino.*" The yellow arrows point the way across a bridge over the fast running, muddy waters of the Rio Bernesga.

After crossing, I see another pilgrim almost two city blocks ahead. He seems to have a slight limp and though he looks to be moving along briskly, I think it's likely I'll catch up to him. Further ahead, I spot another pilgrim walking. Except for them, I have the street to myself. After 10 minutes or so, I'm closing distance to the man in front of me as he draws closer to the first pilgrim. The fellow leading the way is walking much slower now, his gait more unsteady with each step. I'm getting concerned for him. Suddenly he staggers, loses his balance, falls on his side then rolls onto his pack becoming tangled up in the straps. The pilgrim directly in front of me rushes toward him as do I. We find him confused and his eyes are glassy, his face red. He is repeatedly mumbling something about "*agua*" and as he does this we smell a strong odor of alcohol. The other pilgrim gives me a knowing look. We pull him over to a wall and prop him up against it. We place his pack beside him and I fill his water bottle from my spare. Just as we begin to consider our options, he promptly falls asleep. We both agree there is little more to do. This is how I make my acquaintance with Mark from Australia. He asks if I'd like to walk with him. The Camino provides.

Like many Aussies, Mark is friendly and funny and also blessed with a warm, genuine smile. In his mid-40s, he is ruddy and muscular, wearing a wide brimmed hat, tank top under his pack, zip-off shorts and some well-worn hiking shoes. Mark began his walk in Saint Jean Pied de Port as well, though he has not taken any rest days since starting the Camino. A few days ago, his left knee began to hurt, but he senses it's just a strain and nothing to be concerned about. He has been averaging over 30 kilometers a day because his time here is limited. At home he is a building contractor in a partnership with his brother who is holding things down, and Mark doesn't want to take undue advantage. He tells me he was undecided about where to go until two weeks before leaving home. It was either the Camino de Santiago or a long hike in Nepal, but he needed to get away after the ending of a long term relationship. "Wouldn't you know she took up with a mate?"

He vents about this for a while but not in an obnoxious way. It seems after more than 470 kilometers, the walk has been helpful with sorting things out. He admits his behavior wasn't the best with her. He said he could be depressed and angry sometimes, so he knew it wasn't good between them for a while. It seems to have been more hurtful to him that she started another relationship and with a friend no less, before breaking things off with him. Of course, he says, she'd like them to be friends, but he doesn't think that will be likely.

His kids, a 16-year-old son and a 15-year-old daughter from his former marriage live with him full time as does his brother, so they are well looked-after. He tells me the children practically pushed him out the door, knowing how much he needed to go away for a time and work this through. When he talks about his kids and brother, he softens and smiles and becomes quieter, the way men will do when they love deeply.

I can't help but notice how Mark is so comfortable discussing his life and his shortcomings. He's willing to take responsibility for his part in his troubles, and this sort of thing breeds trust in me. He asks what brought me to walk the Camino de Santiago. I tell him. I tell him everything.

"Christ, mate. That was quite a year you had there. It's good you came to walk. And I thought *I* had problems."

"Nah man, it's not like that. Whatever we bring to the Camino is important—matters to us."

"I guess so, yeah."

I have a feeling about this guy.

"You know, Mark, I've also got a past little something in common with our friend back there."

He looks at me sideways and grins. "Right. I might just have that too."

"I'm gonna guess you stopped drinking?"

"Oh yeah. Decided I wanted to live instead," he says laughing.

"How long has it been for you?"

"Eight years," he says. "You've stopped as well?"

"Yep. Been many years now, but it's all about the one day thing."

"Right. I hear ya."

"You a friend of Bill?" I ask to discreetly inquire if he's in AA.

"I am, but it's been a while since I've been to a meeting. I'm thinking that probably has something to do with my relationship problems too."

"Well here we are, my friend. My favorite topic is 'gratitude.' How's that?"

"Gratitude then."

Gratitude is a sweet little trap door of a meeting topic because it will always lead through so many good things. The real art of it is when we learn to be grateful even when our hearts are broken. My new friend and I can certainly join here. We tell our stories and we learn our stories as we walk along on this rolling little meeting of ours.

We walk past bodegas on the outskirts of Leon and through Virgen del Camino, finding the only modern church on the Way where a lovely older lady stamps our Credencials and insists on hugging us. At last we walk out onto the great Meseta under a clear big sky, the sun now getting high and hot. We walk through wheat fields and wild grasses and the first mustard we've seen in quite some time. Endless horizons beckon as we follow the blond dirt and fine stone crunch of the road. In the late morning, we come upon a refreshment stand that provides fruit and juices for donations. The timing is perfect because it's really heating up and there is little to no shade. We rest here a while and I ask Mark how the knee is holding up. He tells me it's doing well.

About 17 kilometers from Leon, we enter the Camino village of Chozas de Abajo. Here, we find a café with tables on a large, shaded porch. Both of us are famished and go for a hearty *bocadillo* with a slice of a Spanish omelet (more like quiche) on the side. We sit close to a table of three German women, Eva and Hannah, twins in their early 20s, along with their mother, Deidre. Contrary to the way many Europeans walk the Camino in sections, they began in Saint Jean and plan to walk to Santiago, then to Finisterre on the Atlantic coast. Both girls are outgoing and friendly yet respectful. Their mother is more reserved, perhaps because she is nursing what sounds like a case of tendonitis in her lower legs. The way they tell it, Eva and Hannah are inseparable on the road, but Deidre prefers to be alone and tends to walk slower, lagging behind them. They normally stay in touch by cell phone, so it's unusual for them to be together like this in the middle of the day. We share our Camino stories, none of us in any hurry to leave here. As I enjoy the warmth of everyone's company, I realize how unique a day this has been in my time on the Meseta. Once again I've whispered a wish and the Camino has provided.

From Chozas de Abajo, it is just over four kilometers to Villar de Mazarife, my destination for the day. As we approach the town, I ask Mark if he'll be staying here tonight or continuing on.

"I've still got some walk left in me today, so I think I'll head on to Villavante. Looks to be about another nine or ten kilometers and my guidebook shows an *albergue* there."

"Been a real treat walking with you, Mark. Thanks for the great company and the meeting. I hope you have a beautiful pilgrimage."

"Same here, Stephen. It's been great. When I remember you, I'll think of gratitude. *Buen Camino*, my friend."

"Me as well. *Buen Camino*, Mark."

We hug as best we can while wearing packs and I watch him as he begins to walk away from me.

"Hey! That limp of yours is looking better," I say.

He turns around smiling broadly, and putting up his hand, turns again as he heads out of town. I know well that with his pace, it's unlikely I'll see him again.

The *albergue* / hotel here is nice, with a café near the entrance and tables scattered throughout a shaded courtyard. I check-in to my room and as I soak my sweaty clothing in the sink, I realize there is no hot water. After notifying the staff, I start wondering how this gets fixed on a Sunday, in Spain, in a village near the western edge of the Meseta. A hot shower begins to take on great importance to me, but then I recall my bronze friend sitting on the Plaza San Marcos back in Leon. I decide to take a nap and hope for a shower later.

The nap fixes everything. I wake up feeling restored and then enjoy a long, warm soaking in the shower. The only thing lacking here is decent wifi, so I'm relieved of posting for the night. The phone has great reception, so I call Dianne and fill her in on the day.

After dinner, I take a stroll through Villar de Mazarife and note the storks nesting on the mudbrick bell tower of Iglesia de Santiago. Like so many of the small towns I've seen on the Meseta, this place carries the energies of isolation and desertion. Still, I feel comfort and peace in the soft, warm tones of the light and the cast of long shadows.

Tomorrow, I will walk 32 kilometers to Astorga. There is a town about 15 kilometers along the way, Hospital de Orbigo, which marks the end of the Meseta's wide open landscape. Can this really be? Change winds are blowing softly again as they once did in Burgos.

> *There is a whispered promise,*
> *Of ascension and relief.*
> *As circles close and the sun rises,*
> *Sleep coming to call then awakening.*
> *Tears that fall on aged cheeks will soon dry,*
> *If only left untouched.*

I have not used an alarm to wake up since the first day of the walk in Saint Jean Pied de Port, and after 24 mornings on the Camino this continues to be the case. I leave the *albergue* under another cloudless sky with light slanting in low from the east, the shadows as long as the walk ahead. It is cool and crisp with a promise of great warmth as the final steps on the Meseta fall behind me. I'm alone again for this, and all is as it should be. There is no one near me for a final heave of emotion on these grassy plains. As before, its cause is unknown to me. There are no echoes out here. The sounds come from my throat and then simply end as if in some kind of a vacuum. Maybe they just hang in the air for someone else who walks behind me to hear later. Silly I suppose, but one can get to thinking like this out here.

After a few hours and 10 kilometers of walking a long, straight stretch of the road, the town of Villavante, my first rest stop of the day, appears to my right as the yellow arrows lead me in. Mark likely stayed here last night and I wonder how his knee is doing. I leave my pack and sticks at an outdoor table of a cafe, then go inside to order at the counter. Back outside are two groups of pilgrims chatting with each other from either side of me. To my right is a table of three Australian women who appear to be in their early 60s, and to the left an American man perhaps in his young middle years with a woman just a bit older, American as well. I'm really not paying close attention, but what I do hear is quite funny (naturally—Australians are involved). At first I thought the Americans were a couple, but it seems they have formed a friendship while here and are walking companions. The banter is like background music to me and it's mostly between the women. The man is very quiet. Finally he gets up, puts on his pack and leaves, simply waving goodbye to the Australians and tapping his friend on her shoulder. She smiles in response and continues chatting.

One of the Aussie women asks the American if she is going past Santiago to either Finisterre or Muxia on the Atlantic Coast. She matter-of-factly says yes, to Muxia to spread the cremated remains of her younger sister she has carried from her home in California. The Australian women wait to hear more, but that is all she will say. Her way is quiet and dignified and absent of any desire for pity. If I never get to know her or see her again, I have all I need to deeply admire her; this from a brief conversation overheard in a small town out on the fringe of the Spanish Meseta.

Lightness returns to the interchange between these women. The American sees to it. It's time for me to go. Getting up and slinging the pack on, I feel it right to say something to them just as another round of their laughter subsides.

"It's been lovely listening to you all, really. I'd like to thank you for the floor show." The women all laugh again.

Looking quite directly at the American woman who carries the ashes, I nod my head and simply say, "Blessings." I can see the grief in her eyes.

She returns a reticent smile.

I begin walking the final five kilometers to the end of the Meseta. Though I had hoped for a lovely, sunlit quintessence of grasses and wheat, one more quaint hamlet, some quiet breeze and maybe a farewell song from a Cuckoo or two, the walk is unremarkable and mostly in proximity to roadways before I see signs of Hospital de Orbigo. After stopping at another café for a quick snack, I proceed through town and come to a very long Gothic bridge that crosses a river. The bridge extends across a large open field beyond, and into another section of the town.

There is only about a kilometer of flat walking beyond the western boundary of Hospital de Orbigo before the Camino folds itself into low rolling hills. Once again, I find myself at a crossroads—a choice between the traditional route and the shorter one which sacrifices scenery. The larger implication lies in experience, though. Who may I meet and what might they say? What will I see and how might it affect me? I recall the last crossroads. It taught me that whatever choice I make, I'll be guided. There is no need to worry. Intuitively then, I follow the longer traditional road and soon pass through the town of Villares de Orbigo.

Not long after, I find myself in the momentary throes of genuine judgement of my fellow pilgrims for the first time since the day I arrived in Saint Jean Pied de Port. Then, I had decided that one of my fellow pilgrims was a *tourist*, implying he was of some lesser station than me. Now it seems I am confronted with this yet again. As the Camino enters the hills, the path narrows. Ahead, I see a large group of perhaps 20 pilgrims, a mixture of middle aged men and women, clustered together and walking considerably slower. Immediately I notice they are wearing day packs—smaller, lighter versions of backpacks that carry only what one might need for the day's walk. Their clothing is a mixture of the quick-drying variety most of us wear and the blue jeans and sneakers one might expect of more conventional travelers. Almost none of them use walking sticks. At the head of this group is a fellow dressed as I am and carrying a full backpack. He seems to be in charge. I have seen a few of these groups before around the larger cities of Burgos and Leon, but not out on the open road. They are on a Camino tour, an expensive itinerary-driven guided experience where busses are used to deliver pilgrims to specific points along the route for day walks. Overnight accommodations are typically in finer hotels, with about twelve stops before the final drop-off at the outskirts of Santiago de Compostela for the final walk to the Cathedral. It strikes me as a bastardization of the Camino, sheer profitmaking, impure, unclean, unworthy and not traditional. Conveniently, I forget about my cell phone, my tablet, and the posh hotels where I slept on rest days. I forget about *The Spirit of the Camino* printed on the back of my Credencial that suggests I "appreciate those who walk with (me) today." Most of all I forget my exhausted medieval friend on the Plaza San Marcos. I wonder how he would react to his fellow pilgrims on the narrow path before him.

"Have I just been paying lip service to the idea that there is no wrong way to walk this road? People taking the bus, sending backpacks ahead, the tours—none of these things

have ever bothered me before. Why am I being this way today?"

"Are you angry?"

"It feels that way. It also feels like I could cry again for no good goddamn reason."

"So what are you afraid of?"

They hear my footsteps as I approach, and every single one of them makes way for me to pass. Every one of them wishes me a *"Buen Camino."* Every one of them smiles warmly. I slide past and greet them as if they too had walked 500 kilometers, because we are all on the Camino de Santiago. And because they are human, each one carries a burden; a burden that would make a 500 kilometer walk seem like nothing. There is a part of me that wants to hold them and tell them how the pilgrim road is a place where miracles happen; how I found our road to be a very thin place indeed. There is a part of me that would ask them to pray for me when they get to Santiago de Compostela. And there is a part of me that would beg their forgiveness of my judgment.

Though hilly, the farm country I walk through is wide open and expansive. I eventually pass an old man who I can see out beyond the edge of a freshly tilled field near the crest of a hill, stepping through high grasses. He stops, hands on his hips, and surveys all that surrounds him. This all belongs to him. I can tell by the way he stands and bears witness to the place. He reminds me that inevitably we must stand alone in our own fields to consider what has been planted and what has grown. The reckoning is unavoidable.

The sun is high, hot on the back of my neck and my shirt is wet. The farms are beautiful, but the dry, dusty road becomes challenging with many short ascents and descents. My legs are fatigued and there is still a long way to go before reaching Astorga—maybe another 10 kilometers from here. This walk is different and unlike the Meseta. It is vague and claustrophobic and leaves me uncertain about everything. What I feel deeply is that I need help. I hope this feeling passes soon.

The Camino climbs once more to a long, level plateau of sorts. Ahead of me, a crowd of pilgrims, some on foot, some on bikes, are gathered around a wall or structure of some kind along the right side of the path, and I can make out a refreshment stand in the front of it. As I arrive and turn to face it, there is a wall to the right, and an open space in the middle revealing a yard of fine stone and small tree plantings. To the left side is a covered sitting area against another wall. The stand contains a variety of fresh fruits and bottles of juices with cups, and after placing my pack and sticks against the wall, I approach it. There is a man walking around speaking to people who seems to be the proprietor. He wears shorts, a tee shirt and sandals. His brown hair is in a short ponytail and he has a scruffy beard. Tanned and weathered, he has an oddly youthful appearance, but I can't guess his age. As I help myself to a cup of juice and a hunk of watermelon, he approaches me.

"*Muchas Gracias,*" I say to him. "*Esto es tan bueno.*" (Thank you, this is so good.)

"Oh you are welcome my friend," he says in English. "It is good you are here. Thank God!"

He looks at me directly and earnestly with pale blue or maybe gray eyes that startle me with their depth and intensity. He squints as he speaks to me revealing crow's feet beside his eyes.

"I believe it is very important for the walk that you are nourished and find rest. Very important, yes. Take your time here. There is no need to hurry. Enjoy."

"Thank you," I say weakly, realizing now that I need to sit down. Assuming this is a *donativo*, I look for the box and finally find it almost hidden behind the juice bottles. I sit near my pack against the wall and watch what is happening around me as I eat and drink. I was about to fail when I came here. I don't know how, exactly. But now I'm nourished and centered. I am feeling rest like I've not felt in some time, maybe ever. I sit here knowing I've found a thin place where an angel keeps watch.

His name is David. He moves fluidly among those who stop here, and I soon realize that through no great effort, he makes his way to everyone. He offers welcome in whatever language is required. When he speaks in English, I hear him say it is about sharing. Everything here is about sharing. It is his practice and his purpose. He lives here nearly year round, sleeps on a hammock, and he provides. It is that simple. He is reflected in everything about this place and in the eyes of the pilgrims as he speaks to them. They soften, they smile, they rest. And then they mount their bikes or slip on their packs and move on as more arrive. He calls this place Casa de los Deoses (House of the Gods).

It's my turn to go and I seek him out once more. I thank him again for everything as I can begin to feel his energy. The air around him vibrates. He pulls me near and hugs me. When he is close to my ear he whispers, "*Buen Camino*, my friend. I wish you a beautiful life."

Blessing: Noun
  1. the act or words of a person who blesses.
  2. a Divine favor, mercy, or benefit.

Astorga is six kilometers away. Continuing along the plateau, my innermost self has been quieted, if only for the moment. I don't know what to think, so I just walk. I walk along this dry and dusty way with the sun at my neck, reflecting on the peace that has just touched me; this human being named David, likely as close to a living saint as I've ever met.

CHAPTER 14

A T THE WESTERN EDGE OF THE PLATEAU, a stone cross, Crucero de Santo Toribio, overlooks the small town of San Justo. The base of the cross is littered with hundreds of stones left by pilgrims. Beyond, I see the spires of the Cathedral in Astorga, and a clear view to the Cantabrian Mountains ahead. I've walked very slowly since leaving David and Casa de los Deoses. That peace will likely be with me for some time. I know with certainty I will never forget being there until memory itself leaves me, and I've a vague sense of having passed through some kind of portal.

At the bottom of the hill is a statue of a more modern pilgrim. This one wears a backpack, a wide brimmed hat, short pants with side pockets, and hiking shoes with socks that go halfway to the knees. His muscular body leans on a walking stick as he drinks from a jug and stands next to a fire hydrant which is a working fountain. I replenish my water and walk into San Justo, stopping at the first café I find. I am craving hearty food. Other than the fruit and juice offered by David, I've had nothing to eat since stopping in Hospital de Orbigo, and the walk has been difficult.

After packing in some carbs, protein and a couple of Cokes, I finish the walk from San Justo into Astorga. I resolve that 30-plus kilometer days are behind me for good, especially now that hills are back in the picture. Depleted as I face one last climb into the city, my legs move as though they're made of lead.

Locating tonight's accommodation proves easy and as an added bonus, it seems I've arrived before the laundry service cut-off time. This is cause for celebration. My clothes are in dire need of washing and I just don't feel like doing it myself. There is enough time to clean-up, explore the city for a little while, eat an early light dinner and fall into bed for a long, deep sleep.

The bells of the municipal building on the plaza just outside my room awaken me. I look out the window to find another cloudless sky for the 20 kilometer walk to the town of Rabanal. Morning prayers today leave me mindful and I dress slowly, almost as if I was donning vestments. The freshly cleaned clothing feels so good against my skin. Breakfast is available here, so I load up at the outset of the trek. As I eat, I remember David's words about the importance of nourishment.

Leaving the hotel, I feel energized and my pace is brisk moving through the streets of Astorga. I pass the famous, neo-gothic Gaudi's Palace and the still-closed Cathedral as I leave the city. Walking on, I stop for a moment of reflection at the tiny Ermita del Ecce Homo in the village of Valdeviejas just beyond the western edge of Astorga. Soon, I'm on the open pilgrim road. My stride is long and relaxed, the sticks tap along beside me, and the sun warms the back of my neck as a gentle breeze cools my face. I'm gliding along now as my friend Heinrich once showed me on the road to Pamplona.

Today's walk is very straight and will gradually climb about 400 meters by the time I arrive in Rabanal. Always before me to the west are views of the hills and mountains ahead, the Camino's silent promise of ascension. There are picturesque towns and villages along the way today and I resolve to rest and eat in each of them. The first is Murias de Rechivaldo, located about five kilometers from Astorga. The Camino's dirt path changes to patterned stone as I enter town. A small garden occupies the middle of a plaza and just ahead I see the red tables and chairs of a café on both sides of the shaded street. Though not feeling especially hungry, I sit here for a while and nurse a *café con leche*.

The road is tedious after leaving here, and I find myself walking a bit slower than usual. I don't know why I've slowed, but the weather is perfect and I have plenty of time today so I don't need to push. Santa Catalina de Somoza announces itself with red tile roofs and a rustic church tower along with the requisite stork nests, all visible just above the trees that surround the place. I stop at the café of an *albergue* in the center of town. There is a line at the counter and knowing this may take a while, I wander toward the rear of the building and find a courtyard lit by the high, late morning sun. It is quintessentially Spanish with a stone floor, potted plants lining the lightly colored brick walls, and a garden with a fountain at the center. A balcony lines the space above with separate rooms located along its length and a wooden staircase with tile steps leads up from the courtyard. It enchants me, and I make a note to stay here should I return one day to the Frances route.

After four more kilometers of the gently climbing road, I pass through El Ganso. It is a curious, forlorn place, mostly in crumbled ruins. Here, I find a nearly deserted Tex-Mex bar, replete with Texas Two-Step music blaring from within. I would not have expected to find this sort of thing out in the countryside of Spain, and after taking a quick look, I move on.

Ahead of me I see a female pilgrim walking alone who looks familiar. I recognize her as the American who is carrying her sister's ashes to the ocean at Muxia. There is something about the deliberate movements of her walk that suggests I give her room; that I not overtake her or engage in conversation. I consider this to be my best way to honor her purpose here even though I want to know more about her Camino. Before long, she disappears into the rolling hills ahead.

Later, at the bottom of a small ravine some pilgrims have clustered around a local fellow dressed in the garb of a Templar. Perched on his leather gloved arm is a great falcon. For a donation, he provides a spare glove which allows the apparently tame bird to move onto the pilgrim's arm. From within the group surrounding him, I hear a female voice call my name.

I turn to see Eva and Hannah, the German twins that Mark and I met on the road to Villar de Mazarife two days ago.

"Ladies! Nice to see you again. How are you two doing? How's Mom?"

They join me on the path. "We're well," they say together, then laugh.

"Twins," I say smiling. "You guys wanna walk for a while? I'm on the way to Rabanal."

We establish who each of them is, and they tell me they're heading to Rabanal as well. Diedre's leg is troublesome today, and she is a few kilometers behind. The girls will secure their beds, and she'll join them later.

Hannah leads the way and quickly moves ahead by 20 meters or so as we navigate a tricky stretch of forested road that is flooded in parts and forces us into the brush. Eva and I exchange some stories and talk about our respective experiences with David. Apparently, he had a similar effect on the girls and their mother. Eventually we rejoin Hannah, who is emerging from the brush into an open area. We pass a field where a few horses stand near a fence by the road. Unable to resist, they both go to the horses. We are just outside Rabanal. I say goodbye and continue on, thinking I may see them later.

Rabanal is a way station—a place to collect oneself before climbing to an emotional and geographic high point on the path at Cruz de Ferro, the place where burdens are said to be left. During the 12th century, a Knights Templar outpost was located near the Iglesia de Santa Maria de la Asuncion, a church currently operated by Benedictine monks. Every evening, the monks offer a pilgrim blessing with vespers service sung in Gregorian Chant. I've anticipated this experience since before leaving home, and I hope it will serve to prepare me for my time tomorrow at Cruz de Ferro.

As I check in at my accommodation, the young lady working at the front desk gives me my room key and earnestly urges me to attend the pilgrim blessing this evening. After performing my usual chores, I venture out for some exploration of this beautiful town nestled in the foothills of the Cantabrian Mountains.

As my good fortune would have it, the church is located directly across from the hotel on a small plaza. It is constructed of randomly sized stones, stacked and mortared such that it creates the impression of great fragility; that maybe a good wind could take it down. Its tile roof, once red, is now stained and weathered to a dull brown orange. A monastery is located across from the church, and its stones are more uniform in size, more tightly fitted than those of the church. The roof is dark gray slate. To the rear of the monastery is an *albergue* run by a British confraternity.

Entering the darkened Iglesia de Santa Maria de la Asuncion through the entrance on the right side of the church, I take a seat in the last row. Two other pilgrims are here, and it is absolutely silent. The sanctuary is small, with the altar in front and congregation seats to the rear taking up an equal amount of space. The curved plaster roof over the altar is supported by walls made from a mixture of stones that creates the effect of being in a cavern. Scarlet red carpeting covers the creaky wood floor. Along both sides of the altar are carved wooden seats, perhaps for a choir. The only external light comes from three small windows behind the altar. It is cool and dark along the back wall where I'm sitting. I close my eyes to pray, and prayer comes easily. Mostly it is of thanks, also for a full experience of vespers later on, whatever that may entail; a prayer to be present in the fullest sense.

After leaving the church, I stroll toward the southern edge of town. As with almost any place along the Camino, old farms dominate the landscape. Beyond the pastures bordered by crumbling, ancient stone walls, green hills roll into the distance and great snow-capped mountains lie beyond them. A cool wind blows now and the sky grows overcast. Low cumulus clouds quickly overtake the blue. The air suddenly feels raw. It could rain soon. I arrive back at the hotel as the first drops fall.

At the community-style dinner, I am seated by the host at a small table already occupied by a gentleman from Paris. Henri is in his early 40s. He is bicycling on the Camino for the third consecutive year; this time planning to go as far as Ponferrada before returning home to his children. He speaks serviceable English, but his thick accent forces me to focus in order to understand him in the din of the crowded dining room. He seems distant and detached, his expression flat. Though I'm finding it difficult to connect with him, an inner urge compels me to try. After polite preliminaries, he tells me that he arrived in Rabanal too early to check in and continued to Cruz de Ferro, a little over seven kilometers away. It was beautiful there today, he haltingly tells me. There is a catch in his breath as he says this.

Though not normally this forward so soon in a conversation, I've a sense he needs to say more, and ask him what has brought him to the Camino these past few years. He looks to the glass of wine before him. His shoulders lift and drop ever so slightly. Behind his wire rimmed glasses his eyes moisten as he looks to the ceiling. He starts to speak softly and I must lean in closer to hear him.

"Only five years ago my wife died. She had a cancer and was gone very quickly. There was little time for us to say goodbye, so I come here to do this. I left a stone this year at the cross. I try to say goodbye this way. It is all I can do."

"Oh my," I say, leaning back in my seat.

"You have had a loss also."

"You can tell?"

"In your eyes," he says.

I feel the flush, the heat coming across my face. I don't know why it is happening now but there will be no stopping this. Grief does not care about crowded rooms or the company of strangers. It does not care about the potential for my embarrassment. It does not care that nearly six years have passed; that I somehow think I should be doing better by now. I squeeze my eyes shut for a moment but it is futile. There is nothing I can do but see the reflection of myself in Henri's face. Uncomfortably, he drinks his wine, and my tears come. I take a deep, unsteady breath and let it out. Then I take another. I try to speak but it is too soon. More tears come.

"My son," I finally say. "And others as well. And a marriage that ended. There was just so much to let go of at once."

I take the napkin from my lap and wipe my eyes. It seems to be passing, thank God. Perhaps 30 or 40 seconds have gone by, but it felt like so much more.

"I am very sorry for all of your loss."

"Merci" I say, trying to smile.

He picks up the wine bottle before him and gestures toward my empty glass.

"No, thank you. Not for me."

"It can all seem so…cruel. Yes?"

"It can," I say. "How are your children doing with this?"

"It has been difficult. My parents, my wife's parents have been very good to us. They help care for the children. My son was seven years and my daughter was only two years when it happened. She really does not remember but asks questions. My son has suffered greatly. Everyone carries a great burden."

"Your stone at the cross today?"

"For us all," he says. There is finality in his tone. My distant friend and I have spoken enough of this.

Our conversation drifts to matters of the road and the differences between walking and riding. We are coming up for air. The difficulty in connecting returns for me, and I sense it's the same for him. I look around the full dining room. There must be at least 50 pilgrims here, many of them in animated conversations. Most were likely strangers to each other before they sat down. How perfect are the fates which placed Henri and me together at this table if only for some moments? After dinner, I stand and shake Henri's hand. I have no doubt that I will never see him again. My wounds freshly opened, I will go to the church for the pilgrim blessing. In the morning, I'll climb to Cruz de Ferro to leave the stones of burdens I still hold. All is as it should be.

Later, I arrive in the church early enough to have a seat, but I choose to stand in the rear with some others instead. How I wish my reasons were altruistic, that I'm standing to be considerate of others. I must be honest—my emotions are fragile. If I'm to have another release, I want to be in the back of the room. I observe as pilgrims arrive. We are so very diverse. Some seem to be amused or curious, others deeply devout. Appearances are often deceiving. At the appointed time, an older man wearing the monk's hooded robe, along with two middle-aged women enter the church and sit in the carved chairs along the wall to the right of the altar. A younger man, also wearing a robe, enters and stands before us. He says nothing, but waits for the murmur of the crowd to settle. When it is absolutely quiet, he speaks in Spanish for about five minutes. Pausing, he then speaks in impeccable English. He invites anyone who may be experiencing difficulty of a spiritual nature to remain after vespers. They need only to stay in their seats, and the priests will come to see them.

He then offers, "We are here to pray; to pray for your pilgrimage to Santiago de Compostela and for communion with the Holy Spirit. We pray to God. And God is here because you are here. If you are familiar with these prayers, I invite you to join in. If not, enjoy the peace of God in this place."

He turns and takes his seat opposite the other monk and two women. They begin to sing the first line of prayer. The Gregorian Chant's call and response is beautiful and haunting. Its mysterious Latin washes through me and stirs memories of church past. Closing my eyes, I think of my mother. Her presence becomes real to me. I speak to her in the echoes and spaces of the chant. She does not answer but only holds me. I have never felt this close to her outside of dreams. My mind wanders, and I entertain the idea that perhaps I'm being called back to Catholicism as I walk to Compostela. Is this how it would be? How would I discern between the play of mind and the call of something deeper? I let this go for now and allow myself to be held, to be washed through, to be lifted, to be somehow prepared. Perhaps 20 minutes have passed as the final lines of the prayer are sung and the last echoes fade. It seems to end on a minor note—something unresolved like a painting that holds a leaping ballet dancer in midair forever.

Most pilgrims leave the church, but several stay, presumably to speak with the monks. I stay as well in the quiet to contemplate the day now passed. I did not expect to react as I did to Henri's observation at dinner; that grief is in my eyes, although this was not the first time it's been noticed. Also, I've spoken about Keith's death in greater detail before without shedding a tear. Why tonight? Maybe I'm not doing quite as well as I'd thought. Maybe grief just loves to blindside. Maybe the time has come to let go the burden.

I step out into the night's chill air, into a soft, steady rain, and walk across the glistening stones back to the hotel. After posting home, I lay in bed, thumb through my guidebook, and settle on the page that describes the profile of tomorrow's walk. It will pass the mythical village of Foncebadon and on to Cruz de Ferro. Staring at a photo of the Cross atop a mountain of stones left over hundreds of years, I fall asleep with the book on my chest.

CHAPTER 15

A CHILLING BREEZE BLOWS through the open window and wakes me. Looking out as I close it, I see the sun is shining. I pray and stretch, then dress slowly in the clothes I washed after yesterday's walk. Next, I empty the backpack completely so that I may retrieve the small bag of stones from the very bottom, kept there to protect them from all manner of harm or loss. I sit on the edge of the bed and consider each.

There are six of them. All can fit comfortably in my open hand. A couple are not mine. One is a pale gray stone given to me by a friend and the other a garnet that Dianne asked me to leave. The remaining four stones belong, in every sense of the word, to me. Three represent the bookends of my lineage—my mother and father, and my son. I harvested them from the ground where they are buried. I was at the cemetery in early autumn, many months before the trip. The markers lay flat and flush to the ground. Because the ground tends to encroach at the edges of the markers, I go there twice a year to trim it back with a hand spade. Though I don't correlate the contents of the graves with who these people were, it sometimes saddens me that this care will end with me; that their names will be obliterated in time by the earth itself. At my mother and son's marker, two small stones appeared and Cruz de Ferro came to mind. Moving over to my father's grave, I found the other.

There is another stone. It represents the others. Life has presented the opportunity to be of some assistance to others; to share, to feel, to listen. People often need to be heard—really heard. And I have heard a lot—beautiful things and horrible things, joyful, uplifting things, and devastating things. I know they have taught me about courage and so much about my own nature. So maybe this stone, gathered from just outside my home, left at this place and at this time, can be more like the closing of a circle that holds forgiveness and peace for them. At least it seems to be a kind thought.

For me, there is a larger idea surrounding this matter of leaving stones, though. Any life thoroughly lived will have a large measure of regret and tragedy—the ruins of experience and relationship. I was a far from perfect son. I was a far from perfect father. Two divorces are the clear evidence of my abilities as a husband. I have a spotty record as a friend. My list is long. There is a ruthless parade of memory that reminds me that life has been littered with the residues of inflicted pain. Dreams of my own making and dreams shared with others will always be with me. But the pain and guilt and shame that I thought I had been long rid of, no longer serve me. They need to be cast away as stones on a pile.

Yet oddly, I feel apprehensive sitting here in my rustic hotel room in the village of Rabanal on this beautiful and breezy morning, about to embark on a ceremony of release at Cruz de Ferro. My stones have been with me since long before they were ever unearthed. Will letting them go be possible? If I can, will it be the end of me? If it is the end of me, can a finer self be realized? Part of me says, "Let them go for God's sake—it's only a gesture." Another says, "You'll never be the same."

> "Therefore, if anyone is in (the) Christ, he is a new creation. The old has passed away; behold, the new has come."
>
> 2 Corinthians 5:17

I place the stones in a zippered pants pocket and repack the bag.

Today's walk will climb. Beginning in Rabanal, it will pass through the ancient village of Foncebadon, then up to Cruz de Ferro. Leaving there, it will continue to the highest point of the Camino de Frances route, just over 1500 meters at Pena de la Escorpia, before a steep, three kilometer descent into El Acebo. There is much before me, but I'm unhurried.

The climbing begins as soon as I step outside the front door of the hotel and onto the stone road leading toward the countryside. It soon changes to a dirt path, making its way through emerald pastures near the edge of town and into open landscape dotted with scrub brush and low trees. The distant snow caps to the south, nearer lime green hills, the yellow and lavender wild spring flowers of the fields are the rooms through which I move. There is warmth in the beauty, and it staves off the chilling breezes. My walk is relaxed yet purposeful.

After five kilometers pass, Foncebadon comes into view against the hills. The wind suddenly starts howling. Had the sky been threatening instead of the perfect blue it is today, I might have seen this as an ominous welcome to this mysterious place. I cross a paved road and continue on the dirt path, following the yellow arrows into the town. Most of the buildings of Foncebadon look to be in various stages of crumbling ruin with loose piles of rocks punctuated by decaying timbers sticking out at odd angles, elegies of utter collapse. Just ahead is an *albergue* with a café, so refuge from the wind is at hand. There is a large group of younger pilgrims gathered in front, eating and laughing, seemingly impervious to the cold. I hear two voices call out, "Hi Stephen!" I wave and smile to Eva and Hannah, and ask if their mother is inside. One of the twins rolls her eyes and tells me she has just now left Rabanal. Inside is warm and inviting. I make my way to a space near the rear where I can drop the bag and sticks, then head to the counter for the usual.

The village of Foncebadon is 2000 years old, going back to a time of pre-Roman, Celt settlers. As with most of these places along the Camino, the atmosphere carries all the weight of its history. Here it seems more palpable than most and I can understand why writers have ascribed mystical and ominous experiences to this lonely, ruined outpost in the foothills. But even though the pilgrimage has shown me old things, there are places like this that bring time into focus for what it is—nothing and everything. I can close my eyes to imagine what was, yet only open them to now.

I leave Foncebadon behind and begin a brief but steady climb of a little more than two kilometers to the high pass over Monte Irago, home of the ancient cross. I stop several times along the way, looking back toward the village and taking in the views so reminiscent of my first day walking through the

Pyrenees. It is noticeable how differently my body feels during this climb. My breath and steps are easier now, which is good because hills will be with me until the walk ends in Compostela. The dirt path comes alongside a paved road for the final stretch as the cross finally comes into view.

Ancient Celts had a habit of marking the mountain passes with piles of stone, or *cairns*. The Romans also marked high passes by leaving mounds of stones called *murias* in honor of the god Mercury, the patron of travelers. History is unclear about *this* pile. At some point, the large wooden pole was erected as a pagan monument, but as the Christian pilgrimage became prevalent, an iron cross was added to the top. Those walking to Compostela began the custom of leaving stones on the pile; either brought from home or collected earlier along the road, to symbolize the sins and burdens they wished to have expunged by their act of pilgrimage. Prayers of forgiveness, release, and contrition are offered here as the stone is dropped.

Stones are perfect metaphors for sin and burden. They are abundant and have weight. They are very difficult to break and are made only over great time. We stand on them, and they somehow seem to support us. They are of the earth and often bear rough edges. As a child daydreaming in catechism class, I would wonder if there were stones or dirt in heaven.

The path leads directly to the cross. A split-rail fence runs along the right side where there is a large open area of grass and a chapel. I slowly drop the pack and leave it and the sticks propped against the fence. There are several pilgrims on the mound. Respectful of their time to be here, I walk slowly around the base of it and feel its energy which is not subtle. Centuries of forgiveness and release could hardly be. The wind has laid down a bit. The sun is warmer and the sky is still the deepest blue.

I approach finally and climb up, stopping halfway. I open the side pocket and remove the six stones. About two feet from the base of the post, I kneel down and hand-brush a small spot in the dirt to place them. When does a handful become a fistful? Tears come as I realize there is no way I can let these go yet. I extract the written prayer from the notebook in my back pocket. It is the prayer I wrote at the church in Leon—a prayer for letting go. There is a familiar feeling with me now. It's the same feeling we get at the cemetery when the funeral has ended and it's time to go; when all the beliefs about the truth of the Soul and the illusions of the body flee from us, and we are left to sit there abandoned utterly. I can't let them go. God help me, I just can't. I feel the flush, the heat across my face once again.

Suddenly in an unholy torrent, the collective burdens flood over and drown me. From long before the deaths of my parents and son, of Bobby and Pop, before the end of Sharon and me and all Alicia has gone through. From long before things went so wrong with Kathryn, before the ruins of relationships of decades past and the carnage of the drinking years, back in time I go. Time—everything and nothing. Through the longest tunnel I go to find the darkness in a childhood no eight-year-old or six-year-old or two-year-old should ever be a party to. Close the door and lock it tight behind me, tight as a fistful. Just drop the fucking rocks for God's sake.

"How are you? That's not a greeting, you know. I'll wait for the long answer."

"I hadn't planned on this. I thought there would be peace here. But thank you. I know you're concerned."

"Always. Remember now, it's very thin here. Things are often not how they seem. I promise you all will be well. Be courageous."

"I believe you."

"One more thing if I may…"

"Yes?"

"Breathe."

Before I left home, I read how a pilgrim does not usually find what he expects on the Camino de Santiago. But a door has been opened, not closed. This, it would seem, is a beginning of something—something long forgotten. Resistance is likely futile anyway. So then. My way or its way? What will it be? I've learned well that sometimes the best prayer of all is to simply be willing. Finally, I carefully place the stones in a sort of circle. I read the words I wrote in my notebook. I take a photo, then stand and step back a few feet. I take another photo that includes the base of the post and the stones surrounding my own, then pick up the pack and the sticks and find a spot on the grassy area. Laying down, my head and shoulders leaning on the pack, I consider a Cruz de Ferro that now contains those stones. They will be here forever. I watch pilgrims come and go for an hour or more. Now there are more stones. Quieter, less chaotic images pass across my mind now; images of a life that has dreamed of such burdens. And where *does* a dream begin or end?

Swinging on the pack, I walk to the base of the mound for one last close look and follow the Camino arrows west and away. I only turn around to glance back once more.

The Camino continues to follow beside the paved road for a while as I walk dutifully, almost robotically, slowly escaping the gravity of Cruz de Ferro. Ahead, a woman appears as though she is waiting for someone. Looking across the roadway to the left, I see her companion as he returns to her, his camera still in hand.

Crossing the road, I have to walk in a little before I can see it. As I approach, something faintly murmurs to me and asks that I simply enjoy what is before me. Directly ahead is a field of grasses and scrub brush overcome with clusters of small, lavender flowers. There must be thousands of them. The field gently rolls down to a stand of pine trees and distant from them, visible over their tops are sharply sloped pale green hills blossoming with spring growth. In the longer distance, perhaps five or ten kilometers away and perfectly framed by the pines, are snow-capped mountains still holding to a season now passed. Above all this is a blue so deep I can imagine the night. Settled atop the horizon is the slash of a loose, pale cloud, flimsy and perfect. Standing for a long moment, I wonder if I've been given recompense by the divine.

The descent into El Acebo begins three kilometers prior to reaching the town and thankfully there is a food stand at the top—the perfect place for a lunch break. What follows is the longest stretch of downhill walking I've yet done, and never have I been more grateful for the trekking sticks that brace my knees against the almost constant slope. With less than half a kilometer to go, I round the top of a hill and see the slate roofs and stone buildings sharply below. My legs are very tired, almost shaky. The Camino descends ahead at a frightful angle, and though I can see other pilgrims negotiating the grade, I am almost seized with a kind of fear that I've not experienced on this pilgrimage. I fear losing my footing on the steep slope. I fear rolling an ankle, or worse. I fear slipping off the path and tumbling uncontrollably down the ridiculously steep grade of this last hill. I fear an injury that could end my walk right here. I fear. Now what?

Dianne told me once in a phone call that she thinks I am courageous. I hope she's right. Like that first day of driving rain, climbing in the Pyrenees when the task before me seemed nearly impossible, I remember the prime directive of pilgrimage: No matter what, just keep walking. Now, every step down the hill is a meditation, every plant of the sticks well considered. An eternity of steps passes. Gingerly, I make it to the bottom, to the very edge of El Acebo. Fear, it seems, has passed. Within 30 minutes I'm standing in a steaming hot shower.

My accommodation is another combined *albergue* and hotel. It is newly opened, located at the farthest end of the town, with a commanding view of the valley in the far distance where I will be tomorrow in Ponferrada. Depleted, I sit on the lawn, view the foothills before me and consider this day now passing. The source of the fear that gripped me on the hillside eludes me, so I settle on gratitude. It is all I have left in me now. I am exhausted by grief and fear and things newly remembered.

Dinner is another community affair, and my table companion is a German woman. She is somewhat matronly and is close to my age, timid and quiet. After twice asking her name, I'm unable to hear her answer. I try to make conversation, but she is reluctant to engage. I don't think she is unfriendly, but maybe preoccupied. I understand. Dinner continues in a respectful silence as I can only wonder about her story.

After posting home, I try to read but my attention is scattered and wants only to return to the cross. I believe I've passed through yet another portal on the Camino de Santiago at the mystical mountain pass of Cruz de Ferro. Nothing ended today. Nothing was really resolved. Something deeper has surfaced. I believe my alchemy waits to the west.

Early morning scattered clouds hang low-slung over the foothills and dollops of sunlight splash across the landscape toward the distant valley floor. I am feeling optimistic about my walk. It's as if something is new beyond morning. I head down the dirt path's gentle grade that leaves El Acebo for the hills and small villages along the 16 kilometer trek to Ponferrada.

After about three kilometers, I pass through Riego de Ambros, which is deserted except for a handful of boisterous roosters that welcome me. Soon after, in what seems like the middle of nowhere and from behind the trees, I hear music. I follow the sound of reggae to an outdoor café, and find a friendly proprietor who promises me the best coffee on the Camino. As I drink it, he speaks freely about the life he shares with his wife and dog in the neat stone cottage nearby, and how he loves every pilgrim he meets.

"Every one?" I ask.

"Every one," he replies. "And no one complains here. Everything I make is so good!" he says, grinning.

In the enchanting Camino town of Molinaseca, I come upon two pilgrim couples, one a bit older than me and the other in their late thirties. They are unmistakably Americans, engaged in conversation at yet another outdoor cafe. I place myself at a table that forms a triangle between us, and wait for my moment until I finally ask, "So where are we all from?"

Tom and Emily are from Santa Fe and are walking the Camino on a retirement adventure. Ken and Elise are from Miami. All began the Camino in Saint Jean Pied de Port. As it turns out, Tom was born and raised in New Haven, Connecticut where I went to grammar and high school. We reminisce briefly about our old neighborhoods, and enjoy the comfort reciting familiar street names can bring when so far from home.

I ask Ken and Elise about their Camino. Both well educated, they decided before marrying that they wanted to live fully and travel well. After some years of working at conventional jobs and saving, they sold their condo, put only the most essential belongings into storage, got rid of the rest, and have devoted themselves to a vagabond life as they travel America and the world. Far from self-centered or indulgent, they try to bring love and service wherever they go. For them the pilgrimage is an exercise in reflection and adventure before heading off to the Philippines for a two year Peace Corps commitment. Though we make no immediate plans to walk, I'm hoping the Camino brings Ken, Elise, and I together again. We leave as Tom and Emily continue eating. Our return to the Camino proves to be a tedious, mostly suburban trek into Ponferrada, and we string-out along the way. Well before arriving, we've lost sight of each other.

The imposing, legendary Knights Templar castle looms large before me on the way to my accommodation near the center of town. It is early afternoon, *siesta* time, and the sign at the castle's entrance tells me I can gain access after 4:00 o'clock. In the meantime I check-in, shower, and head off to a laundromat.

All along the Camino, I've been drawn to places like this, though it's rarely the historical facts that interest me. I recall walking through the grounds of the Citadel on the hilltop in Saint Jean Pied de Port, and standing on the 10th century cobblestones of the bridge in Puenta la Reina as I watched the Rio Arga flow below. I'm reminded of passing through the Cathedrals of Burgos and Leon and the numerous medieval Spanish churches where I've prayed and contemplated. I remember walking past the Ermita Virgen de la Pena in Tosantos, carved into the cliff above the town, and the lonely ruins of the Mozarabic monastery at the edge of the field before Villafranca Montes de Oca. To touch and feel the old meaningful places like the *albergue* in Carrion de los Condes where Saint Francis slept, walk through the ancient air of Foncebadon, and kneel on the stone mound of Cruz de Ferro and add my own, brings me to the experience of my place in time's passing. Far from feeling separate from it as I walk through time, I sense I am being folded into its fabric.

Before coming to Spain, I'd thought the Knights Templar to be mostly mythical or at least enigmatic. Consequently, I have no expectations as I enter the castle and walk around, following the directions on a map I've been given with my admission. As I explore, it occurs to me that something about this place is odd. Most of the castle has been renovated to the point where the refurbished areas appear much too tidy and clean, like new construction would. The map points me to a remote, untouched section.

After crossing an expansive open area, I see large sections of the ground have been excavated, presumably for an archeological dig. The castle was built over older Roman and Celtic fortresses. Ancient foundations of thick walls lie unearthed, tempting the imagination to retrace a thousand years. Beyond this is a massive wall crowned with embattlements, untouched since it was built, with grasses and vines sprouting from the top and sides. Though not yet crumbling, it seems less than sturdy—its potential for collapse more plausible. At one end of the wall, there seems to be a way through.

I now face three more tall walls with towers at the corners, similar in age and condition to the one through which I've just passed. Together, they form a huge courtyard. No one else is here. The sun is lowering in the clear, late afternoon sky, and the walls cast deep shadows. The light is softening, early evening on the way. Steps on the outermost walls lead to the embattlements and walkways on top that were probably used by sentinels. The air within these walls is different, feels different in my lungs. In the silence I swear I hear echoes. Each time, I stop. I look around. But nothing is there—only walls and grass and clinging vines and a measure of decay. Sadness overtakes me. I don't know why. I can't connect to it, but tears are welling. It's as if something is speaking to me, pleading with me, begging me for release from walls under siege. Faint, single notes of distant trumpets reflecting on the walls hang then fade in thickened air. Despondency settles in as does despair and deep disappointment and fear. It begins to feel like I'm standing in a vortex where what lingers here has joined with the stuff of my own heart. The Knights kept deep secrets here. Then they were captured and tortured; forced to confess to things that were untrue. That's what legend says. Where *does* a dream begin or end?

"To sleep, perchance to dream; aye, there's the rub."
William Shakespeare

Tomorrow, I'll walk from the plain of this valley to Villafranca del Bierzo, deeper into the hills and west, ever closer to the region of Galicia and the city of Santiago de Compostela. But am I walking toward some ending?

CHAPTER 16

L EAVING PONFERRADA proves to be a pretty walk. After passing the Templar Castle and crossing the Rio Sil, the yellow arrows guide me through a park that follows alongside the river. There is a touch of humidity in the air this morning, rare on the pilgrimage so far, and I'm already feeling a bit sticky under the pack. The sky has been promised clear again after the early light fog burns off. The good fortune of having had so many stretches of fine walking weather has never been lost on me. Though there have been some gray, drizzly days, I've only had two full-on soakers since leaving France. Galicia lies ahead though, and it is known for being wet. After a few kilometers, I arrive in the suburb of Compostilla as the Camino takes me along the sidewalks of residential streets and through the archway and courtyard of a public building. I'm longing for a soft dirt path and the comfort the soothing crunch of my steps will bring. The open country will feel good again after being in the close quarters of the city.

There are seasons to walking the Camino—long seasons and shorter ones. There is the season of a single day. Maybe rhythm is a better word. Today feels more like a simple walking day, a movement from here to there; some more steps to take. I'm learning the art of pilgrimage is to at least try to keep everything in the step, to always hope for something yet not expect anything. Though it's difficult to avoid anticipation, the wisdom and intelligence of the Camino de Santiago is not a thing to be mastered or argued with. The best I can do is submit to its ways and know that only good will come, though sometimes with a price.

Further along, I am in Columbrianos, another suburb. Having now walked over five kilometers, I stop for breakfast. The humidity has lifted, the sky is cloudless, and I feel renewed. After passing through Fuentas Nuevas and Camponaraya, I'm finally released into a spacious landscape for a six kilometer stretch to Cacabelos at the western edge of the long valley of Ponferrada. It occurs to me as I pass these beautiful farms and vineyards that I have nearly 600 kilometers of steps behind me.

By the time I arrive at the outskirts of Cacabelos, hunger is calling again. The path turns to pavement and then sidewalks appear as civilization once again encroaches on the Camino. Passing a row of buildings, I see a chalkboard sign at the entrance to an alleyway. I can't read the Spanish message, but suspect it advertises a café. Turning down the alley, I'm soon sitting on a shaded second floor balcony at a table which overlooks a lushly planted courtyard. I drink a few colas and eat a delicious, oversized omelet until I can't eat anymore. Ordering a coffee and sipping it slowly, I consider some of the pilgrims I've known over the past month. I wonder where and how they are.

My lunch companions from the first day in Saint Jean Pied de Port come to mind. The only ones I've seen have been Robert and Sarah on that first day of walking the Meseta. The last I saw of Greg was when we walked to Estella and he pulled ahead. I assume that barring injury, he is nearly a week ahead of me now—likely within days of walking into Santiago. I think of the promise I made to Heinrich when we parted in Burgos about buying him a birthday dinner at the end of the pilgrimage should I see him. I wonder if I will. I keep watching for him and always smile when I recall that starry-eyed look he gave me when I last saw him in Castrojeriz. Bill, whom I first met in Roncevalles, the great adventurer I suspected of having serial carnal experiences across the north of Spain comes to mind. At our last interaction in Leon, I saw the changes the Camino had brought to him, and saw as well the limits of my own suppositions. And what of my old friend Romy? Perhaps he is close to or maybe has even already arrived in Santiago. He seems to have pressed ahead, suggesting something of great import must be calling him. And I wonder how the Canadian Girls are doing—how long Jeannette's silvery roots might be by now? My thoughts turn to Percy, whom I've not seen since Sahagun and his friend Dani, whom I've never met. Are they each other's purpose or distraction? The German twins and their mother touched my heart. It's unusual for generations to willingly mix like that these days. I first met them when I was with Mark the Australian, here to walk off the hurt of betrayal, but holding his own in gratitude. And for some reason that quietly enigmatic nameless German lady from dinner the other night has been crossing my mind as well. I still hope to run into Elise and Ken. I love how they live. And oh yes…the lady who carries the ashes. We had an understanding... something in our eyes.

Returning to the street, I walk west through Cacabelos, across a bridge and into the open countryside that puts the great valley of Ponferrada behind me. From here to Santiago de Compostela there will be many hills, and soon, the infamous climb to the mountaintop village of O Cebreiro. Ascension beckons once again.

The countryside is replete with vineyards and new growth cherry orchards that carpet gentle hills. The rocky red soil plays against the trees' deep, summery green and colorful wildflowers abound. In the distance the mountains of Galicia, still two days of walking ahead, seem so very close. They call to me and motivate my every step. At the hamlet of Pieros, an easy choice presents itself where the path splits. My guide book suggests veering right because it is prettier if only a bit longer, so I go that way.

Shortly after the split, I see an orchard of short, stubby cherry trees and just beyond it the ground rolls into a low hill. It is topped by two trees with long, branchless trunks that rise into dense foliage, flat and banyan-like. Together they shade a small, white stone sided home with a weathered tile roof. Beyond lay more distant hills, and further on, the mountains. There is something oddly familiar here, and it's not the first time I've felt this way on the Camino. Something in my chest gives way and opens, as if in my past this lonesome place once welcomed me home after a long and tiring journey. Where do feelings like this begin? Did an old transcendent dream lost from memory bring me here some time ago? For long moments I lean on my sticks under the clear blue sky, bathed in warm sunlight, and immersed in the reverie of a life here.

My surroundings suggest I am approaching the end of the day's 24 kilometer walk at the beautiful town of Villafranca del Bierzo. The road shifts from dirt to pavement and then to stone as I descend from a final hill. Soon, I find my way to the main plaza and my accommodation for the night.

After checking in, I wander through town and observe the beauty of its botanical gardens and pristine medieval architecture. Villafranca del Bierzo is quaint and pretty and clean, nestled cozily into the foothills that envelop it. A soft rain begins to fall and cuts my wandering short.

Sleep proves elusive. The memory unearthed at Cruz de Ferro comes to mind, and its haunting reminder of what has stalked me for so long, from my very earliest days. Darkness beyond the dark of night descends as the old familiar faceless horsemen of guilt, remorse and shame again visit, all asking me, daring me, to justify my very existence. That I should ever experience freedom and happiness on the Camino becomes something absurd; something of which I am undeserving.

*   *   *   *   *

Bless the innocent,
Cain and Abel both.
Am I my brother's keeper?
So I am to wander the earth then, the one who remains.

I was the first of us, born in 1956 to parents who had between them many disparate characteristics. One of the more significant differences was in their particular combination of blood types. At that time, this incompatibility brought with it potentially devastating consequences in bearing children. Our family was so affected. Twelve years later, a medication given to mothers during and just after pregnancy eliminated the problem entirely, but that came too late for us.

As my body formed within my mother's womb, our blood naturally mixed, and because our types were not compatible, her body responded by forming antibodies; proteins designed to attack and destroy something which does not belong. In my mother's case, this formation of antibodies was something that happened slowly over time and so did not adversely affect her first pregnancy. I was born without immediate consequence. I was born to live and breathe and walk the earth. But the consequence remained behind with my mother, to be enacted upon the children who followed.

There is a black and white picture that was taken of me when I was two years old. In it, I'm seated on a stone bench in front of Saint Vincent's Hospital in Staten Island, New York. I was born there as was my father. I've always assumed the picture was taken by him, though I have no idea what may have brought us there. I appear to be smiling and looking toward the sky. Judging from my clothing and the foliage in the background, it is likely springtime and close to my birthday. On the surface of it, that's about all—a photo of a little kid sitting on a bench.

But what of the child's Soul, the truth of him that lies beyond the limits of form and maturity and mental comprehension? Does he know what has just transpired? Does he know that about two months before this, in the very hospital he sits before, his mother gave birth to another son? Could he be aware that his brother did not survive beyond two hours of life? Could he know why? Could he know that a corner has been rounded from which there is no return? That his family would experience the loss of a baby girl four years later during the eighth month of pregnancy? Could he ever have known that two years after they would all share the experience of yet another girl born and gone within minutes? And what of his parents and their experience of loss no one is designed to accept? Could he know on some level beyond cognition that he would one day know a similar loss as well?

*   *   *   *   *

Sleep please come for I am so tired
Release me to good rest I pray
That I may dream again more dreams tomorrow.

Sleep was minimal last night. Befogged, I can't think straight. Walking through the town of Villafranca del Bierzo this morning, a choice presents. Should I travel over the hills, or through the valley? Now within a kilometer of another split in the Camino, I just can't decide. The valley route makes sense because I'm tired. Yet the high road beckons. I recognize the split as pictured in my guide book. A stone road veers to the right from the paved road and launches immediately up the side of a steep hill, but I notice something. The signs indicating the split have been removed. Black paint has been drawn over a yellow arrow on the surface of the stone road heading upward. It appears the high road has been closed. I'm relieved.

The Camino follows along a little-used road, behind crash barriers placed there to protect pilgrims as they walk. There is a numbing sameness about the landscape, hills with dense forest rising on either side from the road, curve after curve. It's a gray day, feeling a bit close, with some light rain possible, and I'm a little depressed. It's one of those days where one can more easily see how the interior life is projected outward. My guide book explains the road today will be on pavement all the way to my destination at the small village of Herrerias. Today, there will be no soft crunching of my shoes on dirt.

The first village I come upon is Pereje and here I find a café for breakfast. I should have eaten before leaving Villafranca del Bierzo, but in my fog I simply walked out of town. I watch my fellow pilgrims come and go, a bit envious of the ones who smile and laugh.

Herrerias is a pretty hamlet, tucked into a small valley beside a river. During the 17th century, life here was centered on smelting iron mined from the hills. Today, as with most Camino towns, its purpose is derived from farming and service to pilgrims. My accommodation is a small, comfortable hotel situated at the edge of a pasture near the river, with an inviting café where I spend the late afternoon posting home and talking with Dianne.

Once again, it seems another wound has been laid open. The ancient wisdom that has brought me here has seen to this. I'm now in the season of the pilgrimage where there is reckoning to be had. The ways of the world have not worked. Acceptance, I've been told before, is my answer. Really, I'm left no other choice unless I want to fool myself some more. And so I surrender to my wound which is easy today because I'm so tired. It's a beginning I suppose.

My eyes open on a Sunday morning with the barest hint of first light beyond my window. Utter exhaustion has allowed for uninterrupted sleep. I remember that the hotel does not serve breakfast until 8:00. Since I need an early start today, I pray, stretch, and pack. Soon I'm standing on the road as a rising sun splays its light through the low broken clouds, and traces of an eerie mist surround the hilltops. Though there is an early chill in the air, there is promise as well and I head off through the town for the long, arduous climb to O Cebreiro before me. At the hamlet of LaFaba, three steep kilometers ahead, I'll eat breakfast.

Crossing a bridge as I leave Herrerias, the path takes me into the dense woods. The air is still, the tree branches unruf-fled, which renders absolute silence for a time until I hear the faint sounds of movement ahead. I encounter a middle-aged French pilgrim walking with his dog, a road-worn German Shepard who is leading the way through a now very narrow Camino path. The Frenchman speaks in a thick, heavily accented English, telling me how he and his friend began their walk in the city of LePuy, which lies over 600 kilometers to the east of Saint Jean Pied de Port. There they joined the Frances route, and at this point in their Camino together, have logged over 1200 kilometers. When I express my admiration for such a journey, he simply says, "It is our Way."

The climb becomes nearly vertical at some points, requiring hand-holds on tree roots and rocks. The going is slow and stren-uous, and it requires great care and attention. These woods are still wet after an overnight rainfall left everything slick under hand and foot. My companions and I walk and climb mostly in a good quiet. After nearly two hours, LaFaba reveals itself just as a soft new rain begins to fall.

The Frenchman tends to his dog outside as I tuck into breakfast in a cozy café. The climb up from Herrerias was by far the most intense I've yet experienced on the Camino. It seemed as though it would not end. Though there is an easier paved road I could have taken, it is not the traditional marked route and would have likely left me unfulfilled. Ascension is best felt in both body and soul. I'm grateful to have come this way and relieved that the steepest portion of the day is now behind me. There is still over five kilometers of steady climbing ahead before reaching the top.

CHAPTER 17

I look up to the mountains.
Does my strength come from the mountains?
No, my strength comes from the Eternal,
Who made heaven and earth and mountains.
Psalms 121: 1-2, The Song of Ascent

I LEAVE THE FRENCHMAN and his dog in LaFaba, and wish them both a *Buen Camino.* They are together outside the café, and the dog is laying down having just eaten. Sometimes, love is as palpable as a tuft of fur beneath a stroke behind the ears that simply says, "We will never part. Not ever."

The brief rain passed and the broken clouds, though low over the mountains, now allow the sun to mottle the beautiful green patchwork of deeply sloping pastures. The foothills are behind now, and mountain views surround me in the steady climb. Today's walking challenge is long stretches of mud from the rains that fall almost daily in this part of Spain, and sometimes I must walk through brush to avoid it. My hope is that the path will dry as I climb higher.

I pass farm yards, muddy and pungent with the odors of urine and manure, and slaughter too. I look at the animals, especially the cattle, and wonder if they know. I've heard the shrill cry of animals being harvested all along the Camino, and in it there is a distinct tone of terror. Though I trust that each being has a perfect purpose, this is the first time I've witnessed the suffering. I try to find some beauty in this much as I've found blessings in my own pain, but it's difficult because the animals are innocent.

Soon I see an elegant looking stone marker on the side of the path. I pause for a long moment to observe a passage of great significance to me. I have been walking through the region of Castilla Y Leon, the largest in all of Spain, since leaving Santo Domingo de la Calzada. Just over 400 kilometers have passed. This marker signifies that I am crossing into the region of Galicia, the last on the Camino. It extends west from here to the Atlantic Ocean, north to the Bay of Biscay, and south to Portugal, forming the northwest corner of the country. Most important to the pilgrim is its capitol city, Santiago de Compostela.

The region of Galicia was originally settled by Celts and the hilly, rugged landscape and wet climate are reminiscent of Ireland. One noticeable change is the architecture, where roofs are made of slate or thatch, less so with tiles. The further one travels across Galicia, the more seafood dominates the diet, and the signature dish here is boiled octopus. I've been anticipating the experience of this region since before walking the Camino, and crossing its border almost has the feel of entering another country.

As I climb, the views become more breathtaking, but ascension is again calling me to my inner life, to the thin place that waits patiently. Discreetly, it opens up as I hoped it eventually would.

* * * * *

They had names. My brother, born when I was two, was Edward. I was told he put up a good fight, but did not see his third hour. They would not let my mother be with him. She was told it would be upsetting to her and of course, as was the practice then, she had been anesthetized. I doubt my father was allowed either, but I don't know. We did not speak of many things, and this probably topped the list. After we moved to Connecticut, and four years past my brother's death, came the next. She had not been officially named because after eight months of gestation she didn't survive. Her name would have been Carolyn. She was removed from my mother a month later during what amounted to a medical procedure at around the same time of the Cuban missile crisis. My youngest sister Karen was born two years after Carolyn, I think during the spring. I remember being kept out of school. She survived only moments. While my mother was still in the hospital, my father and I visited with a priest for guidance on how to arrange a Catholic burial for a newborn. He had my father sign paperwork and said he would contact a local undertaker who provided services under these circumstances at no cost. They would see to everything. Not to worry. Let us pray.

I've long considered the shared journey of my parents. How, for example, does one honor the dogma of Catholicism yet maintain intimacy in a marriage, knowing that a failure of "rhythm" could lead to the demise of another human being? Did they talk about this? Ours was not a family culture given to conversation about the things that troubled us. What about the sheer magnitude of the loss of three children? Was it the Faith that saw them through? Near the end of her own life, my mother once spoke of "carrying death itself" in the case of Carolyn. She said it so matter-of-factly. And what of their thoughts of their first born? What were their views toward this passive instigator of the destructive potential of immunology? Was this their lesson in the concept of unconditional love, or was something darker lurking in the collective unconscious?

Faceless are the names, yet part of my earthly consciousness for as long as I can remember. Alone in my childhood room, I sometimes had conversations with them as if they were there. Edward and Carolyn and Karen; their names have haunted me to my core because I blamed myself for so long, so very long. I wish I could remember how old I was when my parents decided to inform me of the connection between the fact of my existence, and the biology which led to the demise of my siblings. I only know I was young enough to not remember when, and too young to not blame myself. Raised Catholic and as an only child, the only place to go was self-centered guilt.

* * * * *

The climb to O Cebreiro is deep into its fourth hour. Of all the sights I have seen since beginning the pilgrimage, this is where it seems heaven has come closest. The path is flattening, and up the hill to my right I hear the faint hiss of tires on a roadway.

Just over eight kilometers of contemplative climbing is about to end as another experience of the thin reveals itself in this high place where the valleys and mountains are laid out in a seeming endless view beyond me, off to a horizon so far away. The gentle sky above hints at higher possibility, a kind and easy breeze is blowing. And once more I have stepped through.

My body straightens and a feeling in my throat and chest heaves up. A sound tries to escape but cannot. The memory of that eternal step on a distant roadside in Morris, Connecticut returns in an instant, as a timeless circle comes 'round. After climbing since first light for over eight kilometers, the first three of which were as severe as anything I'd known, a realization now washes over me that my body feels as though it has just risen from sleep, rested and perfect and absent of fatigue. It defies the experience of 600 kilometers of walking over mountains and hills and across vast plains. It feels as though I have not walked a single step. It feels as though I have transcended. My pack is weightless. I am weightless. I am at the threshold of the village of O Cebreiro in the region of Galicia, Spain. The distance between two eternal steps and nearly four years of time closes to a single breath. I feel as if I have been anointed.

There is a final point in the climb where the roadway meets the Camino on the doorstep to the town and I turn to consider the summit view. After taking a photo, I sit for a few moments in reflection. Walking in this ever-changing body through a world of merciless change, I have been touched by something changeless. It has conferred cleansing and healing and forgiveness in an absolute way. It is beyond language, but here to be known by me forever. From a roadside near my home to a mountaintop in Spain, from inhale to exhale, right foot to left. How else to say this?

I cross the road and step onto the stone street of O Cebreiro, ancient and mystical. The wind blows harder here and the crisp air brings to mind the fall in New England. I head straight away to the church.

My body still feels charged as I enter Iglesia de Santa Maria la Real, a reconstructed medieval church that had been destroyed in the 19th century. I place my pack and sticks against a wall in the vestibule, obtain a *sello* for my Credencial, and walk the center aisle toward the altar. I stop near the front at the third row of pews. My body genuflects slowly and deeply, knee fully to the floor, pausing before standing and sliding into the pew. Sitting here, I am aware that I have not genuflected in 46 years. Then, it was perfunctory, an approximation at best. This time it was not. I have no idea why I did it, but to express reverence seems fitting.

The energies of forgiveness and gratitude and peace sit with me. Though I know more must be revealed, for the moment at least I can rest in this grace that infuses me. My parents come to mind. Mom would have loved this place, much as in Rabanal during Vespers. Why do I think of them at times like this, in places like this? Do I hear the faint and distant echo of some vague sense of my lineage calling? Could that be? Am I being summoned? Far from convinced, I'm still amazed it is even in the realm of possibility; the burden of such long standing resentment finally lifted in this most Catholic of places. Forgiven, I forgive. I wander through the church and offer yet another genuflection before a sacrament I can barely remember.

In front of a side altar, an oblong engraved stone is set into the floor and roped-off. The name of Father Elias Valina Sampedro is engraved on it, and here his remains are buried. It was he who had the idea of the painted yellow arrows. Though I have momentarily strayed a few times, because of them I've never been lost. With my eyes trained to find them in both city and wilderness, their good guidance reassures me.

Clouds sail overhead in the blustery air as sunlight shines and fades, then shines again. Finding a dark, nearly empty cellar café, I order some food, settle into a small corner table and extract my guidebook to review the elevation changes for the remainder of today's trek. Because of the transcendent experience of the climb, I feel as if my walk begins here. I have only 12 kilometers until arriving in Fonfria. Though there is a brief descent from O Cebreiro, the path undulates throughout the remainder of today's walk and I commit to taking it slowly.

Walking away from the village, the stone road returns to the dirt path and into the trees. I'm compelled to consider my siblings again. It is not the first time I've tried to come to terms with feeling responsible. Some time ago I realized I'd been dealing with a good measure of survivor's guilt, but I was never able to be at peace with it. Whatever walked with me as I climbed to O Cebreiro holds something more. It is not finished. Its grace comes in perfect waves. Its timing is impeccable. Come to think of it, that could be said for my old friend grief as well. But this holy presence that looked to me through the eyes of cows in France, listened to me as a genie on the wind in the Pyrenees, and held me so close in a dreamy field of golden mustard outside Pamplona, has always been with me, and in more forms than I can imagine. It sits with a two year old boy on a stone bench as he looks to the sky.

The Camino trends downhill as I head westward through wooded mountains. I come upon the small village of Linares and from between the buildings near its center I see spectacular valley views with distant peaks and a dramatic sky of broken clouds and blue. Soon, on the town's narrow street, a herd of cattle meanders through and I must make way. The cattle pass and I watch them fade from view, again wondering if they know their fate. Their eyes told me little.

At Alto de San Roque, a sign informs me I'm at a height of 1270 meters, about the same as O Cebreiro. Here, a bronze statue of a medieval pilgrim braced against the blowing winds, left hand on his hat, right hand driving his walking stick, greets me. The area is lit-up with spring wildflowers of every color and as is the theme today, more long views of the lush mountains and valleys of Galicia. Soon, I pass a marker telling me there are but 153 kilometers to Santiago.

By the time Fonfria comes into view later in the afternoon, the day has taken on a raw feel, and I'm ready to stop. Tonight's accommodation is a combined *albergue* and hotel with both a cozy café and washing machines available. The community dining facility is in a classic Galician *palloza*, a round, stone building topped with a conical thatched roof. I'm told by the young man who checks me in that our dinner will be plentiful. After showering, I wash clothes, drink coffee, and post home.

At dinnertime, a relaxed procession of pilgrims ambles down a dirt path and into the *palloza*. The large interior has one very long table which is curved to follow nearly half of the circular outer wall, and another, shorter, straight table toward the center of the room. We take our seats by the order in which we enter; first on the outer side of the longer table, then the inside, with the remaining pilgrims filling the shorter table. About 70 or more could be served. Wine and water bottles are placed at frequent intervals along the table. The dining room is staffed by a small army of women who wear long skirts made of denim. As soon as the last pilgrim takes a seat, the women bring out the bread, crusty and fresh and delicious. Next, they serve huge kettles of soup made of a clear broth with various seafood and vegetables. We eat family-style as the room resonates with a blend of languages and the clink of dinnerware.

To my right is a Frenchman who speaks no English whatsoever. Opposite me are some Australians who are happy to learn I don't drink wine. Large chunks of our interchange are lost to the noise even in the short distance across the table. To my left is an older French lady. She is pretty and dignified, and I suspect quite likely older than she looks. Perhaps she is in her 70s. Her English is quite good, and her energy seems kind. Her name is Annette.

As we eat our soup, I politely inquire about her Camino and where she began. Annette says she made the pilgrimage twice before, once walking the Norte route along the Spanish coastline at the Bay of Biscay, and lastly along this route, the Camino de Frances. This time, she is staging her walk differently, stopping only in the smaller villages, and tells me it has allowed for great contrast in her experience. Her attention is drawn away from me for the moment as she turns to her companion. The soup was delicious, and the women who are serving offer seconds from another kettle before collecting the bowls.

Between courses, I ask Annette what has brought her to walk the Camino three times.

"I have lived a long time," she says. "There is always something to mourn, something to think about, no?"

"I would agree with that, yes. Many things called me here, but loss is part of it all, I'm afraid."

"Yes," she says. "I know this."

"Excuse me?"

With a light touch on my forearm, she turns more toward me, looking at me directly yet softly. "I sat at the table next to you during dinner in Rabanal. I am so sorry, but your grief was unforgettable. I cannot imagine such loss. You seem to be very strong. How is this?"

I have to collect myself for a moment. I did not expect this, though by now I should be less surprised.

"You are even kinder than I first thought," I say, slowly gathering myself. "I hope my difficulty in Rabanal didn't cause you too much discomfort. I was taken by surprise then, much like now!"

We both laugh a little as I tell her, "I'm grateful the Camino has seated us together. I don't know about being strong, but I do feel looked-after."

"Yes, yes," she says, smiling warmly. "Looked-after. This is good. I feel that way too. God provides, and so does the Camino."

She holds up her glass, and we toast to it.

As we eat the main course, a hearty lamb stew, our conversation turns to more practical matters and her need to speak with her companion (in French) as well. She shares some tips for dealing with the more crowded conditions on the road coming after my next stop in the city of Sarria. This is the point on the pilgrimage where one can walk the least distance on the Camino and still obtain a Compostela document. Universities across Europe are letting out for the summer, and many of the students will head there for the five day hike into Santiago. In fact, walking the Camino either partially or in its entirety is almost becoming a rite-of-passage for young Europeans. The character of the pilgrimage is said to change significantly during these late stages, and Annette tells me patience, tolerance, and non-judgment will go a long way.

After dessert, I say goodnight to Annette and thank her for being so generous and kind. I also thank her companion as best I can for sharing her friend with me. It would be lovely to see her again along the way or perhaps in Santiago. I've a feeling we have much in common. But as with most everything now, I'll just leave it to the Camino.

I opt for a stroll around Fonfria before turning in for the night. Sunset often eludes me. It occurs well after 9:00 o'clock, when I'm often quite tired and already in bed. Tonight, I feel summoned by the dusk. Its tones are warm and the twilight renders a gentle mercy on the day. I wear its peace like a soft, warm sweater, walking beyond the town past messy farmyards and pastures so green they seem wet; walking in the good company of forgiveness and hope and relief. Faith may be calling as well.

> "Only six days of walking to go from first light tomorrow. It's hard to believe. And no pain."
> "In the body."
> "Yes. In the body."
> "Any surprises?"

"Are you kidding me?"

"Yes. I am."

"I've missed you. I thought you'd forgotten about me."

"Are you kidding me?"

"Yes. I am."

CHAPTER 18

THE EARLIEST LIGHT appears as a brilliant golden sash low atop the eastern horizon, spreading and fading as it bleeds off north and south. I've walked about a kilometer and past a hill after leaving Fonfria to view the sunrise. Around me the light in the air is morning blue under a deep gray canopy overhead; my mood, reflective and hopeful.

Today's walk through the hills of Galicia is a long ramble—about 28 kilometers to Sarria. There I will join the new pilgrims, who either by choice or necessity will walk only the final hundred kilometers over the course of five days into Santiago de Compostela. We will share the Camino, my new friends and I.

The light warms with the air and the blue fades as the clouds break up. Nothing stays the same. The walk today is very quiet. My thoughts are focused on surrendering to ways I cannot name but are clearly all around me and hidden in plain sight. With the mountains to my back and only hills before me, the guidebook says no more dramatic climbs lie ahead. I have mixed feelings about this, for ascension has been good to my pilgrimage. These gentler hills are increasingly reminiscent of where I live in Connecticut, and a longing for home is setting in. It is good to know that when I return there, I'll be easily reminded of Galicia.

By the time I arrive in Triacastela, nine kilometers have passed. My legs are tired and I'm hungry. At a café, I set my bag near a table and go inside to order. There are a few pilgrims in line and only one young lady working, which is not unusual in Spain. What is unusual is she seems stressed and a bit over-whelmed. She glances toward me as she serves the others, and I try to smile kindly. It's all I have at my disposal to impart compassion, and it feels inadequate.

As I eat outside, I'm approached by a pilgrim who must have been behind me in line. He is balancing his plate, cup, and saucer, and asks if he could join me. He introduces himself as Edward from Wales, takes a seat and almost immediately begins complaining about the poor service here, as well as the last few *albergues* where he has stayed. At first I think he must be just a benign curmudgeon, but when he begins to grouse about his ex-wife and makes inquiries about American politics, I start looking for my exit. It does not come. We end up leaving together, until he mercifully decides to look for an accommodation in town. Relieved, I bid him farewell in short order. I think it is quite a statement about the walk that it has taken me over 30 days to find my first genuinely disagreeable pilgrim. I ruefully wonder if the Camino placed him with me as some sort of preparation for what might follow after Sarria.

I walk through hamlets and villages with names like San Xil, Montan, Calvor and San Mamed. Easy hills, emerald green pastures with grazing sheep and cattle fill the day as the Cuckoos still sing their lovely song. I've learned they can only be heard during the springtime.

Sarria appears suddenly and jolts me out of my reverie. There is little transition between the countryside and bustling city, and I am overwhelmed in the midst of tall buildings, traffic, and urban noises. For a short time I lose sight of the yellow arrows. A mild panic rises. I retrace my steps and find them again which settles me instantly.

I continue to follow the Camino through the city, then rounding a corner I am confronted with the Escaleira da Fonte. I believe this must translate into something like Stairway from Hell. My tired legs must now carry me and my pack up at least a hundred steps. Normally a compulsive counter of things, I pass on this. Grumpiness is setting in.

Arriving at my accommodation, a pension, I find the door is locked and no one answers the bell. Anxiety is knocking at my door and I'm annoyed as well. I breathe. I call the number in my notes and someone named Paolo answers. After sharing my plight with him, he apologizes and tells me to wait, that he will be there, "very soon."

"How long?"

"Very soon."

I am not confident. Checking the time, I realize Dianne would likely answer if I call. I need a sweet distraction right about now, and as predicted, she answers. As I share my situation with her, the worry begins to dissolve. After about 15 minutes, Paolo arrives, profusely apologetic. I realize my condition has improved because I'm feeling badly for him as I try to offer assurance that everything is okay. Soon I'm showered and napping happily.

The light in late afternoon is warm and lustrous, reminiscent of the band of light that topped the eastern horizon this morning in Fonfria. But toward evening, the tone will become more tired and evoke a coming rest. It's interesting how many colors the air itself can seem to take on—infinite really. I see this burnished golden light more frequently now that I think of it, especially at this time of day. Is it because the summer is coming soon? As the light steps down and mellows, I know it will shift into some soft, deepening reds and then, when the sun sinks just under the hills, a blue tinge will inform the air; the cool exhale of a day ended.

The shadows seem longer than usual this morning on the way to Portomarin, though I don't know why. My own is spindly like a vaguely familiar alien. Although my shadow is a distortion, it reminds me about eating enough calories. Nothing along my route out of town has been open. I'll be sure to stop at the first place I find. The road turns to dirt almost immediately after I pass the Monasterio de la Magdelena, and in leaving Sarria the transition is as abrupt as yesterday's arrival.

The sky is spectacular, the clouds high and broken, splayed out in shades of golden yellow, blue and grey. The pastures are wet and lush, shimmering with dew. In the valleys, the mist is cool and collected and waiting for the sun to chase it clear to evening. It could rain at some point today—there is that close feeling in the air. During the springtime this deep into Galicia, it is a rare day when it doesn't rain; nothing harsh or wind driven, but a soft rain that falls lightly and swirls about and instills a kind of peace.

Though I started early today, I'm still surprised how few pilgrims are on the Camino with me. I reason most of the new additions are likely younger, perhaps recovering from a festive night in Sarria. I had pictured mobs choking the road, but I suppose it will happen gradually. A few kilometers pass, then an *albergue* with a large café attached appears in the hamlet of Vilei.

After about 12 more kilometers of walking, a placid Galician rain suffuses the day. It's just wet enough for the pack cover, but the poncho remains stowed. The rain adds to the forests' and hills' lushness as the emerald deepens in its affinity for the gray light. Sections of the path become muddy though, and require my close attention to footing. Soon, the hamlet of Mercadoiro is before me. It consists of a café with an *albergue* above it, the perfect stop for lunch.

The lone building is a restored 18Th century structure and probably the most unique café in my Camino experience so far. After leaving my pack and sticks under an overhang, I step in to the rustic space, greeted by dark wood with stone walls, and a friendly young lady behind the counter. I order my food and then notice an absence of tables. Not wanting to eat in the rain, I ask if there is some place to sit inside. The girl points to the wall a few feet behind me where there is an opening about 4 feet high and wide, roughly the size of a fireplace. Squatting down, I see a dark, sunken dining area. The challenge will be to balance plate, cup, and saucer, while crouching low enough to pass through the opening without banging my head. Soon I'm at my table eating, watching a couple of my older fellow pilgrims bang their heads as they come through. Strange as this place is, it is extraordinarily comfortable and cozy. An hour or more passes before I finally leave for the remaining five kilometer walk to my destination.

The beautiful Camino town of Portomarin as it is known today is my age. In 1956, it was relocated from valley to hillside in order to allow for a dam project that flooded its former location. The historical buildings were relocated stone by stone, including the unique block-shaped Iglesia de San Juan/Nicolas which has characteristics of both a church and fortress. During the spring, the water level in the Rio Mino hides the remnants of old Portomarin and its roman bridge, but pilgrims crossing the river into town during the summer and fall can easily see them.

After checking-in to my accommodation, a harder rain begins to fall. I do my chores and post home while it passes through. During the late afternoon, I stop for an early dinner at a restaurant which overlooks an easy bend in the river below. I feel a stab of homesickness as the view reminds me of a place along the Connecticut River. I think about home and Dianne; how I miss them both, and how I know I will soon be missing Spain.

The morning road switchbacks down a hillside at the edge of Portomarin, past a rusting old footbridge, before scampering up and out of the river basin on the other side. By the time I reach the top, a thin sweat covers me, and the air is still a little close from an early rain now passed. In a meadow beside the path I pause. Painted into the scattered clouds above is a perfect rainbow. I divine from this a fair and lovely omen that smiles on the walk today. My heart fills up, for to not feel hope in the face of this would be unbearable.

Today's walk is a little over 25 kilometers to Palas de Rei. Santiago draws closer with every step. After a few kilometers, I catch up with a younger couple ahead of me. As I approach to pass them, I offer a cheerful "*Buen Camino*" and they both reply in kind, but call me by name. Surprised, I turn toward them and see Ken and Elise whom I first met in Molinaseca. It seems as though it has been so long since I've seen them, but it's only been six days. They are heading to Palas de Rei as well, and we decide to walk together.

It's been a while since I've walked with others. The last time was with Mark as I left Leon to begin the final stages of the Meseta. Though I feel there is much to tell them, my first impulse is to listen and to hear about their walk since we last met. I value this above my need to share mine. There will come a time when it feels right to add my own, to hear my own again.

Just before I ran into them again today, they'd been discussing their next adventure in the Philippines for a two year Peace Corps commitment. They speak almost reverently of it, full of hope and promise and innocence. I admire their attitude, and the way they've chosen to live life together. For them, it seems to be about adventure, motivated by extending love through service. My elegant nomadic friends have done this sort of thing many times before. It is their way.

A soft rain falls. Ken and Elise talk about the people and places of their Camino; how life has slowed down and allowed it all to saturate their souls. Eventually we become quiet as we enter a deeply wooded area. Pausing for a drink of water, we stand in the midst of the deepest Galician green. Barely above a whisper, Ken observes that if we were to be still for 20 minutes, moss would likely grow on us as it has on most of the tree trunks. We're oddly alone, and it's absolutely silent, otherworldly. We look about in wonder before we slowly move along.

On the path ahead, a group of pilgrims is clustered where the dirt has pooled into mud, and scattered wet stones are the only places to step. Among them, are two older women who seem to be Sarria walkers, easily distinguished by their smaller packs and white sneakers. One is very frail and steps precariously on each stone, using a single walking stick along with her friend's steadier arm to maneuver. They allow the more nimble to pass them. Ken, Elise, and I make our way to a dry spot just ahead and stop to wait for the two women. Others have done the same. By the time the women make their way slowly toward the end of the worst of the muddy stretch, about ten of us have gathered to make sure they pass safely. As the older lady takes her last step to the dry part of the path, we all spontaneously break out in cheers and applause as both of the women light up, smiling like children do when they've been brave.

The road is finally becoming more crowded. The promised masses are appearing. We have to adjust our pace more frequently because our newer friends do not yet know the finer points of Camino etiquette, such as not blocking the entire width of the path. Still, good cheer rules the day.

At a crossroads, a large number of pilgrims gather at a refreshment stand and *albergue*. Both are operated by donation and manned by volunteer *hospitaleros*. Propping our packs and sticks against a wall, Ken, Elise, and I turn to get some drinks as a fresh faced, heavy-set young American approaches and introduces himself as James from Texas. He tells us he's in his second year of school to become a minister, had recently heard of the Camino, and thought it would be useful to his education to come here and interact with pilgrims for a few weeks. He has no intention of making the pilgrimage himself, but loves meeting new people and learning what moves them to walk. We take turns speaking with him, and are struck by his sincerity and easy manner. I tell him he will be a wonderful minister, and his congregation will be blessed to have him.

We bid James farewell as the sky suddenly becomes threatening. There are a few more kilometers before Palas de Rei, and we'd like to get there before the clouds open. Within the hour we enter town, saying our goodbyes as the first drops begin to fall. We plan to finish the pilgrimage in a few more days and will try to find each other then. I hope to see my friends again at the end of the road.

For this evening, another pilgrim meal, another pilgrim bed, and some easy, gentle sleep as rain falls into the night. Only three days remain.

> *"I'll bet you knew I'd say this, but I really don't want this to be over."*
>
> *"Who says it will end? You may just find the end is really a beginning."*
>
> *"I can see the possibility."*
>
> *"The possibilities are infinite."*

CHAPTER 19

Palas de Rei comes to life as I cross the roadway from the hotel and join the Camino under a cloudless sky. An early sun is on the rise, casting deep shadows. I can feel their chill, but my brisk pace and the pack's weight soon warm me. The forecast calls for a perfect 65 degree day during my short 15 kilometer trek to Melide.

Because it is still early, the path is uncrowded, but by mid-morning they will be with me. Though I welcome those who have joined the walk, the experience has changed. I'm easily distracted now; unable to reflect and contemplate as I freely did before Sarria. I consider though, the early insights and revelations while walking through Navarre and LaRioja that spoke of oneness and unity among pilgrims and others. There is a season to be with my thoughts, a season to be with others. I know there will yet be a time to hear these thoughts, and in a voice more genuinely my own.

Walking in the bright luster of a clear day removes the soft wetness from the greens of Galicia. It assigns a newer, sharper focus to my surroundings and whatever may be revealed. I trust that it serves the walk. I've come to know that every sound, every breeze against my cheek, every insect in flight, every sweet aroma, is there to be noticed; that not noticing would change everything because every single thing is part of a whole. So let them come, each and every pilgrim, each and every little thing, come rain or shine.

A few kilometers after leaving Palas de Rei, I notice the pain. Just below my right knee and sharp with every step, it greets me and demands my attention. I experiment with planting the right foot toe-in, then toe-out, walking on the inside and outside of my foot. The pain varies little. It is likely a common shin splint—tendonitis. With only two more days remaining, I finally have physical pain. Just like a real pilgrim should. I am convinced that this minor leg pain is here to remind me there has been none before this. I'll give it a dose of Ibuprofen later on in Melide if need be. That should take care of it.

The easy green hills of the countryside bring me to the small village of San Xulian, the hamlet of Mato-Casanova, and the towns of Laboreiro and A Coto. Farms and rustic churches share the Camino with rolling, lush meadows and cool, deep forests. There are stretches of the road that are so crowded as to resemble conga lines, but the newer pilgrims bring their energies of innocence and enthusiasm which reminds me of how the walk felt to me back in the Pyrenees with Greg, then with Heinrich.

Just ahead is a medieval roman bridge that leads into the outskirts of Melide and the town of Furelos. Now within two kilometers of the end of walking for today, I stop into the Iglesia de San Juan for a bit of refuge from the crowds and a few moments of prayer. It has become a matter of habit. These churches of the Camino, especially the humbler offerings such as this one, have the effect of centering me. Their dark, stony coolness, mysterious and candle lit, continues speaking to something old within me, a silent reminder of the comfort of my mother's faith.

Within the hour, I'm checked into my accommodation, a room in a simple pension on a quiet, shaded side street. After rinsing out my clothes and posting photos with some words, I wander around this beautiful Camino town. Even though it is the middle of *siesta*, I'm able to easily find an ice cream cone, an addiction that has followed me across the Camino.

A park along the main thoroughfare proves to be the perfect spot to watch the world pass by. A slow, steady parade of memory from the last 750 kilometers of walking scrolls across my mind. Faces and landscapes, countless Spanish churches and small villages, cathedrals and green wheat and chest heaving sobs alone on the Meseta, Cuckoo birds and echoing cowbells, are with me here to be known, to be recognized, or remembered, or reassembled. Some assembly required.

It's hard for me to look at an octopus as a fish. There is something sorrowful about it in its beautiful gruesomeness, lifeless in a tub, and waiting to be boiled in a copper kettle. Copper is critical to the Gallego preparation—renders something to the flavor, I'm told. I notice my anxiety as I prepare to order the dish, partially because I tend to be a picky eater, and partially because of some vague empathy for the octopus. The plate of Pulpo Gallego is before me at last; inch thick chunks of a tentacle (they use a scissor), drizzled with olive oil, sprinkled with paprika and coarse ground sea salt. It is delicious, though I carve the suckers off as one might discard the gristle on a piece of beef. Traditionally, the dish is served with a bowl of ice cold wine, but even though I pass on this, I consider myself initiated to the ways of this place.

After dinner, I walk some more and to my chagrin, the shin pain persists. I stop into a *farmacia* and speak with a lovely young woman who wears a white coat. I ask for the Ibuprofeno, but first she wants to know my symptoms. Once I explain the nature of the shin pain, she nods and asks which dosage I would prefer. On the way back to the pension, I pop a couple of them with another ice cream cone and call it a night.

Lying in bed, reading the guidebook's few remaining pages, I indulge at last in anticipating my arrival into Santiago. I know it has been inevitable, but there is still an element of disbelief. I'm hoping the weather holds, that this tendonitis improves, that I will meet old friends, and that I will have the opportunity to see the Botafumeiro, the large incense burner, during the pilgrim mass at the cathedral. I'm hoping there will be no questioning my Credencial at the Pilgrim Office as I present it for my Compostela certificate. I'm hoping, it would seem, about almost everything. Soon, my eyes grow heavy with sleep and the book falls to the floor from my chest.

> Penultimate: Adjective—
> 1. *next to the last.*
> 2. *of or relating to a penult or the next to the last syllable in a word.*

In the dim grey light of morning, I stand up carefully beside the bed and place all of my weight on the right foot, then lift the heel up. There is no pain, not even a faint soreness. The only way to know is to walk on it. I can't help but think the problem has been resolved. A 25 kilometer trek to Salceda will confirm this.

As I have for 35 mornings now, I pray, stretch, and shoulder the pack for another day of pilgrimage on the Camino de Santiago, heading west in a purposeful movement toward Compostela. I start early under a sky painted with some high clouds that diffuse the sunlight, still low on the horizon behind me. The air is cool as I wend my way through the blue-shaded streets of Melide. Every step, just like the last million or so, takes me over ground I've never seen, and leaves behind a place where I will likely never be again. These steps are dwindling, and I'm almost reluctant to take them.

My surroundings after leaving the city limits again remind me of home; the dewy sloping pastures, the freshly tilled springtime fields, and the cool shadows of the forest. Soon I am upon the village of Boente and stop for breakfast. There are few pilgrims on the road with me this morning, and only two others join me in the café. Starting this early provides at least a measure of solitude before the crowds fill the Camino by mid-morning. I've walked five kilometers so far and my leg feels good as new. There is a beautiful energy about my walk today, a feeling of hope and promise. Something good is in the air. It makes me want to hasten along to find it.

Bless the Lord, O you his angels, you mighty ones who do his Word, obeying the Voice. Psalm 103:20

After 13 kilometers of walking in perfect conditions, I enter Arzua, a major stopping place full of *albergues*, hotels and cafes. The Camino is crowded and pilgrims cluster all along the sidewalk through town. I step onto the street to loop around a group that has blocked the walkway. As I continue on, I hear a voice behind me.

"Stephen! Dude, is that you?"

Turning around, I see Romy grinning wildly and moving toward me. We hug clumsily in that ungainly, pack-wearing way.

"Holy shit, I can't believe you're still on the Camino! I'd have thought you'd be in Santiago by now. Last I heard you were doing 40s to get there."

"Aw man, yeah I did…been there already. Come on, let's walk and I'll tell you the story. You never know what the Camino is gonna hand you."

He looks over his shoulder toward the people he was just speaking with. "Hey gotta go now. See you guys tomorrow in Santiago. *Buen Camino!*"

"Before I tell you all this, how's your Camino going?" he asks as we begin to walk away.

"It's been wonderful. There are some people I want to ask you about that I haven't seen, but first I need to hear more about what you've gotten yourself into."

"Cool. But you're into Santiago tomorrow, right?"

"I am."

"Weather is gonna be dogshit, man. Calling for a lot of rain through to like noon."

"I hadn't looked and I don't care," I say. "Santiago de Compostela tomorrow for me."

"Me too. So anyway, here's what happened. Right after I saw you last...I think it was Calzadilla de la Cueza, right? I got a call from an old friend from home; this younger girl I used to work with. Got to know her and her family, you know?"

"Anyway," he continues, "she was following my posts on social media and it sounded really good to her. She's going through some serious stuff in her life, and she asked if she could come over and walk with me—thought it would do her some good, and wanted to do the Camino from Sarria to Santiago so she could get a Compostela certificate. She couldn't get a flight right away, but I didn't want to lay up waiting for her. Long story short is I had to haul ass to Santiago, then take the bus back to Sarria to meet her."

"And so now you're walking the last hundred kilometers again?"

"Yeah, I am."

"So where is she?"

"About half a kilometer up ahead," he says. "She's slower than me so we'll catch up to her soon."

"You sir, are something else entirely."

"Seemed like the right thing, man. You know as well as me, Stephen, nothing happens out here by accident. So how far are you going today?"

"Salceda, then a 28 into Santiago in the morning," I reply. "How about you?"

"We're going to Arca."

"Okay. Roll call. The ladies from Canada whose Camino you saved—Allison and Jeanette."

"They got into Santiago not long after me. They were on a crunch for time. Couldn't even take any rest days. By now, they're home."

"How about Percy?"

"Yep," he says. "Got hooked up with a lady…I think her name was Dani? Haven't seen or heard about him."

"I had a feeling. What about Bill? I think he's from Alabama…retired federal guy? Last I saw of him he was in Leon with a leg that was hurting him."

"I know who you mean. Likes the ladies, right?" I nod. "Haven't seen him since before Leon."

"Did you meet Heinrich? Tall German guy? And Greg, a Canadian?"

"I think I last saw Heinrich in Castrojeriz or maybe a little after that. I'm not sure. I don't think I know the other guy."

"You sure have met up with a lot of pilgrims, Romy. Everybody seemed to know you. I sure did enjoy that talk we had back on the Meseta."

"Same here, man. Same here. But I'm gonna remember you for springing me and the French dude from the hotel lobby in Hontanas," he says, smiling.

We both laugh and walk quietly for a while.

"Tell me about walking into Santiago at last."

"I guess it's different for everybody, but for me it was kind of an anticlimax in an odd way. And you know I'd come up from Portugal once before. But it's kinda weird. I think I expected some kind of rush after all the walking. I'll admit I got a little teary, though. But hey, you'll find out for yourself tomorrow."

"Tomorrow. My God."

"Hey man, there she is taking a break ahead. I think I'm gonna walk with her for a while if that's okay. Come on and I'll introduce you."

She looks tired, but it's more likely from whatever weight is on her heart than from walking. With a far-away gaze, she sits on a rock and leans against a tree. Her pack rests in front of her. We approach, and I meet a very quiet Megan from San Francisco. She has trouble maintaining eye contact and remains seated. I don't think she wants to chat.

Romy turns toward me.

"Hey Stephen, been great running into you. Maybe tomorrow in Santiago?"

"Sure hope so. *Buen Camino* to you both."

Romy and I hug as Megan nods toward me and smiles weakly.

Perhaps he will return home to San Francisco and then on some future day while walking in his silence on a beach, my friend will reflect on the numerous lives that crossed his path along an ancient road in Spain, on the perfect timing of such crossings, and on all the unintended outcomes. In doing so, will he realize his own miraculous and perfect course to each of them? Is this how it will happen? Will it only be in hindsight? I wonder in my own quiet moments, if we can even know the language of that voice which calls us to touch another's soul; if the knowing of this would simply ruin everything. Maybe we're all angels, benevolently removed from such understanding so we may act well and truly.

The road is more crowded since passing through Arzua. A mild agitation stirs as I once again slow to a crawl behind a large group that blocks the path, until it occurs to me to look at this another way. What if I'm being slowed down? Accepting the road as it is today is a calming idea, and it would seem the road wants a slower walk from me, at least for now.

No matter how far down the scale we have gone, we will see how our experience can benefit others. (The Big Book, Alcoholics Anonymous)

I've been picking my way through the moving clusters of pilgrims for most of the morning and in to early afternoon. Footsteps land all around me. The sound of them joins my own; boots on dirt, a perfect song of the road. Muffled conversations fade in and out of my hearing. I passively wonder what they are saying.

The pace of my walk brings me alongside two women who wear light packs and fresh looking clothing. They are engaged in conversation, but passing by I wish them both *"Buen Camino"* anyway. It's a forgivable interruption. They respond together, but then one of them adds, "Now there's a Saint Jean pilgrim."

I look back toward them. "You're right, but I'm almost afraid to ask how you can tell."

They laugh, and I introduce myself to Joan and Tricia, close friends and college instructors from Pennsylvania who are here leading their latest group of upperclassmen on an international studies trip. Both seem younger than me by about 20 years and carry an energy that is friendly and inviting. We fall easily into walking together as I ask them about the course they teach, and what is required of their students who walk the Camino. As I suspected, they began in Sarria so the class members will be able to receive a Compostela certificate when they finish. As older students, they are mostly autonomous save for a mandatory discussion at dinner each night and an 11:00pm curfew. For the teachers, the trip itself is not too taxing.

As we walk, I join in their light conversation about students, friends back in Pennsylvania, and about their work and social circles. They speak with each other in the soft tones and familiar ways of women who have become especially close over time. Sometimes they use certain words and phrases in a parlance all their own, likely cultivated during late nights spent in far flung hotel rooms and across their kitchen tables. Everything about them suggests they have few, if any, secrets between them.

Joan asks me about my pilgrimage, if I'd be willing to share why I came to walk. I ask if she'd prefer the long or short version. She insists on hearing it all. As she says this, I notice Tricia easing a few steps ahead of us. I proceed to tell of the stuff that brought me here; of losses and sadness, tragedy and baffling change, anger and confusion. I tell of accepting and embracing and letting go, of feeling strangely grateful for it all, and of surrender to what is and to my Source. I tell of emotional crucifixions and resurrections of hope and a miraculous calling on a country road. I tell of having no expectations of the Camino, trusting that whatever it chooses to reveal will be perfect and right, for I believe it to be the way of the Divine. And for some reason I cannot name, I mention my recovery from alcoholism. Maybe it's for context I tell myself, but I've spoken to very few along the Camino about this. Joan listens to me without interruption. Tricia remains a few steps ahead.

When I'm done, we're all quiet for a while before Joan finally speaks.

"I think I know why we ran in to each other. That's quite a story you have there. I'm so sorry. I feel like I've just had my guts pulled inside out."

"Well...you asked."

"You know, I caught the recovery in everything you said before you even mentioned it. I've heard the language before, but never like that, never outside a meeting. That people can actually live that way..."

I look at her.

"I used to go with my ex-boyfriend a lot back when I thought going along would help him."

"That worked out well." Tricia says flatly without looking back.

Joan tells me how it was for her. She tells of his addictive use of alcohol and cocaine, and how it made her feel. She tells me of lost trust and lost hope, and an absolute conviction that if she could only love enough, it would all go away. She tells me about feeling betrayed by his utter inability to keep even the simplest promise. She tells me about the fights and the chaos and the isolation.

"Then I figured if I can't beat it, well... So I started drinking and using with him, but I just couldn't keep up. It was insane. I don't know how anyone could have possibly kept up."

"I thought I'd lost her," Tricia says, now looking back toward me. "Really thought I'd lost her."

"So," Joan says, "When I failed at that too, I went to the other extreme when he got a DUI and the lawyer told him to go to AA. I took charge of that for him so he wouldn't fuck it up and have to go to jail. He was good until the case went away, then he went right back to using, only worse if that was possible," she says. "What finally did it for me was finding out he had started smoking crack because his nose was all torn up, and that he was using with other women."

She sighs deeply.

"It's been six months and still, God help me, there are times when I want to call," she says wistfully. "Just to see if maybe I could help this time without getting sucked into his twisted life."

"Sounds to me like if you substitute his name for alcohol and drugs, you're feeling just like he is. It seems we can become addicted to the addicted," I say as gently as I can. "Just so you know, you never had a chance at fixing him. It's simply too powerful, and that dance can go on until there's nothing left of you. If you don't believe anything else I tell you, please do believe this and just keep moving away. Eventually you'll start to feel better, maybe find a healthier distraction. But at some point, it would be a good idea to look at what attracted you in the first place so you never have to go through that again. Maybe," I say, "it's time to heal from all this."

Tricia just looks back at me with a half-smile. Joan tells me it's been suggested.

I notice a stone marker indicating 27 kilometers remain before Santiago de Compostela and I suddenly realize my walk tomorrow will be 28.7 from Salceda. Lost in our conversation, it would seem I've over-walked. I need to backtrack about a kilometer, then turn south off the Camino for about half a kilometer to get to my accommodation.

"Ladies, please do enjoy the rest of your journey. Thank you for your wonderful company. Apparently it was hypnotic," I say smiling.

Tricia gives me a quick hug and says, "Take care, my friend."

Joan considers me for a moment. "To me this seemed a bit one-sided, but thank you so much. I won't forget this, and I'll think about what you've told me." She hugs me, then stepping back says, "And for the record, I could tell from the worn shoes and how you carry the pack."

My accommodation is an inviting hotel and albergue just off the Camino and nestled into a crook of pastures. Recently restored, the building retains a rustic farmhouse sensibility. This place is called Salceda, but I can find no sign of a village or hamlet in my late afternoon wanderings along dirt roads and through grassy jade meadows.

The final night on the Camino is upon me and this seems to be the perfect place to spend it. I'm considering what my final photo for posting should be. I'm searching for something with a bit of irony, and if I can poke some fun at myself as well, then even better. Standing in my room, I consider the surroundings. Three walls are plaster painted off-white, and one is an accent wall made from stones and mortar. The hardwood floor plays visually against the stone. Before coming to walk, I promised myself that if I was going to share words and photos online, they would both be in the first person. I have not posted photos of myself since stepping on to the Camino, much to the chagrin of Dianne who has regularly chastised me. This photo needs to say goodbye, and to remain consistent with the first person, cannot include me. I place my pack, strap side out against the stone wall, cross the walking sticks in front of it, put my hiking shoes in the foreground, and shoot. I'll post it after I arrive in Santiago. Tomorrow.

I turn the lights out and check the weather for the morning. Romy was correct—a hard rain early, then fading to drizzle by noon. I want to arrive in Santiago by 1:00PM to allow time to join the line for the Compostela at the Pilgrim Office. Very long waiting times have been reported for the past week or more. I need to leave before first light to do this. Wet then. And so it is.

I close my eyes and consider the walk that brought me here, this loaded matter of movement, and its many implications. Now what? Does a light come on when I walk into Santiago de Compostela, all of life's mysteries revealed at last? Are all of my sins forgiven? Is absolution to be found before the bones of the saint as the Church promised so long ago? Maybe not. More likely it will come in a whisper, best heard in the silence of the soul.

"I've been wondering how long I'll have to chew on all of this before it makes any sense."

"Is that what it has to make?"

"Is it so wrong to want to know why things happen?"

"Wondering why may be the wrong question. Might want to consider how instead."

CHAPTER 20

T HERE IS A SKYLIGHT in the vaulted ceiling directly above the bed, and the rain taps hard on it with a wind driven rhythm. Though still warm and dry in my bed, I feel a sense of abandon as I consider the walk before me. My shoes and socks will be soaked, the water will wick-up my pant legs and soak me through. Hopefully, the pack will stay dry under the fitted cover and poncho. But none of it matters because the walk ends today, and today I will leave all of myself on the road if need be.

I leave through the darkened lobby. The rain has slowed to a drizzle, but I know this will be temporary. The gusts and heavier rains will return. A palpable urgency wells from within, and the quick pace I choose feels right. At least for now, my body agrees. My focus in this pre-dawn darkness is the arrows. This is not a good time for losing the road. The quicker pace and the poor visibility could conspire to lead me astray. I resolve to take great care. Soon, I intersect the Camino and turning left, spot the first yellow arrow. The sky opens. Just over 28 kilometers remain.

I saw a pilgrim last night before turning in, a woman about my age who stayed in the room next to mine. Passing in the hallway, we had smiled and nodded to each other and I sensed we were kindred spirits. This morning as I left, I dropped my key on the front desk next to hers, and I wondered how far ahead of me she was. But after two kilometers of walking without seeing her, it's as if she has dissolved into the rain and the Camino. It is mine to walk alone.

Further on, I come upon the warmly lit glow of a cafe directly beneath a street lamp that illuminates the steady downpour. Other than the young lady working here, there is only a man and woman drinking coffee and conversing in French. Both smile at me. Leaving my pack, sticks and poncho just inside the door, I settle into a *café con leche*, thick toast and croissant. As I eat, I sneak a look at the Doppler radar image on my phone. It's not encouraging, and I decide not to do this again because it is pointless.

There are some specific documentation rules to obtain the Compostela certificate: In addition to the stamps at each stop along the entire Camino, two stamps per day must be collected while in the region of Galicia. Also, two stamps must be obtained on the final day prior to entering Santiago. I must be sure to secure these. This will also fill all the panels on the Credencial del Peregrino. My plan in place, I return to the road.

There is a dull, gray first light that bleeds through the rainfall. My shoes already soaked, the wetness travels up my pant legs like a fuse. There is little to do but put my head down and open my stride. A few more kilometers bring me to the village of A Rua and a crowded café with a self-serve stamp. The worker is overwhelmed. I stamp my Credencial, leave without ordering, and head toward the town of Arca.

The rain continues unabated as the not so distant rumble of a jet engine from the Aeroporto de Santiago de Compostela interrupts the steady pattering of the rain. The path turns into the woods toward the village of San Payo, then on to Lavacolla for my final coffee stop on the pilgrimage. Before leaving Lavacolla, I obtain one last stamp. The remaining open panel is reserved for the Pilgrim Office to affix theirs. About ten kilometers remain before I stand at the Cathedral.

I encounter some surprisingly difficult final hills before they eventually flatten to a plateau, and the rain fades to a drizzle then stops. The sky brightens to the extent that I confidently stow the poncho. Passing the television complex on the outskirts of Santiago, I hear young men singing far behind me, out of sight. It is the sound of youth and joy, a victorious call and response to celebrate the end of a very long walk. Listening to their obstreperous singing, I recognize the rich voice of Spain, a thousand years of history, and an unquenchable human spirit.

From the overlook of Monte de Guzo, I can see Santiago de Compostela laid out below like a feast. Countless pilgrims have stood here over the millennia and fallen to their knees at the end of a journey so much more difficult than my own. I contemplate the relief rendered into the bronze face of the medieval pilgrim back on the Plaza San Marcos in Leon, his eyes closed, his head tilted back. Here at last, my friend. We are here. Our walk to Santiago is almost over.

From Monte de Guzo it is all downhill. Curiously, my upper back aches between my shoulder blades. I've never had tension there before, and I'm looking forward to removing my pack soon. I walk through the streets of San Lazaro, the outer, modern part of Santiago before the Old City looms ahead. It is not walled as in most Spanish cities, but the architecture is suddenly medieval, the surfaces of the streets now stone.

I think I can spot one of the Cathedral's spires between some buildings ahead of me as I approach a busy, teeming plaza lined by shops and cafes. The arrows are coming easily now, and I see where they are leading me. It's a little like walking through the murmuring chaos of a Moroccan Kasbah, and I'm getting sensory overload. From a group of tables along the plaza, I hear a familiar voice above the crowd.

"Stephen!" Romy pops up from his seat and comes for me, arms open. "Good job, man! You've made it! You must've gotten soaked like we did."

I can't speak. I can feel the tears already, and I know he understands. I manage a feeble, "Yeah."

"Ok, the Mass already started, so you want to get to the Pilgrim Office?"

I nod. He directs me although I struggle to follow along.

"Thank you Romy," I say as I hug him again. "You gonna be around?"

"Yeah, we're not heading out until tomorrow."

I know I'll see him again. How else could it be?

As I get closer to the Cathedral, I hear bagpipes being played under an archway. Haunting notes echo on the stone and greet pilgrims as they enter the Praza de Obradoiro. I pause to listen for a while. I'm sure it is intended as a gesture of welcome, a joyful thing. But for me, bagpipes have always connoted something mournful and sorrowful, so I suppose it is right they are played here as this walk I've come to love is ending. It is a requiem, a farewell to this wonderful labor that will not be again. I walk into the open plaza, turn, and regard the iconic western façade of the Catedral de Santiago, the Cathedral of Saint James. It is partially covered in scaffolding, undergoing cleansing and restoration; like its tired pilgrims, a work in progress.

I feel no youthful urge to jump up and down, or dance, or scream. I'm tired and wet and my back is sore. I swing off the pack and drop onto my right knee. I make the sign of the cross as an offering to Catholicism, lower my head and say a simple prayer of gratitude for my safe arrival.

I show my Credencial to the guard and gain access to the line at the Pilgrim Office. The queue snakes through the court-yard and down two hallways. It seems no one around me speaks English, so I'm consigned to wait with my thoughts and my fatigue. It is a relief to have the pack at my feet at last, freed of its weight. There is no more reason to deny it. I am exhausted.

After over an hour of inching along the corridors of the Pilgrim Office, I'm nearing the head of the line. Approaching the gentleman behind the counter, I'm filled with apprehension even though I know my Credencial is in order. Authority has always had this effect on me.

"You have walked the entire Camino?" he asks quietly as he looks over my document.

"Every step of the way," I say looking directly toward him. He doesn't look up.

He places one Catedral de Santiago stamp in the final panel and another on the opening fold of the Credencial and hands it back to me. As he glances toward me, I drop my donation into the basket on the counter. He looks down as he writes for a while, then slides the Certificado de Distancia across the counter. It officially notes that I have walked 775 kilometers along the Camino Frances, leaving Saint Jean Pied de Port on 20 April and arriving in Santiago de Compostela on 28 May. His head is down again as he writes. My pulse quickens, and I am surprised at how much this means to me. I've never assigned too much value to documents. Yet when he hands me the Compostela with my name written in the mysterious old Latin, it becomes my tangible proof that I have been cleaved into the lineage of the Camino. The old religious hurts and confusion of childhood and the resentments and anger they became in my later years, dissolve into nothingness as the Church now acknowledges that I have completed this most Catholic journey. I don't know if I'm being called back to the religion of my youth, but there is light again. There is light, and there is peace as well.

After showering and changing into dry clothing, I remove the documents from their protective tube, lay them on the bed in my hotel room, and photograph them for posting later. I wonder about what to put in the caption.

I know I have been freely given the gifts of such great generosity and kindness and support. Not a soul who is aware of my walk could possibly be excluded from this. Many have followed through my postings, and every time they look, their beautiful thoughts find their way across an ocean and into my heart and soul. Many have told Dianne they have found these posts to be uplifting, and have been inspired by the Camino's beauty. This was always my highest hope: To simply pass it on, to share what I have found and seen.

These two documents are for us all. I need to tell them this in the caption, because I know without reservation that I have been carried to this place on the power of everything they ever showed me in all of the ways I've known them. And I've come to believe this power to be synonymous with the Camino's mystical energy and its infinite, timeless voice.

> *The bells say: We have spoken for centuries from the towers of great Churches. We have spoken to the saints your fathers, in their land. We called them, as we call you, to sanctity. What is the word with which we called them? Come with us, God is good, salvation is not hard. Love has made it easy.*
> —Thomas Merton, *Thoughts in Solitude*

I wake later than usual this morning. Relief and exhaustion conspired to give me a deep and dreamless sleep, and I've not felt this well rested in a long time.

The Cathedral is a 15 minute walk from my hotel. The city streets of Santiago de Compostela remain deeply shaded and cool, but the sky above the buildings is mostly blue with some low, fair weather clouds passing by. I move into the old city and walk the narrow stone streets that will lead me along to the Praza de Obradoiro. I decide to stroll around the perimeter of the Cathedral. The bells begin to toll as I walk. I've gotten used to the sound of bells, but these carry a different voice. They are neither passive nor ambient. They are portentous and commanding and insistent. Am I being summoned? Called home? Celebrated? As I walk the streets in the echoes of the bells, I wonder if others hear them as I do.

I pass the bagpiper and enter the main plaza, already filling with arriving pilgrims fresh from the road. Some celebrate, especially the young, some just stand and stare at the Cathedral, others lay down using their packs as a pillow.

From my left, I hear a young woman calling my name. I turn to see Ken and Elise coming toward me, their arms open.

"Oh my God, I can't believe it's you! I almost didn't recognize you without your ball cap and pack on," Elise says grinning. She explains they arrived in Santiago yesterday morning during the worst of the rains.

We hug, and regarding them both I say, "Seems we've all cleaned up nicely."

They've been talking with two young German girls who are introduced to me as M and M. Apparently their names are phonetically challenging, so they decided long ago to keep it that simple. Both are in their mid-twenties. Ken and Elise had previously met them on the road much as they had met me. We quickly make plans to attend the Pilgrim Mass together.

As we're standing on the plaza an older German lady arrives from the road who knows M and M. She is smiling so broadly that it takes me a moment to recognize her as the reserved, shuttered pilgrim with whom I had dinner back in El Acebo. Though I'd seen her walking with another lady since, she is alone this morning. She knows me immediately and in her exuberance, hugs me as if we were old friends. The air around her is charged, her face is the expression of joy itself, youthful now and seemingly relieved of the weight it once carried, her eyes sparkling and crisp and bright. After a few moments, she says goodbye and heads off toward the Office for her Compostela, her life clearly touched by this long walk from home. It could be simply the accomplishment and maybe relief, but I know better.

Ken and Elise went to Mass yesterday and were able to see the Botafumeiro used. Though not fired at every Pilgrim Mass,

the five foot high, 175 pound incense burner is always an anticipated part of the ceremony. Its origins go back to medieval
times when it was used not only as part of the High Mass,
but also to overwhelm the stench of a thousand unwashed pilgrims. Suspended from a pulley system, it takes eight red robed
men pulling ropes to launch it toward the ceiling as the pendu-
lum action eventually causes it to swing across the front of the
main altar. It is the final part of the Mass, a form of blessing.
Ken thinks they are using it this weekend, but I don't want
to have expectations. Still, it is Sunday morning so we have a
good measure of hope. He suggests that to sit in the transept
under the flight of the Botafumeiro, we'll need to be there long
before Mass begins.

We sit in a pew to the right side of the altar. As the Cathedral
fills and the crowd continuously murmurs, a man wearing a red
blazer periodically steps up to a lower pulpit, leans into the
microphone, and shushes the crowd. I keep my thoughts to
myself. The Botafumeiro is suspended about fifteen feet above
the center of the altar, so we remain hopeful it will be used. The
organ plays, and my emotions stir. Full, rich, and resonant it
vibrates through the floor and into my heart, summoning me as
the bells did earlier. Old things, old things that still hold sway.

A procession of celebrants approaches the altar from the
main aisle in the nave of the church, and Mass finally begins.
My emotions are reasonably in check until they begin a roll call
of the starting points and countries of origin from yesterday's
pilgrim arrivals. When I hear "Saint Jean Pied de Port, Estados
Unidos de America," it seems as though the entire Camino
experience flashes before me in a holy sliver of time, and I feel

more unified with the world than I ever have before. This Mass, the daily Pilgrim Mass, has been celebrated essentially uninterrupted for almost a thousand years. Today, I am here and folded into its history.

With the Sacrament of the Eucharist completed, Mass winds down. Near a column where the Botafumeiro is tied-off, eight red robed men, the Tiraboleiros, release the ropes. Slowly, the thurible is lowered to a few feet from the floor and fired with incense, smoke immediately billowing from its sides. One of the men grasps the base and pushes it in the direction it will soon fly. The Tiraboleiros then pull down together on their rope ends which join to a single rope extending upward to the pulleys. The Botafumeiro launches upward and then drops as the swinging motion begins. Another pull down on the rope ends and the flight launches even higher. The organ music swells, growling into my bones. The censer reaches nearly to the ceiling at its apex and the speed at which it crosses the altar is almost frightening. The whole of this scene is remarkable; steeped in history and devotion as the people of the earth have found this way to say, "We are this thankful, we love You this much, we lift ourselves to You." And then as in Burgos, from so close within me, there It is. Beyond the vaulted ceiling, the spires, the music, and the soaring flight of the Botafumeiro, from out of the silence, *there* It is.

The haze and fragrance of the incense linger, and pilgrims make their way toward the exits or mill about taking photos. Across the altar in the front row of the opposing pews, facing toward me but not making eye contact, I see Romy. He is alone and staring toward the altar at the larger than life statue of Santiago. His face is expressionless and his hands are folded in front of him. There is a crowd between us, and I have yet to say goodbye to my friends, but I want to run over there. I keep looking through the crowd and can just see him begin to turn away. Now my view is obstructed, although I continue to move about, trying to maintain a line of sight. After a few seconds I can again see the spot where he was standing. Frantically, I look to the aisles around his pew and then toward the altar. But I know he is gone, dematerialized like any good angel would.

M and M say good bye with a quick hug and move toward the exit behind where we sat. Ken, Elise and I make some tentative plans to join again for dinner which I suspect won't happen. I'm left to the remaining pilgrim customs on my own.

The first is to climb the stairway behind the retablo of the main altar which leads directly behind the statue of Santiago. I mount the steps, touch the statue, and say a prayer of thanks to the Saint for my safe passage to Compostela. I hug the hard metal sculpture as if it were alive, and pause for a moment before proceeding down the descending staircase. As moving as this ritual is, what touches me most is looking down at the marble stairs and seeing them worn on either side where others have stepped for centuries before me. How many footfalls would it take to wear down stone?

The final pilgrim custom is no small matter. It is the object of the pilgrimage itself—the relics of Saint James, Apostle of Jesus. I follow a roped-off route from the stairs that leads to the cool, dark crypt beneath the altar. I lower myself onto a kneeler, and face an elegantly illuminated, ornately decorated silver chest. There is absolute quiet of course, but also a depth of quiet dignity and power that startles me.

Here I choose to suspend my skepticism regarding its contents. Are they really the bones of the Saint, or a Camino legend hovering in some vague netherworld of superstition and fact-tinged belief? Was this merely an elaborate story created to inspire the Spanish people in their fight with the Muslims and then perpetuated throughout the centuries? I do not care. Its truth lies in the journeys of those who have made their way here for over a thousand years through mountain passes, deep rolling hills, and seeming endless, unshaded plains through all manner of weather. It lies in the kindness afforded them by strangers and each other, the infinite stories and purposes that called them here, and the mysterious intelligence that carried them on its power. The truth of it lies in every realized revelation of every pilgrim who ever walked. It lies in their utter surrender to the ways of the road. Whatever is contained in this reliquary has served Creation exceedingly well. And so I pray and honor those who came before me and those who will follow. I honor every thought that comes to them on their own country roads of home that lead them here.

There are few things I really do know, but I know I have not traveled here alone. I've walked with both living and dead and have carried them so close as to be my very breath. Stones have been left behind along with a river of tears and cries of anguish on open plains that left no echo. I've recalled and relived hurts both given and received in the course of this life. Yet all along this way I've walked, there has been a vague something holding me into itself, swirling around me with every step, and imparting itself to me ever so gently. Though I still can't be sure, it seems at least one thing I've taken from this road has been some kind of forgiveness; a forgiveness so deep and so pure that I now wonder if there was ever anything to forgive.

"*Seems to me there is more to consider, don't you think?*"
"*In what way?*"
"*It feels like I'm ending on a minor chord.*"
"*I see. Would you go to any length to find your major chord?*"
"*I suppose so, but what do you mean?*"
"*Would you go to the end of the earth?*"

CHAPTER 21

IT FEELS STRANGE to be moving across the ground so fast, well beyond the speed of a walk. The bus hugs the Atlantic coastline of Galicia and heads toward the small fishing town of Cee (pronounced SAY-UH). From there I plan to walk the rest of the way. I mention the pronunciation because the woman who sold me the ticket at the station in Santiago corrected me when I apparently said it wrongly, so it must be important. The sun is brilliant today and the air is summer-warm. I'm anxious to slip on the pack, open the sticks, and go walking. I've missed it terribly over the last several days. The song of Compostela was sweet, but now it's time for new music of salted breezes and gulls and waves; a return, perhaps a centering.

I've checked the maps and know exactly where I can join with the path. It passes the harbor, and the bus stop is a stone's throw from there. The warm air envelops me as I step onto the sidewalk and fetch my pack from the luggage compartment at the bottom of the bus. I shoulder the bag with a well-practiced movement, extend the sticks, and head straight for the water's edge. A small beach faces the harbor and crescent shaped bulkheads extend from either end. Beyond them, some work boats rock gently at their moorings. Sedate waves lap at the sand just before my shoes. I squat down and dip my hand into the water, then touch my tongue for a taste. Is there anything more ancient?

It's mid-morning, so before leaving town, I stop for a late breakfast at a café with outdoor tables and a full view of the harbor. It's a good time for one last look at the guidebook and maps. I'm less sure of myself here than I was on the Camino Frances and have been told this road is not as well marked.

The path disappoints me a little as it heads inland, into the woods for a while. I'd hoped to keep the ocean more in sight. After a few kilometers, the trail opens onto the coastal highway which I'll follow for a short time until I pass into Sardineiro de Abraixo. I slow my pace to look at a small harbor and the ocean just to my left. Under the cloudless Spanish sky, I cannot remember a time when I have seen a deeper blue reflected on the water.

Back into the woods, its shade is a welcome respite from the mid-day sun. The path is yielding the same soft crunch under foot as so much of the Frances route did. The road as always is perfect. It's a good time to be reminded of this, for I must trust it absolutely despite the scant markings. With the sun almost directly overhead, I have completely lost my sense of direction in these woods. A few more kilometers pass before I emerge and descend a hillside toward the coast. Across a large bay I see my destination: Finisterre, the end of the earth.

From the hillside, perched about twenty meters above the water, Cabo Finisterre is laid out like the last great finger of the land pointing west toward uncertainty. Logic once told those who lived here long ago, that across the water there could only be an abyss, a frightening nothingness existing mostly in nightmares.

Now, my eyes focus along the length of the Cape all the way to the lighthouse, still some six or seven kilometers away. There is a long beach at the bottom of the hill, and I'll walk along its edge into the town of Escaselas, then on to Finisterre, known here as Fisterra. A few more kilometers of walking on a winding road past there, is the lighthouse and the western tip of Spain. I have arranged to be here for a while to allow the Camino to settle in my pilgrim soul and perhaps reveal more secret things.

The town straddles the narrowest part of the Cape, its waist if you will, from the bay side to the ocean side. The distal end of the peninsula to the lighthouse is wider, covered in forest, scrub brush, and carpets of wild flowers. There are trails that trace through all of it, and it will be my mission to explore as many as I can find.

My accommodation, a hotel *rustica*, is located near the top of a hill with panoramic views of the bay, yet only a short walk from a playa, a beach, on the ocean side. Two skylights illuminate and ventilate my room, and a sea breeze blows through almost constantly. After I settle in, a young lady at the front desk tells me about the newer, main route to the lighthouse along the roadway, as well as the original, more rustic route along narrow paths that begin just outside the hotel. This evening, I will walk to the sunset at the end of the Cape, where the relatively few pilgrims who have come here after Santiago will gather to watch. It is a tradition among those who travel here. Some will also burn their walking shoes and clothing in the spirit of celebration and release.

I've chosen the newer route which has necessitated walking down the hill to join with the main roadway through Fisterra, then following a path which parallels the road to the end of the Cape. It traces the edge of a steep hill that falls off to the bay, and looking south I see the rugged coastline of Spain fade away toward Portugal. A little more than three kilometers from the town, I arrive at the lighthouse.

A southerly wind blows hard and the ocean swells are visible from high on the cliffs. The afternoon light is softening, and a peaceful feel is in the air. I make my way to a leeward spot on the rocks that face the Atlantic. I have seen this water looking east from places like Cape Cod and Maine, from the beaches of New Jersey and North Carolina, but I have never seen it look this big until I've looked west back toward America. It is an eternity of an ocean.

In a cloudless sky, pure and unencumbered, the light deepens to a burnt orange. Pilgrims surround me. We face the light from our perches on the rocks like seagulls align themselves to the wind along the beach. It's as if we are expectantly awaiting hallowed word from something divine just past the sun. The air turns ashen blue and chills in the final sigh of the day as the sun slips below the horizon. But it carries on, still high in the afternoon sky over the lake back at home, chasing the solstice that is coming soon.

I climb back over the rocks toward the lighthouse and the roadway for the walk back to town. A few fires have been started, and pilgrims gather around them for the light, warmth, and comradery. They will toss in some of the things they've used on the road, but it's not for me. I've become attached. I can't let go. It's like the stones of Cruz de Ferro.

At this time of year, sunset is at nearly 10:00PM but the light does not linger long. When I reach town it's quite dark. I pass an old church at the very edge of Fisterra and make a note to come back when it's open. The sturdy pale brown stone beckons as if there may be something waiting for me inside. I climb the hill to the hotel. After over 20 kilometers of walking, I fall onto the bed, exhausted. No longer in the rhythm of the daily walk, such a distance once again bears consequence. A lightly salted breeze infuses the hotel room as sleep quickly overtakes me. Come the morning, I'll still be wearing my shoes.

"Will we find your lost chord my friend?"
"Oh, we must."

I want to go to where the Atlantic comes ashore at nearby Playa Mar de Fora. Two pathways lead from the hotel through scrub brush and grasses to a lookout high above the beach. There are a few picnic tables, and I sit on top of one, my back warmed by the morning sun as I look toward a 50 kilometer horizon that might as well go on forever. I cradle a coffee cup as I ponder my shadow. It is proof enough that I'm here, that the walk across Spain is done, and that home lies across the water.

Wooden walkways scale down the hillside to the beach. I remove my sandals and feel the soft grit of the sand on my feet. Summer is again in the air, and wearing a tee shirt and shorts, I cross the beach toward the hard, wet sand. The water is Atlantic-cold and harsh, but I feel as though I must have it on my skin to finish the walk rightly. I kick through the surf for a short distance before its temperature drives me back to the warm sand. I've arrived at the end of the earth. Now what?

Tall, jagged cliffs bracket the beachhead and large, scattered rocks below extend into the surf. I sit on the sand close to the cliffs and rocks, and listen to the many voices in the waves as they pound ashore. Each has a word of its own, unique and violent and said only once. It is incapable of repetition, so it's important to pay close attention. Once its word has been spoken, it's forgiven and slips back to the ocean barely noticed, feeding itself to the next. On it goes and it never ends. It never ends.

I hear Saint Augustine whispering between the words of the waves.

"It is solved by walking," he tells me once again. "Step lightly over the ground and then cast into yourself, dear Soul. Where do these things begin and where do they ever end? Neither on the country road of home or on some beach across an ocean. So move along now," he says. "For God's sake son, just move along."

So I'll walk here at earth's end. I'll walk again to the ways of pilgrimage. I'll put on the shoes, open the sticks and walk and watch carefully. Walk until the sun drops in the sky, and then rest. Then walk again. I'll try hard to be quiet because the holy self likes it best this way. No distractions, no desires, few needs.

Just pay attention. I'll begin today, a little later this morning when I'll walk toward the lighthouse and move slowly along the paths of the older, traditional route. But now, for just a little while longer, I want to sit here in the warm sand and listen to some more of the beach music.

Less than a half kilometer from the front door of the hotel, the stone roadway abruptly changes to dirt and scattered rocks as it enters the woods. It had been climbing gently all along, but now once under the cover of shade, it launches straight up before a clearing opens after perhaps another half kilometer. I turn around to look behind me. To my right I see part of the bay side of Fisterra where it slopes down to meet the water. To the left far below is the beach where I was and the great blue Atlantic. The sky is cloudless again today; the trees and scrub brush all wear deeper summer greens. Though warm, perhaps 85 degrees, a soft ocean breeze blows and the air is dry. It is as close to perfection as a day could be. I turn back around and continue along the path.

Still climbing, the trail edges along the Atlantic side of the steep hill, and I can see the cliffs of the coastline north toward Muxia. Sometimes the pathway is plain to see, made of fine stone and dirt, and at other times it fades away into matted grass. Turning uphill, I'm forced to clamber along the rocky trail toward the summit. It reminds me of the ascent to LaFaba with the Frenchman and his dog, and I must find sturdy hand-holds to pull myself along. Finally, I make it to a high point on the Cape, surrounded by knee high scrub brush and wild flowers blooming yellow, purple and white. The landscape is strewn with rocks and outcroppings of ledge and I find a place to sit in reasonable comfort facing toward the ocean. Looking outward to the end of Cabo Finisterre, I easily see the lighthouse in the distance and all of the rugged ground in between. Normally, when feeling contemplative, I tend to close my eyes, but I want to burn this image hard into memory so it will last forever and then some.

"Go gently now. No expectations, no agendas. Entire days remain here."
"You know me well."
"I do, don't I?"
"There was a wonderful gift much earlier in the walk. Lasted for just a fleeting moment, but I remember it so well."
"Seems as though it was important to you."
"I think it was very important."

There is something odd about making inquiry of memory. It's just so big and yet the moments remembered have passed so quickly as to be nearly missed. I've walked a million steps over these 800 kilometers, and here I'm trying to locate something that happened in a flash. Yet reflecting on this now, I think it may be the most fundamental thing I was given along this Way. Something to bring home.

It had been a cool, crisp and lovely day as Heinrich and I were about to leave the region of La Rioja. We walked quietly through some gentle hills in the mid-morning, and pilgrims were strung along the Camino as it coursed through the landscape ahead. Sleep had been kind so I was well rested and alert, but then came a spontaneous shift into something…else. It was sudden but not jarring; appearances did not change one bit. That would have been too much. Yet everything else did.

> No longer do I see pilgrims, I see pilgrimage; a movement toward something, a movement away, a movement of Grace. I realize in this moment I am not apart from them, or they from me. I am in no way living in opposition to them. I am them. And in the larger context of life beyond the Camino, all the competing needs and desires, all the conflicting interests, all the wounds inflicted and received, all the differences of body and thought and language and most certainly of religion, are revealed as only mistaken notions of things. Elegies of separation become expressions of compassionate oneness along this thin, magical road to Santiago. Realization loves to dance here, to be glimpsed even if only in the briefest of flashes.

So if this is real, then everything would change. If the world's idea of separation is untrue, and my realized glimpse of oneness is true, then death and suffering and fear are forgiven in one stroke and become things that merely appear to be. But how can one dismiss experience? (So my son only *appeared* to hang himself?) I'll walk on.

I make a long, slow loop of some of the trails that cross over the spine of Cabo Finisterre and eventually return to the path that delivers me to the roadway near the hotel. I've walked maybe seven or eight kilometers, though with no pack to carry and perfect weather it's been easy despite the constant elevation changes.

Evening is approaching and I'm hungry, so I leave the sticks at the hotel, and walk down the hill to the café-lined waterfront. I soon find a place that broils its scallops still in the shell. Simple and delicious, I have another plate before I go. The old port at Fisterra is quiet now. The fishing fleet is either tied-up at the piers just past the bulkhead, or moored further out in the protected harbor. The smells of a lowering tide, the rapping noises rigging makes in the breeze, and the songs of gulls, summon a sense of endings. The light wanes as the sun drops below the hill behind me, shading the town. Across the open bay, the sharply rising hills are still fully lit in a red brick light as the bright afternoon blue of the water is fading. I walk back up and over the hill to take in sunset from the lookout over Playa Mar de Fora.

Pilgrims dot the beach and sit side by side in delicate little strings all facing the sun as it lowers over the ocean and enters a distant layer of clouds just above the horizon. A burnished reflection on the water softens by the moment, and the music of the waves sings even though I can't make out any of the words. As I watch them from high above, my fellow pilgrims on the sand break my heart with their innocence and hope and presence. I have the distinct impression we are all thinking the same thing: How then do we return to the ways of the world? How to do this? How in God's name to do this? Madrid and my flight to New York await me in a week's time.

I've slept well and with my shoes off this time. The first thing that occurs to me is that it is my mother's birthday. She would have been 84 today. It's funny how we say these things to ourselves. She never would have been 84. All is always as it should be. These dates spawn memories, though. This too is as it should be. Her presence has been with me, especially when I've wondered about being recalled to Catholicism.

The Iglesia de Santa Maria das Areas sits at the very edge of Fisterra, the last building of note seen when traveling the main road out to the lighthouse. Thick, brown stone walls, small, randomly placed windows, and a weathered tile roof reflect a church that has withstood over eight centuries of coastal seasons. It holds something for me though I cannot yet imagine what. I've lost count of how many of these I have passed since the Pyrenees, yet this one has insisted I come in since I first saw it.

Inside there is nothing remarkable. The ornate and intricately carved wooden retablo behind the altar is as mesmerizing as any other I have seen, and the dressed statues offer their usual plaintive expressions. The arching curvature of the upper walls creates a sense of being in a stone cavern, though the ceiling over the central nave is made of wood. At the rear of the church, my attention is drawn to a baptismal font in an alcove and the low stone arches that surround it which create a sort of chapel. It feels medieval, and although it is lit with a few slit-like windows and several discreetly placed lamps, torches would seem to be a more appropriate way to illuminate it. I take a seat in the midst of it and close my eyes with the intention of remembering my mother in prayer. It feels good to be here.

But apparently a prayer is not to be. I experience a meditation instead. Shifting into its subdued imagery, I stand at the threshold of this same space, and it is dark and cold as two flickering torch lamps mounted on the wall shed the only light. There is a table to the side, and on it is a large, roughly carved wooden bowl two feet in diameter. Next to the bowl is a folded, dark brown, heavy woolen cassock like a monk might wear. I'm to take off my clothing and wear the cassock. I feel its weight and the scratch of the harsh woolen material against my skin, but I can also feel its great warmth in the chilled air that surrounds me. Intuitively, I pick up the bowl, its considerable weight pressing my hands flat against the bottom, and I look to where the baptismal font would be. There is a small, stone altar instead just a few steps away. I place the bowl on the altar, then lay face down on the stone floor before it, completely prostrate and surrendered. Oddly, I recall that this same position is used in the ceremony of Catholic ordination for the priesthood. In this meditation, the bowl, specifically its utter emptiness, represents all I have come to know over the entire course of my life. I should find this shocking, but I don't. I simply accept it as absolutely true. What follows next is not as clear. The bowl is being filled, but I can't see it because of my position on the floor. I dare not look up. It is not my place to do so. The meditation ends abruptly. I'm calling this a meditation and not a vision. It does not have the quality of a vision even though it may seem that way.

…forgive and you shall be forgiven. (Luke 6:37)

The next morning, I wake to a cool and breezy day, though not raw. The varied sky is mostly overcast with clouds at different heights, and I wonder if it will rain. Some of them are very low, but there are streaks of blue as well. After breakfast, I ask an older lady who is at the front desk today for a map of the roads heading north along the coast. She produces one immediately and points to some landmarks, including an area on the map designated as Castrominan.

"You must go there," she says. "It is quite beautiful. You will not be disappointed."

The route from the hotel takes me through the residential areas of Fisterra and Escaselas before turning me out to a rural landscape of farms and pastures. I realize that I am now on the Camino that runs between Finisterre and Muxia, after I pass a crossroads and see yellow arrows and stone distance markers with engraved scallop shells. Walking several kilometers on a long, straight paved road with very little traffic, I notice the path to Muxia veers to the right, leaves the roadway and heads across an open pasture toward some hills. My sense of direction tells me that to continue on the roadway will keep me more to the coast and so I let the arrows fall away behind me. I have not looked at the map since entering the countryside and have no intention of doing so for the rest of the day. Let the energy have its way and take me where it will.

After a while the paved road bends slightly, and ahead I see a downhill stretch. I stop. There are pastures to my right and a stand of trees on the left. I spot a sandy path heading into the trees and reason that following it should bring me closer to the coastline. I walk in. A clearing beyond the trees opens almost as soon as I enter them, and moments later I'm standing at the edge of an expansive tract of coastal moors that gently rises from the tree line. Worn-in paths trace through the wild grasses and low-lying growth of gorse blooming in subdued yellow. Instinctively I follow them toward the slope's crest.

The wind increases, and I hear the muffled sounds of the surf crashing. I arrive at the edge of rocky cliffs, 20 meters or more above the ocean. Looking north, I trace the coastline toward a still distant Muxia. To the south, the cliffs lead to a smaller beach tucked into a cove that can likely only be seen from this spot. It is a wild and overwhelming, almost otherworldly place, untouchable and unfettered in the sheer power of the wind, the waves pounding in below, and the deep gray overcast above. It surrounds me and swallows me whole. I'd imagined the rocky coast of Ireland would be like this, and I understand now why the Celts felt so at home when they settled here. This place is utterly unchanged since they first arrived. Nothing in my sight was placed here by human hands. All of it has been carved by water and wind and the good and mighty earth.

For now, I walk the cliffs' edges and stand on precarious outcroppings. Leaning only on the sticks, I know one misplaced step would be the end of me, yet they come easily. As I slowly make my way through this wild and primitive place, the experience of walking the Camino de Santiago begins to play out in a different way, in short bursts of memory. They arrive in a sort of rhythm, although not chronologically. The sequence to these thoughts is like some kind of coded message I can't quite seem to grasp. There is another, more obscure logic to it.

My mind struggles to comprehend, but this can only lead me to what I *think* I know. The spirit however, bids me to relax, to look around and breathe all of it. Just look and breathe and let it all be. I need only to pay attention, and perhaps I will see things beyond mere appearances. Above all, I must not press. I must be patient, for I feel a sense of something gathering.

Time gets lost and the sun is of no help today. I have no idea how long I've been walking and exploring before deciding to return to Finisterre. I find my way back to the path through the tree line, to the paved roadway, and retrace my steps all the way to the hotel without stopping. I know I'll be this way again before I leave for home.

I've established a casual circuit on the northwestern coast of Spain: the streets of Fisterra and the waterfront of the town, the many faded trails and rustic dirt roads that thread through the wilderness between the town and the lighthouse, as well as the long beach of Playa Mar de Fora and the moors and cliffs of Castrominan further up the coast. There is daily potential for long, ranging walks that may quiet my mind and allow memory its way, along with the simple lazy pleasure of lying on a beach under the sun's warmth and comfort.

As this final week in Spain rolls along, I'm ending my days now as I begin them; by reading, praying, and attempting meditation, especially *that* meditation. I've been revisiting it mostly to see if something changes. I continue to wear the heavy, coarse woolen cassock, move the large bowl to the altar, and lay face down and vulnerable on the cold stone. What am I meditating on? Is it about a return to Catholicism? I don't think so. It's too obvious, and if I've learned anything on pilgrimage, it's that things are not usually what they seem to be. I suppose I should just be diligent and patient and keep showing up.

Every day there is a new walk, another chance to break the coded message of what these memories have been trying to show me. On one clear and sunny day, warm and breezy, I wade through the waist high scrub brush on the moors of

Castrominan. My thoughts are still. I stop for a moment. It's as if someone has called to me. Even though I'm alone, I look around.

Just as gently as the soft winds brush against my skin, it whispers to me that everything that happened along the Camino de Santiago has been pointing me toward oneness, forgiveness, and returning with these things to the ways of the world. It had told me this before, but my thoughts were too loud. As important as understanding this message is, I now realize the degree of silence that was required for it to be known. And that may be the most salient thing of all.

The following day dawns bright and clear once again. My only goal for today is to lie on the beach. It's all I want to do. Truth be told, it is about vanity. I want Dianne to first see me with a decent tan and I'm giddy at the prospect of doing something hedonistic. After breakfast though, I come back to my room because it's still early for the beach, and decide for now to pray and meditate. I sit in bed, lean my back against the headboard, and close my eyes.

Once again, inside the dark stone walls of the Spanish church, I've placed the bowl and I'm lying on the floor in the warm coarseness of the cassock. The bowl is being filled. This time however, my body vibrates and heat emanates from within me; yet, I feel no anxiety. I have an emotional release, an unclenching of my heart, a freedom from worry or concern or fear. Though my body is still on the stone floor, I'm able to see the bowl filling with a moving, liquid light pouring down from the darkness above the altar. There is a sound associated with the light, but I can't identify it. Awareness returns to the bed in my room. I snap in one motion to a sitting position with both feet on the floor; my hands grasp the mattress to steady myself. Instantly, I'm flooded with the full feeling of blame for my siblings' deaths. In this desperate moment, it is as if I've wrung the very life out of each of them with my bare hands. In the next moment, I realize it was not my fault, had never been my fault, but the terrible heaviness of responsibility stays with me and will not let go. Finally, everything lifts from me as I come to know that there is only one act of forgiveness left owed, just one. I feel held with great motherly warmth and tenderness, forgiven of my one and only sin in all of this...that I had ever *believed* the fault was mine. That I had ever believed it.

A guttural sound erupts from me and I spring to my feet as if I'd been lifted from the bed like a puppet, weightless. I move randomly, almost spastically, around the room, sobbing in the ecstatic relief of it all as over 50 years of guilt dissolves into the nothingness it always was. Could it have been that simple?

For so long, I'd forgiven myself the act of killing my brother and sisters, wondering why it still wasn't enough, why I carried that pain around all this time. I once heard something wise about this sort of thing: If my pain cannot be transformed to something forgiven, then I will certainly transfer my pain to others. To be forgiven of this is to be forgiven of it all and of anything.

Perhaps I'm idealizing some, but I've come to regard the Camino as perfect. It's probably unfair of me, though understandable given all that's happened. But could it have ignored something? Could it simply have forgotten? Something waited on and thought about. Something even conjured. Yet nothing has ever come up around it. It's almost as if it had never been. On some days, maybe in the good quiet of an early morning, it will cross my mind. And often when this happens, random lines from the Prayer of Saint Francis will cross there as well, mingle and blend with it. Maybe that's all there is for now. It keeps bitterness away, but I'd hoped for more. I'd begun to hope when it came up almost magically with Heinrich during dinner that night in Estella. Since then it's gone all dark even though I've tried to play the light on it. Although the perfect forgiveness that was visited on me here in Finisterre was surely all encompassing, it does seem that at least for now, the absence of my remaining child has come to rest on a minor chord.

A calling on a distant past August road, an 800 kilometer walk across Spain and the entire 60 years of a life poured into the crucible of pilgrimage, finally brings me here to this place by the sea at the end of the earth. Now, none of what came here with me is as it was before. Though not necessarily resolved in human terms, it is cleaner and brighter, more likely to shine on my life than shadow it. That this kind of thing could be done leaves me awestruck. But of course, it all began before a calling and will end well beyond time and the earth. God is great.

On one last sunny day in the town of Finisterre, I board the bus bound for Santiago de Compostela. We travel along the coast again and stop in the fishing villages before heading inland. I will continue to drink this in so I will never forget it. Beyond photos or notes or any words I may one day write, I want to remember all of it in the cells of my soul. I pray this may be so.

In a few hours, I'll walk past the Cathedral once more, spend a last night in Santiago, and then take an early train south and eastward to Madrid. Truthfully, I've been a bit lonely for much of this last week in Spain. Thoughts of home have been prominent lately, and I want to return. I really do. It's just…

*　*　*　*　*

As I check in at the airport in Madrid, the official asks all the usual intrusive questions about the details of my life before I'm allowed a final boarding pass and therefore permission to leave the country. The young woman is focused and professional as we talk, observing my facial expressions and body language as I respond to her many inquiries.

Finally she says to me, "Tell me why you came to Spain."

My eyes immediately fill and I feel like I must look away. I know I have to gather myself. I take a breath, then look at her again.

"I'm sorry," I say. "Actually, I came to walk the Camino de Santiago."

For just an instant, she softens. Glancing down for a moment, she looks back to me and hands me the pass.

"You completed it?"

"I did, yes."

She almost smiles. "Congratulations."

I feel the gentle nudge as the plane is pushed from the gate. It bounces along the taxiway for several minutes before turning on to the runway, lining up, and stopping. I want to freeze this moment and stay right here forever, to stay connected firmly to the ground of Spain. I want to walk through the door at Dianne's house and hold her close like I never have before.

The plane is rolling now and soon the nose wheel is off. The main gear thumps and we leave the ground behind. The wings have us now. We fly northwest and directly over Santiago de Compostela on our way to the Atlantic. Home soon.

LATE AUTUMN

MORRIS, CT

I T'S THE TIME OF YEAR when a certain rawness enters the air. The sky takes on a milky winter white, and dusk comes early with the solstice fast on the way. The trees are newly bare; the few remaining leaves are dull brown. At the lake, an early crust of ice forms after a cold snap or two. It's good to come out of the chill after a brisk walk and into a warmly lit, snug and comfortable home. Coffee is usually on and soup is always a good idea. This is a time when I tend to be circumspect and a bit nostalgic. It is no secret around here that I miss the Camino de Santiago and Spain; that they've left a hole in my heart. Yet I've never been so grateful for how much I love my home and all it means to me. Without this, the longing would be unbearable.

I walk nearly every day unless the weather is dreadful. I walk because it is my love and my need, my holy affliction. Should my body fail, it will be my deepest loss. Many days I pass the spot where the Camino first called to me, and there are times when I hear its whisper still hanging in the air. I'm almost sure it is my imagination. Almost. Though many things still occur to me as I walk, it can never happen in the same way it did on pilgrimage. Spain's personality is strong and silent. Echoes persist.

Summer was delightful. The weekend after I came home, Dianne and I got away to the coastal town of Stonington in southeastern Connecticut. It has always been a favorite place of ours and it was her idea that we should go there. She knows how good it is to be near water. I could tell she was concerned that I've changed and will likely change some more. I don't know how to respond to this. I really don't.

For the remainder of the season, I wore nothing other than tee shirts and shorts and a casual tan. It was that kind of summer, free from care, yet knowingly in a benign denial, reminiscent of childhood with the start of school coming all too soon. Something seemed to be drawing close.

I kept running into people who had seen my posts from the Camino, and they would ask if I had started a book yet. Not if I was going to write, but when. I thought this odd because it hadn't really occurred to me past some vague notion. I'd respond by mumbling something like, "Well, I don't really know what that would look like." I quickly tired of this answer, realized I never would know until I began, and finally wrote the first words just a few months ago in early September.

The idea of returning to Catholicism proved a bit pesky. I'd needed to consider it seriously because of its persistence on the Camino which did not let up now that I was home. After looking at it during some walking contemplation, and of course speaking to Father John, I felt what was needed was discernment. I was willing to go to serious lengths. It made sense to me that a directed retreat using the Spiritual Exercises of Saint Ignatius could be the answer. I applied to a Jesuit retreat house located by the sea in Massachusetts. I never heard back from them. Things get lost. I understand. I applied once more. Sometimes, no answer is the answer. I will not speculate. After finally making a true and lasting peace with Catholicism, I wasn't about to stir that up again. I think that was the larger point anyway. Mass is ended, go in peace.

During this time, I spoke with a friend of mine; an intriguing man in his early 80's who has always been a voracious spiritual seeker. He listened to my story about the Jesuits but made no comment, just shrugged. He told me about a new spiritual study group he'd just started attending and asked if I'd be interested. He described their philosophy of non-dualism, of oneness, of forgiveness, of finding a holy silence and of living in this world without the need to be of it. I accepted his invitation. Circles eventually do close and then never end.

The summer walks became the walks of autumn, and daily, I noted the changing colors and changing habits that come with the cooler days. I had arrived at some random conclusions while making my way along these country roads of home. Though they strike me as essential and true, they are not absolute. Few things in this world can be. My view of them will change just as the tides rise and fall, as clouds inform the dawn and dusk, as seasons pass. Here is a sampling of them in no particular order:

It's very difficult to live contemplatively these days. The world seems to conspire against it.

Sunrise is holy. So is sunset because it's always rising somewhere; the circle thing.

There is nothing to be upset about.

I am in perfect safety.

I am at peace; deeply, eternally, infinitely.

I am loved beyond the beyond and then some more.

I am free from all bondage.

These things I am, we are, because it's all shared.

Blessings of the Divine cannot be portioned.

Beginnings and endings of things are highly suspect; the circle thing again.

Silence of thought is unbelievably difficult.

Silence of thought is unbelievably eloquent.

Realization comes out of silence.

We are loved beyond the beyond and then some more. I know. It bears repeating.

One of the common themes that fueled the walks of my fellow pilgrims and my own was feeling some great sense of loss that was usually connected to an ending of relationship with others. Of course, by the time one enters the seventh decade of life, these things tend to have piled up. My last dose of this was heavy and compressed over a very short time. Pain turns out to be but a prelude to something greater, and it is this way without exception given the proper influences. This is an ongoing matter and not one given to clear and tidy endings. But at this point in the proceedings I can say this with all of my heart: it has made for a life of such depth and texture that I would not ever have sought to avoid any of it. There is not a single domain of the life I live that is as it was before the Camino and all that brought me to it. This, I can only receive with gratitude. Going forward, I am to simply rest in our Source from all the mistaken poverty of my humanity. It has shown me a Way to Itself and so I must go in. Praise be.

> *"I suppose you'd suggest this compulsion to write could be an exercise in reliving the Camino."*
>
> *"Well, yes. But still it seems you have a thing to say."*

ACKNOWLEDGMENTS

Heartfelt thanks to the following for their contributions to this work, and for their generous encouragement and patience:

Two who are my bookends—Dianne, my beautiful companion; close as my breath in every step along the way. Siempre has tenido mi Corazon. Hugh, who's been with me through everything for over 40 years. This was no exception. He dreams.

The first readers: Frank Avella, Bill Broden, Lee Cantelon, Bill Considine, Fiona de Merell, Nancy DePecol, Mary Dunleavy, Terri Dyer, Mark Griffin, Hugh Hamblet, Bill Ludwig, Lynn Martin, Terry Sheron, and Dianne Slater.

Tom Lagasse, for his invaluable assistance in shaping the manuscript, nudging me in the right direction during the process of submission, and showing me the value of wonderful editing.

Leslie M. Browning, editor, publisher, and founder of Homebound Publications, who took the risk with a first time author, and lives a life that inspires.

All who followed the postings as I walked, and those who later asked about a book I could not yet see.

Countless pilgrims who have gone before me, walked with me, and will follow. I honor their calling, their walk, their pain, courage, and innocence.

Most of all, from the depth of me, I offer my gratitude to the Source of everything for the magic of the words.

ABOUT THE AUTHOR

Stephen Drew lives in the northwestern Connecticut town of Morris, a bucolic community that surrounds Bantam Lake.

The memoir *Into the Thin, A Pilgrimage Walk Across Northern Spain* is his first published work. He is currently shaping his next book, a novel.

Stephen practices a minimalist lifestyle which includes daily walking, mostly on the roads and paths around Bantam Lake. Hiking here and elsewhere serves as a centerpiece of contemplative living and a connection to Source.

Follow Stephen at www.authorstephendrew.com
and on Facebook: Author Stephen Drew

HOMEBOUND PUBLICATIONS
OFFERINGS

HOMEBOUND PUBLICATIONS
Ensuring that the mainstream isn't the only stream.

We are an award-winning independent publisher founded in 2011 striving to ensure that the mainstream is not the only stream. More than a company, we are a community of writers and readers exploring the larger questions we face as a global village. It is our intention to preserve contemplative storytelling. We publish full-length introspective works of creative non-fiction, literary fiction, and poetry. Join us.

WWW.HOMEBOUNDPUBLICATIONS.COM
LOOK FOR OUR TITLES WHEREVER BOOKS ARE SOLD

SINCE 2011